WOMEN
AT
WORSHIP

WOMEN

AT

WORSHIP

INTERPRETATIONS OF
NORTH AMERICAN DIVERSITY

MARJORIE PROCTER-SMITH
and JANET R. WALTON, Editors

Westminster/John Knox Press
Louisville, Kentucky

Book design by Susan E. Jackson

Cover design by Claire Calhoun

First edition

This book is printed on acid-free paper that meets the American National Standards Institute Z39.48 standard. ∞

For Acknowledgments see page xii.

Published by Westminster/John Knox Press
Louisville, Kentucky

PRINTED IN THE UNITED STATES OF AMERICA

9   8   7   6   5   4   3   2   1

Library of Congress Cataloging-in-Publication Data

Women at worship : interpretations of North American diversity /
  Marjorie Procter-Smith and Janet R. Walton, editors.
      p.   cm.
  Includes bibliographical references.
  ISBN 0-664-25253-2 (alk. paper)

  1. Women and religion—North America. 2. Public worship—
Comparative studies. 3. Feminist theology. I. Procter-Smith,
Marjorie. II. Walton, Janet Roland.
  BL458.W5764 1993
  291.3'8'082—dc20   93-10752

For all women
whose claims of ritual authority in community
make this work possible

and

for all men
willing to listen, discover, and risk

Contents

Contributors

Mary Collins, O.S.B., is Director of the Liturgical Studies Program at the Catholic University of America. Past president of the North American Academy of Liturgy, author of *Worship, Renewal to Practice, Women at Prayer,* and numerous articles, she has been coeditor of the liturgy volumes of the international theological journal *Concilium* and of *The New Dictionary of Theology.* She is writing a book on contemporary Benedictine sisters' communal reinterpretation of traditional monastic liturgies.

Ruth Duck is Assistant Professor of Worship at Garrett-Evangelical Theological Seminary. A United Church of Christ clergywoman, she has pastored several churches. She has edited several books of worship resources.

Sue Levi Elwell, is Director of the American Jewish Congress Feminist Center in Los Angeles and serves as rabbi of the Irvine Jewish Community.

Wendy Hunter Roberts is a Pagan (Unitarian) Universalist. She lives in a converted warehouse in Oakland, California, where she maintains a spiritual direction/therapy practice and a music studio, producing rituals and writing earth-based rock and roll with her musician husband.

Ada María Isasi-Díaz is Associate Professor of Theology and Ethics at the School of Theology and Graduate School of Drew University. Born and raised in Habana, Cuba, she is a mujerista theologian working to articulate a Hispanic women's liberation theology.

Eileen King is a Roman Catholic feminist and founding member of a women's liturgy group in New York City.

Patricia Malarcher is an artist, writer, lecturer, and teacher. She lives in Englewood, New Jersey.

Irene Monroe is a Ph.D. student in religion, gender, and culture at Harvard Divinity School and a recent graduate of Union Theological Seminary in the City of New York.

Diann L. Neu, cofounder and codirector of WATER, the Women's Alliance for Theology, Ethics and Ritual, is a Catholic feminist liturgist and therapist in Silver Spring, Maryland. She has designed many liturgies for national and international gatherings as well as for her own small women-base community in the Washington, D.C., area.

Annie Ruth Powell is a Ph.D. student in systematic theology at Union Theological Seminary in the City of New York, an A.M.E. minister, and current Director of the Christian Community Learning Centre in Brooklyn, New York.

Marjorie Procter-Smith is Associate Professor of Liturgy at Perkins School of Theology, Southern Methodist University. She is the author of *Women in Shaker Community and Worship* and *In Her Own Rite: Constructing Feminist Liturgical Tradition.*

Sheila Redmond works as an HIV/AIDS counselor in Ottawa, Canada, focusing mainly on issues relating to women and AIDS. An independent scholar, she recently received her Ph.D. in Psychology and Religion from the University of Ottawa, her thesis being a study of the impact of Christianity on the recovery process from father–daughter incest.

Janet R. Walton is Associate Professor of Worship at Union Theological Seminary in the City of New York. She is the author of *Art and Worship: A Vital Connection,* coeditor of *Sacred Sound and Social Change: Liturgical Music in Jewish and Christian Experience.*

Ann Patrick Ware, a Sister of Loretto, now retired, has been a teacher of Latin, French, theology, liturgy, and scripture. Professionally engaged in ecumenism, she was for twelve years Associate Director of the Commission on Faith and order of the National

Council of the Churches of Christ in the U.S.A., and she worked for ten years for Church Women United. She is one of the founders of the Women's Liturgy Group of New York.

Margaret Moers Wenig serves as rabbi of Beth Am, The People's Temple, and instructor in liturgy and homiletics at the Hebrew Union College–Jewish Institute of Religion, in New York City.

Delores S. Williams is Associate Professor of Theology and Culture at Union Theological Seminary in the City of New York and author of the recently released *Sisters in the Wilderness: The Challenge of Womanist God-Talk.*

Acknowledgments

Grateful acknowledgment is made to the following for permission to reprint copyrighted material:

Confraternity of Christian Doctrine, for excerpts from the *New American Bible*, copyright 1970 by the Confraternity of Christian Doctrine, Washington, D.C. All rights reserved. Used with permission.

GIA Publications, for "Lucha, Poder, Esperanza" and "Profetiza, Pueblo Mío," by Rosa Marta Zárate Macías, from the sound cassette *Profetiza y Cántico de Mujer,* © 1991, GIA Publications, Inc. All rights reserved.

Lynn Gottlieb, for "A Guide to Celebration."

Rick Hamouris, from "We Are a Circle."

Hope Publishing Company, from "Lord, as We Rise to Leave This Shell of Worship," by Fred Kaan. Copyright © 1968 by Hope Publishing Co., Carol Stream, IL 60188. All rights reserved. Used by permission.

International Commission on English in the Liturgy, for the English translation of *Rite of Holy Week* © 1972, International Committee on English in the Liturgy, Inc. (ICEL); and excerpts from the English translation of *The Roman Missal* © 1973, ICEL. All rights reserved.

International Creative Management, Inc., for material from *Beloved,* by Toni Morrison. Copyright © 1987 by Toni Morrison. Published by Alfred A. Knopf, Inc. Reprinted with permission of the author.

Jewish Publication Society, for quotation from *Tanakh, A New Translation of the Holy Scriptures According to the Traditional Hebrew Text*, copyright © 1985 by the Jewish Publication Society.

Diann L. Neu, for "Women of Fire" liturgy and quotations from *Women of Fire: a Pentecost Event*, WATERworks Press, 1990.

Oxford University Press, New York. From "Crone Song," by Anodea Judith, reprinted with permission of author and publisher; and for quotation from Albert J. Raboteau, *Slave Religion*, published 1978.

Pilgrim Press, for "Prayer of Confession for the Nineteenth Sunday After Pentecost," from *Fresh Winds of the Spirit: Liturgical Resources for Year A*, by Lavon Bayler; published in 1986; for "Prayer of Confession for Pentecost," from *Bread for the Journey,* ed. Ruth C. Duck; published in 1981; and for "Prayer of Confession for the Twenty-fourth Sunday After Pentecost," from *Touch Holiness*, by Ruth C. Duck and Maren C. Tirabassi; published 1981.

Introduction

Marjorie Procter-Smith

The women planning and leading the liturgy are students in a Christian seminary. They are graduating seniors, dissatisfied with the traditional ceremonies, who have chosen to make for themselves and any other women students a liturgy that meets their spiritual needs and addresses their questions as they leave seminary for ministry in a church that is often hostile to them. The women and their families and friends sing and laugh and eat together.

The women planning and leading the liturgy are Christian clergywomen. The liturgy follows the final session of their regional denominational meeting. Its purpose is to bless the clergywomen who are leaving the ministry, some by choice, some by coercion from church leaders, some by a combination of both. The women sing and tell their stories, and weep, and embrace one another.

The women planning and leading the ritual are churched and unchurched, ordained and lay, religious and skeptical. The group of forty or so is meeting for the first time, learning to sing and dance together, to weep and rage and celebrate and laugh together.

I participated in these three events within the space of one month. They embody the energy behind this collection of essays: women have spiritual and ritual needs which are not being met by present-day institutional worship, and women are taking action to meet those needs both within established religious settings and apart from them.

The claiming of this ritual authority, this insistence that liturgy is women's work, has motivated what has aptly been called a feminist liturgical movement in Christianity and Judaism. Like the

1

male-dominated liturgical movement that began in the 1830s in Europe and later spread to North American churches, the feminist liturgical movement is concerned with the vitality and authenticity of our worship. But the two movements differ in several important ways, especially in regard to issues of authority. The feminist liturgical movement, in order to legitimate women's ritual authority, always stands in some degree of tension with official church and synagogue authority.

This tension creates both difficulties and possibilities. For women who choose to remain within their religious tradition, there must be constant critique and frequent compromise. The struggle to remain and simultaneously to maintain a critical stance is reflected in the essays of Part 2, "Transforming the Tradition." Such a position requires a kind of "double vision" that enables women to see the truth of their tradition's ritual practices and also to see what that tradition might become.

For many women, the struggle eventually becomes devitalizing, and they choose to step outside, to some degree or another, their inherited tradition. For some this has meant moving into another religious tradition altogether, particularly contemporary feminist reconstructions of ancient Goddess-centered religions. Others have retained much of their religious identity but have rejected the patriarchal authority structures that have limited them as women and have taken the authority to construct a feminist vision of their tradition. From the storehouse of their traditions they have kept certain festivals or other calendrical observances, certain prayer forms, or certain popular devotions. With these remnants they keep their tie to their tradition, but they place them in an entirely new context, one in which women are central, not marginal. These perspectives are represented in Part 3, "Building Anew."

It sometimes seems as if these different approaches—remaining within a patriarchal tradition, rejecting patriarchal authority while claiming traditional identity, or moving to another religious context altogether—are competing options, or that one or another is morally superior. Such is not the case, however. Each position has its struggles and its costs as well as its pleasures and rewards. Nor are they "stages" in women's spiritual lives. Some women do indeed move through them in a progression, while others find themselves moving back and forth among them or even occupying all of them simultaneously.

So perhaps this book is best understood as a kaleidoscope, offering glimpses of a changing scene of women at worship.

However diverse, all the options evidenced in this collection point to one incontrovertible point. Women have spiritual and ritual needs that are not, by and large, being met in traditional Christian or Jewish congregations. Whether and how contemporary congregations will take this lack seriously remains to be seen, even in the midst of modest change to include women. As these essays indicate, women are pushing the discussion beyond questions of the use of inclusive language and the ordination of women to questions of identity: What does it mean to be a Christian or a Jewish woman? Who decides? How do we worship the deity? Who is the one whom we worship? What is the best way to offer worship? Such questions go to the very heart of our religious identity, which is precisely where women wish to be.

Moreover, when women ask such questions, we are not asking abstract philosophical questions or even aesthetic questions so much as ethical questions. The feminist liturgical movement has pointed out the harm that is done to women by the exclusion of women from ordination or by the use of male-dominated language, as well as by patriarchal liturgical structures. The development of feminist liturgies and rituals is often motivated as much by women's need to recover from deep hurt as by anything. Many of the earliest feminist liturgies were healing rituals.

So perhaps this book is best understood as a kind of healing ritual itself, in the naming of pain and the claiming of ritual authority.

The conversations that prompt and are prompted by these liturgies and rituals are ongoing and open-ended. Out of the pivotal questions noted above arise new questions. As more and more women's voices are included, the diversity of women's religious and ritual needs becomes clearer. Many questions remain unanswered, inviting us to live with them as questions a while longer. Such questions include the meaning, form, and content of prayer. What does it mean to pray? And how do we do it so that women and women's experiences are honored? For Christian women, there are questions about the value of Jesus in Christian feminist worship. What is the meaning of a male savior for women? How do traditional interpretations of Jesus' human suffering and death relate to the suffering and death of women from violence in the home and in the world? What is the meaning of Christocentric liturgies for women? These new, tentative questions, as well as the firmer questions regarding ordination and inclusive language, invite us to create a new language, a new liturgical/ritual language.

Perhaps this book is best understood as an introductory grammar to the learning of a new ritual language.

The contributors to this volume offer some of the necessary pieces to such a project, as well as hope for the possibility of its realization. Mary Collins's essay, "Principles of Feminist Liturgy," gets behind the particulars of individual events to consider the principles and strategies that seem to motivate such events and asks critical questions about those principles and strategies. The essays by Margaret Moers Wenig, Annie Ruth Powell, Ruth Duck, Sheila Redmond, and Ann Patrick Ware demonstrate both the difficulty and the promise of critiquing traditional liturgical practices. The authors are not content simply to criticize, however, but offer practical suggestions for change within their traditions.

The essays of Sue Levi Elwell, Diann L. Neu, Patricia Malarcher, and Ada María Isasi-Díaz demonstrate, by means of very particular examples, the possibilities of creating feminist/mujerista liturgies that retain recognizable links with their traditions but push the boundaries of those traditions. Irene Monroe and Wendy Hunter Roberts present examples of the possibilities of creating new traditions from ancient or non-Western sources.

Delores Williams and Eileen King conclude the collection by offering beginning reflections on two questions with which we are living: What is the value of the image of Jesus for Christian feminist worship? And what is feminist prayer? Williams's introduction of the idea of "resistance rituals" can serve as a useful description of where many feminist liturgy groups find themselves on both these questions.

Perhaps this book is best understood as an invitation to the development of "resistance rituals" of all sorts, both within and without established religious traditions. Perhaps this book is all of these—kaleidoscope, healing, grammar, "resistance ritual." Or perhaps it is something that we, the editors, have not yet imagined, something it can only become when you, the reader, pick it up and encounter the ideas and the questions found in it. It is our hope that, whatever else you find here, you will find hope for your religious journey.

PART 1

Feminist Liturgical Principles

General Liturgical
Principles

Principles of
Feminist Liturgy

Mary Collins

The group of thirty-five Catholic men and women had been meeting since Thursday evening. Late Saturday afternoon, as the meeting was about to end and the group to share a meal and then to scatter from coast to coast, an articulate feminist said, "Why don't we have a Eucharist before dinner?" Then she asked the one priest present among the five men, "Would you be willing?" No one voiced objection, although surprised looks were widely exchanged. The group gave itself twenty minutes to organize.

Somebody went looking for a Bible, another for mass texts, another for bread and wine. A few started to arrange the space; others to arrange the ministries. Only then did the question of shared assumptions arise. Decisions were made ad hoc, and the ensuing liturgical action was a study of horizons in tension.

Most, including the priest who had been asked explicitly, assumed that he would pray the eucharistic prayer. Yet not everyone took it for granted, and there were movements within the group to arrange otherwise. But the Irish-American feminist who introduced the idea of celebrating the liturgy declined to voice a eucharistic prayer for the group herself. A Hispanic woman turned aside an invitation, telling the one who approached her that she had not been participating in Eucharist for some time. Another middle-aged woman declined on the grounds that she never led public prayer unless she had time to prepare, and there was no time. In the end, the eucharistic prayer fell to the priest. Voicing an opening prayer was assigned to one woman, the leading of the prayer of the faithful to another, the closing prayer to a third, and the eucharistic prayer to the priest. He asked a fourth woman to cue him, lest he overstep his role. She did so with occasional nods of the head. One dissatisfied organizer, who had herself declined any leadership role, described the three women who had agreed to voice minor prayers as "candlesticks."

Meanwhile the space organizers had placed chairs in an oblong circle. At the center of the open space they placed a low table on which sat a plate with bread and a goblet with wine. In the milling around, reservations were voiced from many quarters about how the liturgy was shaping up, but only one person left. When it was time, people took places randomly, and ministers performed their agreed-upon parts from wherever they sat. The priest who was to voice a eucharistic prayer for the gathering had situated himself in the middle of one of the long arcs of the oblong circle, as close as he could be to the bread and wine while honoring the spatial organization. But he did not handle the plate and cup until the time of the breaking of the bread for Communion, when two women spontaneously stepped out to the table, and the three of them assisted one another in readying the eucharistic food for the group assembled.

When the liturgy was over, no one was particularly satisfied with what they had done together. Still, there was no major blaming or complaining or questioning, and most seemed tacitly pleased that they had given thanks together in Christ's name, even if the ritual action was full of compromises for everyone. Odd occasions such as these are increasingly common among worshipers, whether Christian or Jewish, as feminist consciousness rises within traditional religious communities. What follows is less a reflection on this particular narrative and more a theoretical account of the implicit principles of liturgical order that are in tension whenever feminist consciousness and traditional consciousness meet as they did in the situation described above. These go well beyond what surfaced in that event.

Feminist Consciousness and Feminist Liturgy

Five principles can be identified as basic to intentionally feminist liturgy. First, feminist liturgies ritualize relationships that emancipate and empower women. Second, feminist liturgy is the production of the community of worshipers, not of special experts or authorities. Third, feminist liturgies critique patriarchal liturgies. Fourth, feminist liturgists have begun to develop a distinctive repertoire of ritual symbols and strategies. Fifth, feminist liturgists produce liturgical events, not liturgical texts. Each of these principles can be explored briefly.

Because rituals are about relationships, *the foundational principle of any feminist liturgy is the ritualizing of relationships that emancipate and empower women*. This involves both symbolically negating the patriarchal culture that has denied and actively suppressed women's power or demonized it, and actualizing redeemed and redeeming relationships that allow women to claim their full power as human persons. While many feminist liturgists readily acknowledge that men, too, have been harmed by the disorder of patriarchal culture, there has been little disposition to engage in ritual strategies that give direct attention to men's experience. The feminist hermeneutic for reinterpreting redeemed and redemptive relationships centers on women's experience.

A general theory of feminist interpretation of culture grounded in women's experience has several moments. This general theory also informs feminist ritualizing, and so it must be taken into account here. The first moment in the process is suspicion in approaching all cultural materials, most especially those considered to be a particular culture's highest achievements. This inevitably involves scrutinizing the relational schemes implicit in the religious symbols and institutions of every culture.[1]

The second moment is retrieval of aspects of women's cultural experience of significant relationships that have been forgotten or suppressed or negated in the creation and transmission of culture. The third moment is affirmation of what has been retrieved, both women's achievements and stories of women's suffering exacted as the price of maintaining patriarchal relationships. In this moment

memories of women's suffering are valued; they become "dangerous memories," providing in the recollections of past (and present)
destructiveness a sharp contrast with the anticipated future. The
fourth moment is constructive; women use their power actively,
negating the authority of the past by creating a present and introducing a future that affirms the full humanity of women and the
value and truth of their achievements. In any particular feminist
liturgy, one or more of these "moments" may be ritualized, in a
symbolic exploration of social and religious culture's oppressive
and liberating relationships.

A second principle for feminist liturgy, reflecting the feminist
challenge to patriarchal order, is that *feminist liturgy is effected not
through elites but through the communal interaction of all the members of
intentional groups.* This principle has consequences for the way
feminist liturgy is created. For while the feminist liturgical project
sometimes involves writing or compiling liturgical texts, the major part of the feminist liturgical enterprise is not textually ori-
ented. It more characteristically involves direct feminist ritual
action, affirming, negating, or transforming relationships by symbolically embodying them.

But precisely because feminist ritualizing very seldom gets
turned into text, either before or after it is done, feminist liturgy
as such is less accessible for examination than are traditional liturgies. Left undocumented, as it regularly is, feminist liturgy is also
less accessible for study than are other feminist cultural productions such as poetry, art, theology, or biblical interpretation. On
what database, then, can an investigator establish empirically
what—beyond feminist consciousness itself—are the principles
for feminist liturgy? Observation, participation, anecdotal reports,
self-reporting from feminist liturgists, and a relatively few published theoretical reflections are qualitatively different kinds of
sources; taken together they provide what material there is for
analysis. However, even the most cursory analysis of the available
materials shows the inherently critical nature of feminist liturgy.
This critical intention might be identified as a third principle.

It is beyond question that the feminist liturgical project is critical.
This is true first of all at a general theoretical level. Ritual theorist

Ronald Grimes has argued that all ritual practice is inherently ritual criticism, because each ritual event is an implicit commentary
on all previous performances of a rite within a tradition.[2] So even
when a traditional worshiping community plans an Easter vigil,
for example, or a bar mitzvah, it looks at its past performances and
confirms them or determines to adjust them according to agreed-
upon traditional and pastoral criteria.

But *feminist ritual practice engages in a quite particularly focused critique, setting out as it does to transform patriarchal schemes of redeemed and
redemptive relationships.* Just how the feminist criticism is enacted in
particular rituals is a matter of strategic practice in local settings;
different occasions in different traditions will call for different
strategies. The skill of feminist liturgists, like that of traditional
liturgists, is intimately tied to their general ritual competence and
their skillful use of the relational schemes of the known cultural
traditions with which they are engaging. In this regard another
ritual theorist, Catherine Bell, makes the judgment that any particular ritual practice—whether it is feminist or traditional—is
competent and effective when it enables all the ritual actors to deploy the ritualized relational schemes in settings beyond the rite
itself.

But Bell's theoretical analysis of ritual practice introduces an
additional perspective on the general effectiveness of feminist ritual action. Feminist liturgy intends to empower women spiritually
beyond the rite itself. But as Bell suggests by implication, feminist
liturgy will inevitably be limited by the relative effectiveness of any
and all ritualizing as a form of human practice; it is effective for
those who have faith. Ritual effectiveness is optimal when the
power-laden relational schemes at issue are perceived as grounded
in divine mystery and when they are concerned with constituting
redeemed and redemptive community for the ritual participants.[3]
Women's personhood, spiritual and social identity, authority, cre-
ativity, destiny—not immediate economic or political power—are
the controlling concerns of effective feminist liturgy.

The spiritual acumen of ritual adepts, feminist or traditional, is
learned, but it is learned through doing, so it is not necessarily self-
conscious. Information about "how to do it" cannot simply be

garnered through interview, for example, or through academic studies, for that matter. Catherine Bell argues that practitioners' general "misrecognition" of the nature of all ritual action is one of ritual's characteristic dynamics. At least one implication is that while patterns have emerged that might be identified as feminist, because they are common strategies operative in the many diverse cultural situations where feminists are ritualizing, judging whether or not they are uniquely feminist requires further reflection.

For example, many feminist liturgies attend to healing of traumas, spiritual, emotional, and physical. Feminist communal healings are often worked through exorcistic rites that confront the various cultural embodiments of violence against women and through rites of invocation that affirm wholeness or through some combination of the two. Narrative, touch, incantation, physical movement from one location to another, and the handling of symbols of malevolence and benevolence are familiar forms of feminist ritualizing on such occasions. Yet upon examination it is clearer that these are not distinctively feminist strategies but general ritual strategies.

So in attempting to identify further principles of feminist liturgy, it can be more informative to look at what conventional ritual strategies for embodying relationships feminist ritualizers commonly avoid or reject as antithetical to the feminist project. High on the list of rejected ritual strategies would be working with symbolic forms that are hierarchical, phallocentric, or that set up spirit and matter dualisms. Such strategies are, of course, stock-in-trade for patriarchal liturgies.

Feminists have begun to develop a repertoire of alternative symbolic forms or relational schemes. In feminist ritualizing the actor strategically shapes polycentric forms rather than hierarchical ones, organizing ritual interaction to acknowledge that spiritual power can be found in many places. Feminist ritual action is often deliberately "headless" to affirm that spiritual power and wisdom have been given to all. Feminist liturgists also draw upon women's own experiences of human bodiliness for orienting symbols of relationship; for example, they typically choose forms that gather and enclose. Further, in feminist liturgies dualisms regularly are transformed to circles and spirals and spheres and squares, symbols that embrace multiple energies in tension. These relational strategies operate for feminists at the level of principle, and taken together they constitute a fourth cluster of general tenets approaching normativity in feminist ritual practice.

There is yet another way, related to the second principle discussed above, in which feminist liturgy is distinctive, and that is in the manner of its production. We already noted that *feminist liturgies are generated at the level of practice;* feminists ritualize together. They seldom produce texts that fully script an event or record it; moreover, only occasionally do feminists reflect upon their ritual practice in written form. This way of operating could be either a matter of circumstance or a matter of principle, for it is certainly not necessary. Feminist liturgists are commonly, if not exclusively, women of the middle class. As literate as their male counterparts, they have often been schooled in the historical liturgical traditions that have been producing written texts for fifteen hundred years and more. If texts served their purposes, feminists could publish texts. They seem not to, as a matter of principle.

Of course, the case might be made that this scarcity of texts is merely circumstantial, reflecting the relative novelty of feminist liturgy. In support of this explanation of why texts are so few, the steady publication of a modest number of textual resources for feminist liturgy in recent years might be cited. But something else seems to be operating. In a literate culture where the publication of texts tends to confer authority on those who produce them and on the texts themselves, it is more plausible to interpret feminist liturgists' failure to produce a full corpus of feminist ritual texts as principled, a fifth principle in this series. Women who have been socialized to look elsewhere for authority are learning to look to themselves and to one another, not to expert authors who have the answers.

Yet I can envision circumstances in which what seems now to operate as a principle—oral or informal traditioning—might give way to the production of texts. So the characteristic atextuality of feminist liturgy may be only a strategy and not a principle.

Beyond the five general principles noted briefly here there are, of course, particular tenets peculiar to particular subgroups of feminists, socially located in diverse situations: Jewish feminists and feminist Jews, ecofeminists and feminists reconstituting matriarchal traditions, Christian feminists and feminist Christians, and so on.[4] When feminist groups ritualize from within or at the edges of the Jewish or the Christian liturgical traditions, they often explore in their ritualizing how, as believers who have appropriated feminist consciousness, they might also adhere in a principled way to the central biblical revelations mediated through the androcentric and patriarchal symbols at the heart of their traditions.

These women typically employ in their ritualizing specific strategies that will either reinterpret or subvert the central religious symbols and metaphors of their traditions because these symbols and metaphors legitimate patriarchal relationships. Sometimes, this feminist appropriation of tradition may be done simply and directly, as, for example, by naming women wherever women's names have been omitted in the traditional proclamations of the names of the mediators of the faith. But more subtle and complex situational strategies have emerged as feminist liturgists operating within the traditions of biblical faith have learned to recognize the complexity of androcentric expressions of revelation. As they have analyzed "the Word of God in words of men," they have noted how androcentric symbols and metaphors have biased and narrowed and distorted religious insight. So both Jewish and Christian feminist ritualizers regularly explore strategic ways to redeem the identity of the living God, whom they continue to trust as the source of their empowerment and the world's salvation. The immediacy of feminist ritualizing often ventures ahead of systematic feminist theological reflection on the mystery of God.[5]

Feminists involved in the retrieval of suppressed pre-Christian spiritual traditions, whether Wicca or the ways of the Native American tribes, for example, will also commit themselves in principle to soteriological centers of power believed to be congruent with the presuppositions of feminist consciousness. These distinctive centers of spiritual wisdom and the symbols and myths surrounding them inevitably influence the ways Wiccans and Native Americans ritualize.

Feminist ritual strategies are most likely to be eclectic when feminist groups are not located directly within a shared spiritual tradition or when group members locate themselves within several traditions simultaneously. In such situations feminists may tend to look to ritual traditions beyond their own as well as inward to familiar ritual schemes. Raiding the symbolic treasures of other people's religious traditions, like imperialist raiding of archeological sites for other people's precious artifacts, has been the subject of some ethical reflection among ritualizers recently.[6] Yet because cultural and religious pluralism is a widespread phenomenon, especially in urban areas, feminist ritual explorations of saving relations often affirm and use whatever forms are congruent with feminist consciousness, wherever these might have originated.

Lack of consensus about the generative center of spiritual power and meaning provides an inadequate foundation for ritualizing. Yet even in apparently secular settings, feminist ritualizers may devise rituals to express a mutual mediation of spiritual power. Here the feminist liturgical project often becomes self-generating, celebrating women's spiritual power without any explicit transcendent reference, devising ritual strategies that find depth and meaning and power in women's experience per se.

Yet again, other feminist liturgists may devise situationally strategic rituals that identify technological society itself, the child of patriarchal culture, as the locus of oppressive relationships.[7] Ecofeminist liturgists can then invite ritual actors to relate to the presence of spirit-in-matter in the universe as mediating redeemed and redemptive relationships between humans and the earth or the cosmos that they share. The distinctive principles, both implicit and explicit, informing each of the particular expressions of the feminist liturgical project—Jewish and Christian, mujerista, womanist, Native American, Wiccan, ecofeminist, and so on—are worth a book-length study. But even this brief preliminary discussion of the feminist liturgical project raises a more fundamental question for reflection.

Liturgy or Ritualizing?
On Naming Feminist Ritual Practice

The phrase "feminist liturgy" itself needs to be examined. "Liturgy" is the substantive term and "feminist" the descriptive qualifier. Is this substantive use of "liturgy" the best way of naming what is going on in what I have also referred to as "feminist ritualizing"? When liturgical studies are pursued in the academy, liturgy is commonly explained with reference to the Hellenistic culture in which the word was coined.[8] In that ancient Mediterranean culture, the word named the people's public service, some but not all of which was religious; for example, both road building and the offering of sacrifices were *leitourgia*. Obligatory liturgies served to maintain the good order, sociopolitical and religious, of the cultural community; that good order was patriarchal, to use our contemporary critical categories.[9]

The word "liturgy" entered the vocabulary of biblical religion when the Jewish religious leaders at Alexandria translated the Hebrew Bible into Greek in the second century B.C.E., producing the version known as the Septuagint. The translators judged that the Greek word *leitourgia* was an apt term to name the Jerusalem temple service conducted by the priests.[10] The Jerusalem *leitourgia* of the priests was restricted to male participants. A man took his place within the temple liturgy according to his status in the covenant community; women's place was on the porch outside the holy place. The Jerusalem temple tradition did not challenge the wider culture's sense of good order as patriarchal order. But *leitourgia* in biblical discourse was explicitly religious activity; it did not retain its broader reference to wider forms of the service of public order.

The early Christian community, familiar with the Greek Bible and its use of the word, eventually chose *leitourgia* to name its own public religious services conducted by its ordained clergy. As the eucharistic action of the early church became more formalized, it came to be designated as "the divine liturgy," and Christian women were forbidden access to the altar or surrounding sanctuary reserved for this central liturgy. Classical Christian liturgical order, like both Jewish liturgical order and the Hellenistic liturgical order, was androcentric and patriarchal.

Up to the present, the meaning field for "liturgy," a term in the vocabulary of biblical religion, has consistently evoked a well-ordered, male-dominated religious world. Even where women have taken liturgical leadership, as at the opening of the sabbath in

Judaism, in the liturgy of the hours in a monastery of Catholic nuns, or more recently in the ranks of the ordained in church or synagogue, the ritual work to be done was prescribed by male authorities. Similarly, someone who set out to do liturgical studies, whether in seminary, synagogue, or university, knew that the territory into which she or he was entering was male-centered. Classical liturgical forms and contemporary feminist consciousness are discordant realities.

Given that long history of consistent usage in the vocabulary of Jews and Christians to designate religious worship ordered on patriarchal terms, what are we to think of the recent appropriation of the term "liturgy" to designate an aspect of the feminist project? Feminist liturgy is directed to ritual subversion and transformation of precisely those spiritual and social relational schemes of traditional liturgies that are believed to constitute good order.

But there are other reasons for examining the suitability of the phrase "feminist liturgy" beyond this inherent tension in the phrase itself. First, the feminist liturgical project is bigger than the efforts of Jewish or Christian feminists to engage their own traditions in a critical way. So "liturgy" may say something too narrow. Feminist liturgists include among their number women whose identities have been shaped within other spiritual traditions. When the feminist liturgists are African-American womanists, are Native Americans, or are persons who identify with the pre-Christian tribal peoples who occupied northern Europe beyond the Mediterranean basin, they understand their task to be one of reclaiming and reappropriating—now through emerging new feminist consciousness—indigenous religious rituals long condemned and suppressed by the dominant Christian church in Western culture. Such indigenous peoples, unconnected with Hellenistic culture, never called their own rituals "liturgy," nor were the rites of indigenous peoples in Europe or the Americas so designated by Christian missionaries. (For that matter, even some groups of Protestant Christians have avoided identifying their public worship as "liturgy.")

Yet that is not the whole picture. As we have already noted, there are feminist liturgists who may be unconnected with either

biblical or indigenous Western spiritual traditions; many are nontheist in their self-understanding. Some ecofeminist liturgists, for
example, may be ritualizing a nontheist consciousness of oneness
within the universe, a spiritual consciousness emerging in resistance to Western technological culture that exploits the nonhu-
man world.

By using "liturgy" to designate all communal ritual activity
performed with a feminist consciousness, feminists have torn—
liberated?—the word from its traditional field of meaning. A feminist liturgy is as likely to ritualize human connectedness to the
Great Mother or the Great Spirit, to Sophia or the spirit of the
universe, as to the ineffable Holy One of Israel or to the Risen
Christ. Feminist liturgy aims to explore and celebrate a new order
of ultimate relationships, one that is saving or redemptive for
women insofar as it heals the destructive disorder wrought by patriarchal consciousness. It intends to go beyond androcentrism toward
inclusiveness and wholeness. Not surprisingly, many classical liturgical authorities, who know clearly that their own liturgical traditions assert male dominance, are apt to pronounce negative
judgments on this feminist liturgical project. They call its contrast-
ing relational schemes "pagan" or "idolatrous" or "heretical," because feminists refuse to cede ultimacy to the male-centered
religious cosmos that such traditional authorities have pro-
nounced ultimate.

But there is a second reason for pausing to examine the suitability of appropriating the word "liturgy" to name the project of
feminist ritualizing, even when such liturgies arise from within
communities confessing biblical faith. Feminist consciousness is
antithetical to the normative tradition of ritual worship to which
"liturgy" refers. When Christians or Jews take up the feminist
liturgical project, they regularly critique the normative liturgical
traditions of church or synagogue from their standpoint as insiders
precisely by introducing the norm of feminist consciousness.
They imagine and explore possibilities of ultimacy that are as yet
unknown in the authoritative worldviews of their own traditions.
The normative salvation narratives and the communal patterns of
traditional Judaism and Christianity alike categorically affirm that

salvation is mediated through chosen males divinely favored; all others are the beneficiaries of their religious mediations and subject to their authority.

The tension between traditional liturgy and the feminist liturgical project is dialectical. Feminists subvert the authority of the tradition by refusing to be devotees of classic liturgical order where men are regents of the divine. Feminist liturgies within the Jewish and Christian traditions locate women where women never were: at the center of things or at the head of things. Or they decenter spiritual power altogether, celebrating its presence throughout a community. At times they use as mediating symbols of divine mystery forms that the patriarchal traditions viewed as "unclean," for example, the blood of the covenant is juxtaposed with menstrual blood; lesbian friendship symbolizes saving communion.

Such reinterpretations of the normative traditions are not groundless or mindless. Both intuitive and systematic reflection on the received traditions of biblical faith precedes and accompanies most Jewish or Christian feminist liturgical celebration.[11] Feminist theological critique ordinarily (but not always) derives its authority from data already available within the particular tradition. These data may be doctrines, symbols, narratives, and practices that have gone unexamined under the weight of naive androcentrism or been actively suppressed in the interests of the official liturgical order. But even when the criteria Jewish and Christian feminists use to evaluate liturgical authenticity are internal criteria—themes found within their own religious traditions—their use rests upon a prior transformation of the critic's consciousness from androcentrism to feminism. The authoritative horizon of feminist liturgy is not the horizon of the spiritual universe that has borne the name "liturgy" up to the present.

A third and further problem confronts the feminist use of the term "liturgy." Does it perhaps claim too much for the constructive ritual work of feminists? Classical liturgies have been associated with orders of relationships that are understood to be authoritative, express ultimate truth, and mediate salvation. Classical liturgical orders celebrate a "right way" of being and doing, a way understood to be in harmony with a divinely revealed design. But little beyond the feminist assumptions of the feminist ritual project immediately involves claims of universal normativity; feminist liturgical activity is typically exploratory, local, and occasional. Having introduced these three reservations about the "fit" between the word "liturgy" and the feminist project—"feminist liturgy" is too narrow, it is oxymoronic or antithetical, it claims too much—I will look at another explanatory frame for speaking about what is happening in this realm of feminist practice. Earlier, I used the phrase "feminist ritualizing" alternately with "feminist liturgy." A further consideration of the category of ritualizing is in order.

As a historian of religions and a ritual theorist, Catherine Bell has proposed that the human behavior of ritualizing is more fundamental than any particular liturgical or cultural systems such ritualizing might generate.[12] She argues that communal ritualizing, and especially that ritual which is explicitly religious—in whatever milieu it occurs, traditional or not—is an active negotiation, construction, and production of relationships that both empower and set limits. What ritualizers are doing in their ritualizing through symbolic transactions is producing relationships that are redeemed and redemptive for those participating in the ritualizing. So ritualizing is always strategic situational practice, grounded in a community of shared faith.

Ritualizers who are recognized as "adepts," or experts, enjoy their competence only with others who share a common culture. In a shared context of meaning, ritualizers take known relational schemes and strategically rearrange them. They give nuance to one element, privilege another, transform the whole; in doing so they effectively display the redemptive schemes by actually embodying them in the course of the ritual experience. This doing or enacting the schemes effectively impresses them on all the ritualizers so that the participants are able to deploy the redeemed relational schemes in appropriate settings beyond the circumstances of the rite itself.[13]

Bell's analysis of all ritualizing as strategic and situational generates a theory that applies equally to the workings of the classical liturgical traditions and to the workings of feminists. Consider first the ritual practice of the classical traditions, Jewish and Christian. Traditionalist ritualizers within a synagogue or a church setting might employ strategies that produce a sense of cultural stasis, but, as Bell argues, these liturgies identified as "traditional" are contemporary strategic productions nonetheless, as contemporary as this week's service. Such practitioners within a tradition use ritual strategies that "produce the past in such a way as to maximize its dominance of the present," to borrow Bell's phrase.[14]

But other competent ritualizers within the same classic liturgical traditions, Jewish or Christian, have long made use of alternate ritual strategies to produce other versions of the relative authority of past and present.[15] They are as adept at authoring and authorizing change in communal relationships through ritual performance as are their coreligionists in serving stasis. Their strategic productions constitute another version of tradition. But up to the present generation, the liturgical traditions, whether in their static or dynamic forms, have operated with androcentric presuppositions. Jewish and Christian liturgy alike have posited a shared culture of male dominance.

Looked at within Catherine Bell's explanatory frame, all feminist ritualizing is also situational and strategic. Yet because the social location of feminists is diverse, this diversity introduces complexity into the feminist ritual project. Middle-class feminists are to be found ritualizing in relationship to synagogue and church; poor women of color may reframe their middle-class sisters' versions of women's experience of biblical faith. But many feminists ritualize outside the cultural frames of biblical faith altogether, as we noted earlier.

Whatever their social location, feminist ritualizers sometimes use, as part of their strategic practice, the negating of every cultural frame, since the cultures in which women find themselves have all served to empower men and disempower women. Not surprisingly, such feminist ritual practice can appear to be formless to eyes attuned to classical liturgical forms and aesthetics. Introducing the explanatory category of "ritualizing" helps to sharpen the perception that the feminist project is not contained within the classical liturgical project, even when some feminist liturgists are engaged in their ritualizing within one of the historical liturgical traditions. The ritual workings of feminists are strategic productions expressing an emerging new consciousness, a consciousness not to be found in any existing liturgical order. The terms has its limits, however. "Ritualizing" is used in social science discourse to name a broad range of styled and repetitive human behaviors, both communal and private, many tied to the mundane and daily, some even pathological. Moreover, even when social scientists examine overtly religious rituals, they tend to disqualify themselves from discussions of ultimacy, whereas much feminist ritualizing commonly intends no less than that. Given the intentions of social scientists like Ronald Grimes and Catherine Bell in their discourse about ritual and ritualizing, the emergence of the word "liturgy" in many circles to name feminist ritual practice may better convey feminist self-understanding. What most feminist liturgists are about is spiritual, cosmological, theological in its intent.

The available vocabulary, whether "liturgy" or "ritualizing," is not fully adequate to the task of naming the feminist ritual project, since liturgical traditions and feminist consciousness exist in tension. Whether the inherent tension will generate conversion within the historical religious traditions and, more profoundly, create new possibility for life on the planet it is premature to judge. Meanwhile, wherever feminist consciousness is emerging, people are gathering to explore ritually and then to embody fully a future of relationships different from what has long been believed to be the truth of things.

Notes

1. Marjorie Procter-Smith's *In Her Own Rite* (Nashville: Abingdon Press, 1990) offers a sustained feminist look at Christian liturgical materials; Lawrence Hoffman's "How Ritual Means: Ritual Circumcision in Classical Rabbinic Culture" (*Studia Liturgica*, Spring, 1992) examines a central covenanting rite from a feminist perspective; for an analysis of the rhetoric of the

Roman Catholic rite of ordination, see my "The Public Language of Ministry" in *The Jurist* 41:2 (1981), pp. 261–94.

2. Ronald Grimes, *Ritual Criticism* (Columbia: University of South Carolina Press, 1990).

3. Catherine Bell, *Ritual Theory, Ritual Practice* (New York: Oxford University Press, 1992), p. 116.

4. Sandra Schneiders suggests such distinctions in *Beyond Patching* (New York: Paulist Press, 1991) when she argues that "feminist Catholics" and "Catholic feminists" have quantitatively different investments in the feminist project; pp. 96–110.

5. See Elizabeth Johnson's *She Who Is: The Mystery of God in Feminist Theological Discourse* (New York: Crossroad, 1992) for a feminist systematic theology of the Christian doctrine of God. Calls for inclusive language to address God in public prayer and the composition of inclusive-language prayers began to press the Christian doctrinal tradition two decades earlier.

6. See Grimes's *Ritual Criticism* for an account of the ethical discussion.

7. Rosemary Radford Ruether's *Gaia and God: An Ecofeminist Theology of Earth Healing* (San Francisco: HarperCollins, 1992) offers an explication of this aspect of emerging feminist consciousness.

8. "Liturgy," M. Collins, in *The New Dictionary of Theology*, ed. J. Komonchak, M. Collins, and D. Lane (Wilmington, Del.: Michael Glazier, 1987), pp. 591–92.

9. Gerda Lerner, *The Creation of Patriarchy* (New York: Oxford University Press, 1986), introduction.

10. "Liturgy," I. H. Dalmais, in *Encyclopedia of the Early Church*, Vol. I (New York: Oxford University Press, 1992), p. 494.

11. See, for example, Rosemary Radford Ruether's *Women-Church: Theology and Practice of Feminist Liturgical Communities* (San Francisco: Harper & Row, 1985); also Penina V. Adelman's *Miriam's Well: Rituals for Jewish Women Around the Year* (Fresh Meadows, N.Y.: Biblio Press, 1986); *WATER*, the newsletter of the Women's Alliance for Theology, Ethics and Ritual, in Silver Spring, Md.; Judith Plaskow's *Standing Again at Sinai: Judaism from a Feminist Perspective* (San Francisco: HarperCollins, 1990).

12. Bell, *Ritual Theory, Ritual Practice*, pp. 81–92.

13. Ibid., pp. 108, 114–17.

14. Ibid., p. 123.

15. See Barbara Myerhoff's account of the "traditionalizing" of contemporary events among a community of elderly Jewish men and women in *Number Our Days* (New York: E. P. Dutton, 1979).

PART 2

Transforming the Tradition:
Critique and Commentary
on Traditional Worship

Feminists who choose to remain within patriarchal religious traditions are sometimes seen as choosing an easier path, the path of accommodation, and are seen as being somehow less radical than women who have chosen to separate from established religions. But as the contributors to this part show, this is an erroneous assumption. The decision to challenge the patriarchy of Christianity or Judaism from within requires a rare kind of courage: the courage to see what is harmful as well as what is good, and the courage to face misunderstanding, accusation, and rejection from representatives of a community that is still beloved.

Margaret Moers Wenig exemplifies this courage in her survey of the positive ways in which Reform Judaism has responded to the concerns of women as well as deeper questions now being raised by Jewish women regarding the authority of Torah, the meaning of Israel, and the naming of God. Similarly, Annie Powell describes lovingly both what African-American Protestant worship is, in her experience, as well as what it might be.

Ruth Duck and Sheila Redmond consider particular aspects of North American free-church Protestant worship: prayers of confession and a Mother's Day sermon, respectively. Both essays focus on the harm done to women by certain liturgical practices that are common in contemporary Protestantism, and both propose possibilities for change.

Traditional understandings of sin and grace have been critiqued by Valerie Saiving and Judith Plaskow, who argued, in studies that are now considered classics in feminist theology, that these definitions failed to reflect the experiences of women. But these analyses never have influenced Christian worship. In light of Plaskow's and Saiving's work, updated now by Rosemary Radford Ruether, Ruth Duck examines prayers of confession as used in Protestant free-church worship for their assumptions about sin and grace, drawing out the theological messages about sin and grace often encoded in such prayers, and how they tend to be heard by men and women.

Sheila Redmond invites us to view Mother's Day from the perspective of those who suffer violence and abuse in the home. North American Protestantism recognizes Mother's Day as one of the major celebrations in most churches, attendance being exceeded only on Easter Sunday (if then). Our current observances of Mother's Day, with easy sentimentalizing of mothers and perhaps, if the minister is very daring, a sermon that suggests that God might be like a mother, are very far from the original purpose of the day: Julia Ward Howe introduced Mother's Day in 1870 in order to issue a call for peace and to reject war. "The sword of murder is not the balance of justice," the proclamation reads in part. "Blood does not wipe out dishonor nor violence indicate possession." This is deeply ironic, considering how many women and children live in a state of war in their own homes, subject to violence and abuse.

Redmond examines a particular Mother's Day service in light of this violence with which millions of women and children live. By focusing our attention on the sermon she demonstrates the denial that surrounds the issue of violence against women, and the way in which this denial is often cloaked in sentimentalizing and glorifying praise of motherhood.

Ann Patrick Ware's essay on the Easter Vigil of the Roman Catholic Church concludes this section. The Roman Catholic Church, in the wake of the liturgical changes introduced by the Second Vatican Council, reformed the Great Vigil of Easter to restore practices more nearly like those in the ancient church. This elaborate and powerful liturgy has been adapted widely within Protestantism, and thus Ware's essay, while focusing on the practice in the Roman church, has implications for others as well. Also, Ware exemplifies the dual vision necessary for women who continue to worship within the established religious traditions. Without denying the power and beauty of the service, she draws our attention to both the marginalizing and the devaluing of women that are deeply imbedded in the liturgy, running as a kind of ominous ground-note against which the melody of the rite plays.

2

Reform Jewish Worship:
How Shall We Speak of
Torah, Israel, and God?

Margaret Moers Wenig

In the past twenty years, Reform Jewish liturgists and worship leaders have responded to concerns of women in a number of significant ways: the ordination of women, ritual naming of daughters, words and songs by women, language about women.

The ordination of women.   The year 1992 marked the twentieth anniversary of the ordination of women in the Reform movement. More than any change in the *text* of our liturgies, this change has had a profound effect upon the nature of our worship. For every time a female rabbi leads worship or preaches, her very presence communicates that women too have inherited the authority to interpret and shape our ever-evolving tradition. That the very presence of women in the rabbinate has, in a single generation, transformed worshipers' perceptions is testified to by an oft-told story: Children reared in congregations served only by a female rabbi have said, upon encountering a male rabbi for the first time, "I didn't know that men could be rabbis!" Liturgical leadership is now open to women. Many other changes have coincided with or resulted from this fundamental change.

The ritual naming of newborn daughters.   Twenty years ago daughters born to Reform Jewish parents were rarely, if ever, publicly named and welcomed into the covenant.[1] Sons, however, were named and initiated through the rite of ritual circumcision.[2] The past twenty years have seen the increasing popularity of covenant-initiation ceremonies for daughters. These are performed at home (like a ceremony of circumcision) or in the synagogue during regular Sabbath worship. Homegrown liturgies are often prepared by the rabbi and parents together. The 1988 edition of the *Rabbi's Manual* of the Central Conference of American Rabbis contains the first official "Covenant Service for a Daughter," designed to be parallel to the ceremony for a son.[3] The current popularity of such rites expresses the belief that the birth of a daughter is as worthy of celebration as the birth of a son, and that a daughter is as much a member of the Jewish people's covenant with God as are her brothers.

The incorporation of women's words and songs in the official liturgies of the reform movement. Both our daily, Sabbath, and festival prayer book, the *Gates of Prayer* (1975), and our prayer book for the Days of Awe, the *Gates of Repentance* (1978), contain prayers, poems, and songs composed by women. The first contains thirteen pieces by eight different women.[4] The second contains eight pieces by seven different women.[5] While women's words make up a small minority of the thousands of words in these liturgies, nonetheless, that *any* words by women appear at all is new and communicates that women's words are now considered worthy prayers for the community gathered for worship.[6]

Inclusive language. In the official liturgies of the Reform movement, and in ad hoc practice by rabbis, cantors, and lay leaders, the oft-occurring Hebrew word meaning "our fathers" is now routinely translated as "our ancestors" or "our mothers and fathers." The names of the matriarchs Sarah, Rebecca, Rachel, and Leah have been added in the English alongside the names of the patriarchs in two of the ten Shabbat evening and one of the six Shabbat morning services in the *Gates of Prayer*. In practice, many worship leaders add the matriarchs' names aloud (in English as well as in the Hebrew[7]) even when they do not appear on the printed page. This practice acknowledges that some women played a role in the formative period of our people's history.

Moreover, in recent years nouns and pronouns for God have been changed from masculine ones to neutral ones to make manifest the belief that women, as well as men, are created in God's image. Though inclusive language for God is not used throughout the *Gates of Prayer* and the *Gates of Repentance*, it is used in the translation of the Torah reading for Rosh Hashanah morning (service II). The traditional translation, "And God created man in His image, in the image of God He created him. Male and female He created them," has been revised to read, "God created us in the divine image, creating us in the image of God."

Following the publication of the *Gates of Repentance*, the liturgy committee of the Central Conference of American Rabbis committed itself to using inclusive language for God.[8]

1972–1992: A Critique

One ought not minimize the extent to which the mainstream of the Reform movement has gone in the past twenty years to respond to concerns of women: women now appear in roles of liturgical leadership; the sound of women's voices and the very words of women are heard in synagogue worship; women are acknowledged to be created, along with men, in the image of God and to be party, along with men, to the covenant with God.

Nonetheless, the mainstream of the Reform movement has not yet fully "heard" women's voices or given them full authority in worship. From the periphery of the movement, women can be heard asking fundamental questions that have serious liturgical implications: What is Torah (revelation)? Who is Israel? and How shall we speak of God?[9]

What is Torah? The reading of Torah is central to our worship. It requires special skills. It is preceded and followed by blessings. Honor is shown to the scroll of the Torah through special handling, special coverings and ornaments. In some congregations the scroll is carried through the congregation while members reach out and kiss it and, after the reading, it is elevated as the congregation stands and sings, "This is the Torah which Moses placed before the people of Israel to fulfill the word of God."[10]

What is Torah that it merits such honor? Is Torah the very word of God? For Reform Jews, the answer is no. Despite the fact that we chant "Baruch ata Adonai . . . v'natan lanu et Torato" (Blessed are You, Adonai . . . who gave us his Torah), most Reform Jews do not believe that God gave us the words of the Torah. According to the *Centenary Perspective* of the Central Conference of American Rabbis, Torah is the "earliest record of our people's encounter with God" rather than the very words of God.

It is this liberal understanding of Torah that has given us license to eliminate from our religious practice regulations that hurt women, such as requiring a rapist to marry his victim or prohibiting a woman from initiating a divorce.

Reform Jews don't consider those regulations to be God's will. Reform Jews consider them to be a reflection of the morality of their ancient Near Eastern world. So we don't enforce them and often don't even read them aloud when they occur in the weekly lectionary. To do so denigrates women.

Nonetheless, Reform Jews still read aloud, as part of the lectionary, *narrative* portions of Torah that hurt women, such as stories in which

—the heroically hospitable Lot offers his daughters to an angry mob intent on rape, to protect his male guests[11]
—a father is rewarded for nearly killing his wife's only son[12]
—women are desperate to conceive, yet when they do, their names are excluded from their sons' genealogies[13]

Such passages hurt both women and men.

Moreover, some women are murmuring, the *Centenary Perspective*'s definition of Torah is misleading. The Torah is not "the record of our people's earliest encounters with God." The Torah is the record of half of our people's earliest encounters with God: the male half. The Torah, and therefore the synagogue lectionary based upon the Torah, is woefully partial. It leaves out, it relegates to oblivion, the history, the perspectives, the earliest encounters with God of the female half of our people.

Following these earliest encounters, how have later women fared in the accumulated corpus or canon of sacred writ? The *Centenary Perspective* says of Torah:

> Rabbis and teachers, philosophers and mystics, gifted Jews in every age amplified the Torah tradition. For millennia the creation of Torah has not ceased and Jewish creativity in our own time is adding to the chain of tradition.

The teaching of women, however, is rarely added to that chain. In Jewish liturgy, readings from the prophets and the study of passages from Mishnah and Talmud are preceded by special blessings. Before the readings from the prophets we thank God for giving us prophets; before reading the Mishnah and Talmud[14] we acknowledge the One "who commands us to study words of Torah." A professor of modern Jewish thought at Hebrew Union College–Jewish Institute of Religion[15] even prefaces each of his classes with that blessing as if to say, "even the words of Leo Baeck, Abraham Heschel, and Martin Buber are words of Torah." Yet, rare is the synagogue in which one will hear words of women preceded by either of these blessings. Women's words do appear among the official prayers of the movement, but not as part of its liturgical canon, of sacred scripture, of Torah. Women may address God, but their encounters with God are not yet considered worthy of ritual reading.[16]

Who is Israel? Jewish worship defines the worshiping community mythically, historically, and culturally. Mythically the worshiping community is descended from Abraham, was enslaved in Egypt, and was redeemed from slavery to enter into a covenant with God at Sinai and to possess the land God promised to them. That definition is manifest in the reading of the biblical narratives that recount those events, in daily prayers that identify the God we worship as the God "of our fathers, God of Abraham, God of Isaac, God of Jacob," and in daily prayers that recall the exodus.

Historically, the worshiping community is a people that survived the Holocaust and found new life on the soil of its ancient land. That definition is manifest in the annual Holocaust Remembrance Day and Israeli Independence Day observances and in the Reform movement's Yom Kippur afternoon service "From Creation to Redemption" in *Gates of Repentance*.[17]

Culturally, most Reform Jews define themselves as Ashkenazim. This self-definition is manifest in styles of liturgical music[18] and in the language used for preaching and for translations of Hebrew texts.

Some women are increasingly dissatisfied with limiting our definition of the worshiping community to the mythic, historical, and cultural understandings of Israel. They argue that the worshiping community is also a community of men, women, and children, Jews and even non-Jews, who lead routine daily lives, struggling with jobs, families, and bodily existence. The official liturgies of the Reform movement insufficiently reflect those realities. For example:

1. In the prayer for the new month, inserted in the service for the reading of the Torah on the Sabbath prior to each new month, the petition for *parnassah* (livelihood) was eliminated by the editors of the *Gates of Prayer*.[19] In times like ours, when some members of our congregations are losing their jobs, when some elderly find their pensions provide insufficient support, when some disabled young and middle-aged women and men are unable to find work, the petition for livelihood bears inclusion. Such an addition arises not so much out of a belief that God will provide jobs for people but in order to acknowledge their presence in our midst.

2. The editors of the *Gates of Prayer* also eliminated the prayer for the sick from the supplements to the service for the reading of the Torah. In practice, many rabbis recite a prayer for the sick borrowed from another movement's prayer book. However, its absence from our own prayer book gives the false impression that our worshiping community does not include people who are ill or those who care for them.

These two specific examples illustrate a general problem in the definition of Israel as reflected in our worship. Our worship defines us mythically, historically, and culturally, but it disregards our bodies. Our bodies play a significant role in shaping our identities as individuals,[20] yet we are asked to leave our bodies at the door when we enter the synagogue to worship as part of the community of Israel. Reform worship ignores the body when it permits little movement other than sitting and standing on command. Reform worship ignores the body when it fails to acknowledge experiences such as menarche and menopause, sexual abuse, or rape. Reform worship ignores the body when it presumes that all worshipers are heterosexual, fertile, and able-bodied.

Only a few mainstream Reform congregations acknowledge the presence of lesbian and gay worshipers by celebrating Lesbian and Gay Pride Sabbath, by naming the children of lesbian and gay couples in the synagogue, by consecrating the unions of lesbian and gay couples, by honoring lesbian and gay couples with *aliyot* to the Torah.[21]

Only a few mainstream Reform congregations provide sign language interpretation or assistive listening devices for hearing-impaired worshipers. Some sanctuaries are accessible to those in wheelchairs. Some offer large-print prayer books for the visually impaired. But for the most part, Reform worship is accessible only to the fully able-bodied.[22]

Some women are attempting to rectify the disembodied nature of most Reform worship by composing blessings for menarche, laments for rape, and rituals following miscarriage and abortion and by incorporating more gesture and dance in regular worship:

—As a master's thesis, Cantor Karen Webber choreographed a dance for the portion of the *Gates of Repentance* titled "From Creation to Redemption."

—Many rabbinic students at the New York campus of Hebrew Union College–Jewish Institute of Religion now enroll in an elective course, Dance Midrash.

—In the New York area, a Jewish liturgical dance company, the Avodah Dance Troupe, has danced in a number of Reform congregations.

—In one congregation the liturgical canon of "prophetic" readings is expanded to include a passage, from Toni Morrison's *Beloved*, that celebrates the body and acknowledges the need for bodily freedom:[23]

"Here," she said, "in this place, we flesh: flesh that weeps, laughs; flesh that dances on bare feet in grass. Love it. Love it hard. Yonder they do not love your flesh. They despise it. They don't love your eyes; they'd just as soon pick em out. No more do they love the skin on your back. Yonder they flay it. And O my people they do not love your hands. Those they only use, tie, bind, chop off and leave empty. Love your hands! Love them. Raise them up and kiss them. Touch others with them, pat them together, stroke them on your face 'cause they don't love that either. . . . This is flesh I'm talking about here. Flesh that needs to be loved. Feet that need to rest and to dance; backs that need support; shoulders that need arms, strong arms I'm telling you. And O my people, out yonder, hear me, they do not love your neck unnoosed and straight. So love your neck; put a hand on it, grace it, stroke it and hold it up. And all your inside parts that they'd just as soon slop for hogs, you got to love them. The dark, dark liver . . . and the beat and beating heart. . . . Hear me now, love your heart. For this is the prize." Saying no more, she stood up then and danced with her twisted hip the rest of what her heart had to say while the others opened their mouths and gave her the music. Long notes held until the four-part harmony was perfect enough for their deeply loved flesh.[24]

How shall we speak of God? In 1992, the Central Conference of American Rabbis published *Gates of Prayer for Shabbat: A Gender Sensitive Prayerbook*, the first Sabbath liturgy for the Reform movement to use "inclusive language" for God. The editor offers it as a contribution toward the reshaping of the "language of our liturgy so that it will reflect our view that masculine language and exclusively male assumptions [about God] ought to give way to a broader, more inclusive expression."[25]

For some, however, calling God "Source of mercy, Fountain of life, Eternal One, Divine Presence, Teacher, and Friend" is not yet inclusive enough. At worst, even though the liturgy now uses "Eternal One" for "Lord" and "Ruler" for "King," people still *think* of God as male. Why else would many still scream "Idolatry!" when a *female* image for God is used? Eliminating masculine pronouns and names for God does not eliminate people's well-established masculine *associations* with the word "God." As a five-year-old girl put it, "'God' is [still] a boy's name."

At best, gender-neutral language, while removing a barrier to women's identification with God, does not encourage either girls or boys, women or men, to see themselves in God's image. For we are not gender-neutral. We are male or female. For this reason, many see the new gender-sensitive prayer book as only an interim step toward a Reform liturgy that will one day be inclusive enough to include feminine as well as masculine metaphors for God.

In twenty years, Reform Jews have learned how *not* to speak of God. We have only begun to find the words to speak of God in a new way. We need not only new *names* for God but also richly developed metaphors and stories, narratives about God that we can read liturgically over the course of many weeks, year after year. We need narratives that will give "God of our mothers" as much resonance as "God of our fathers," narratives that will give "Our Mother" as much resonance as "Our Father." Rather than eliminating anthropomorphic metaphors for God, some women argue, we need more of them. For these are the metaphors "that come from a place deep within human experience."[26] These are the metaphors that enable us to speak of the complex dynamics of relationship: of loyalty and betrayal, love and loss, presence and absence, offense and forgiveness, separation and reunion.[27]

Moreover, while we need metaphors and stories that express the dignity and power of women and men, we also need metaphors and stories that acknowledge our lack of power. For though we are created in God's image, we are not God. How we speak of God and our relationship with God will communicate not only how inclusive we can be of women but also how honest we can be about life and death.

Conclusion

In the past twenty years, the official, published liturgies of the Reform movement have consciously attempted to be more inclusive of women: ordaining women as clergy, initiating newborn daughters into the Covenant, including prayers and songs by women, referring to the matriarchs and removing masculine pronouns and names for God. The movement now must struggle to incorporate women's newly emerging understandings of Torah, Israel, and God.

Notes

1. Two of the earliest published liturgies marking the birth of a daughter appeared in 1973. "On the Birth of a Daughter," by Daniel and Myra Leifer, and "B'rit B'not Israel: Observations on Women and Reconstructionism," by Sandy Eisenberg Sasso, in *Response*, Number 18, Summer 1973.

2. I do not know what percentage of Reform Jewish parents actually observed the rite of ritual circumcision. Nonetheless it was a part of official Reform Jewish practice and appeared as "Service at Circumcision" in the 1961 *Rabbi's Manual* published by the Central Conference of American Rabbis.

3. Even the titles of the two ceremonies are parallel: "Hachnasat ben l'vrit / Covenant Service for a Son" and "Hachnasat bat l'vrit / Covenant Service for a Daughter."

4. The notes to *Gates of Prayer*, found in the companion volume *Gates of Understanding*, credit Molly Cone, Hannah Senesh, Nelly Sachs, Kathleen Raine, Elizabeth Barrett Browning, Muriel Rukeyser, Alas Lukas, and Katharine Lee Bates (for "America the Beautiful"). The acknowledgments at the beginning of *Gates of Prayer* indicate that poems by Amy Blank and Denise Levertov were also included. I cannot find them in the notes, however.

5. Using the notes to *Gates of Repentance*, in the companion volume *Gates of Understanding II*, I have found contributions from Joanne Greenberg, Ruth Brin, Mollie Golomb, Edith Sitwell, Madame Blavatsky, and Katharine Lee Bates (for "America the Beautiful").

6. Of course, since the sources of the prayers in these published liturgies appear as notes in separate volumes, a worshiper would have to *recognize* that a given poem or prayer was the work of a woman in order to appreciate the significance of its inclusion.

7. In 1992 *Gates of Prayer for Shabbat: A Gender Sensitive Prayerbook*,

edited by Chaim Stern (New York: Central Conference of American Rabbis, 1992), became the first official publication of the Central Conference of American Rabbis to include the names of the matriarchs alongside the names of the patriarchs *in the Hebrew*.

8. See Herbert Bronstein, ed., *A Passover Haggadah* (New York: Central Conference of American Rabbis, 1974); for Chanukah, Elyse D. Frishman, ed., *Hanerot Hallalu* (New York: Central Conference of American Rabbis, 1989); and *Gates of Prayer for Shabbat: A Gender Sensitive Prayerbook*, 1992.

9. The most thorough presentation of these challenges can be found in Judith Plaskow's *Standing Again at Sinai: Judaism from a Feminist Perspective* (San Francisco: HarperCollins, 1990).

10. *Gates of Prayer*, p. 439.

11. Genesis 19:8.

12. Genesis 22.

13. Genesis 25:19.

14. From the second and fourth or fifth centuries respectively.

15. Dr. Eugene B. Borowitz.

16. I myself know of only two Reform congregations in which the lectionary is expanded to include modern *haftarot* (prophetic readings), including writings by women: Beth Am in New York City and Congregation Sha'ar Zahav in San Francisco. At Beth Am, the custom of reading modern *haftarot* was suggested in 1985, by then president Judah Rosenfeld, who said he borrowed the idea from the Reconstructionist movement.

17. *Gates of Repentance*, pp. 410–49.

18. Western European art music, North American folk music, and the recently revived Eastern and Western European cantorial tradition and prayer modes.

19. *Gates of Prayer*, p. 453, omits the word *parnassah* (livelihood), though alludes to it in translation, with the petition "May we have long life, a life of peace, prosperity, and health."

20. Consider the title of a book canonized by the women's movement: *Our Bodies, Ourselves*.

21. An *aliyah* is the honor of being called up to recite the blessings before and after the reading of the Torah. Many synagogues give this honor to (straight) couples (as well as to individuals).

22. Bruce Black, "Jews with Disabilities," *Reform Judaism* 21, no. 1 (Fall 1992), pp. 4–8, 48, 49.

23. At Beth Am, in New York City, this modern *haftarah* is read every year on Shabbat Shira when Exodus 15:20, in which Miriam leads the recently freed Israelite slaves in song and dance, is read from the Torah.

24. Toni Morrison, *Beloved* (New York: Alfred A.Knopf, 1987), pp. 87–89.

25. *Gates of Prayer*, p. v.

26. Sally McFague, *Models of God: Theology for an Ecological, Nuclear Age* (Philadelphia: Fortress Press, 1988), p. 80.

27. My own extended description of God, "God Is a Woman and She Is Growing Older," was an attempt at just such a narrative. It was published in *Reform Judaism* 21, no. 1 (Fall 1992), pp. 26–28, 44, 45, and has been used liturgically in synagogues around the country.

3

Hold On to Your Dream: African-American Protestant Worship

Annie Ruth Powell

Wilma Rudolph, an African-American woman, contracted pneumonia and scarlet fever as a child, which left her crippled. Rudolph's greatest dream was to walk. In fact, so strong was her desire to walk that she often "felt" as if she were walking, running and playing with the other children as she watched them play from her front porch.

Rudolph's family members were "dream-makers." They offered her the utmost encouragement to pursue her dream to walk. Her brothers massaged her legs; her mother traveled a hundred miles to take her to the doctor. Rudolph's family never let her feel as though her physical impairment was burdensome to them. Their loving attitude provided an environment conducive to healing.

With the help of her dream-makers, Rudolph's dream became a reality. At eight years old, she could stand; at twelve, she could walk, run, and even play basketball with her brothers. Later, she became the first woman to win Olympic gold medals for the hundred-yard dash, the two-hundred-yard dash, and the four-hundred-yard relay race. A triumph for an African-American woman!

"Hold on to your dream," urged Rev. Gloria Bennett, guest preacher at St. Mark Church. The community understood what she meant. They had witnessed the fulfillment of dreams like

Wilma Rudolph's. In fact, their new church building itself was the realization of a dream.

St. Mark Church was organized in 1828 by a group of former slaves. In 1906, the congregation became a part of the African Methodist Episcopal Church (AMEC) family founded by Richard Allen in 1787.[1] The present contemporary structure, the steeple of which can be seen from far away, is located on Northern Boulevard in Jackson Heights, Queens, New York. This multi-million-dollar edifice was dedicated on April 9, 1988, as an abiding witness to the Christian faith in Queens and in the world. But the building alone is not enough to realize a dream.

The people envision a church that is the center of the community's life, where they can come together for *all* their needs: worship, food, community organizing, drug counseling, and many others. However, African-American women want even more. They dream of a place where they can gain spiritual insights for their *daily* lives, for the grinding regularity of work and the unending task of providing for others. They want a place where their emotional needs are met, a church that goes out to the community and invites the community to come to it. They imagine a church where people are intent on breaking the chains of fear that trap African-American women in feelings of unworthiness and low self-esteem and that convince them of their inability to achieve intellectual success. They dream of a church that is committed to the total well-being of women, including their call to preach (to do something more than missionary activity).

The Sunday Worship Service

A typical Sunday morning worship service at St. Mark begins with the ministers' entrance to the pulpit, where they kneel to pray. Then the choir, made up of men and women, gathers at the rear of the church and begins singing. On the particular day when Gloria Bennett preached, they sang "Holy Ground."

"What is it," I wondered, "that makes us perceive this place as holy?" I thought of the exodus of Israel and how African-Americans relate that exodus to our own movement from slavery into freedom;

of God's command to Moses and later Joshua, "Take off your sandals. The place where you are standing is holy ground" (Ex. 3:5; Josh. 5:15, NIV). "We are standing on holy ground," we sang. Do these African-American Christians gathered here believe this ground is holy? Several choruses of the song were sung. The more we sang, the more reverent I felt, and I sensed that the people around me did regard this place and this moment as holy. Perhaps it did not have as much to do with the place as it did our purpose. For like Moses, Joshua, and contemporary women, our purpose was to meet God here in worship.

After the prelude, the choir led the congregation in singing the processional, "Glorious Things of Thee Are Spoken," an old favorite in the AMEC:

> Glorious things of thee are spoken,
> Zion, city of our God;
> He whose word cannot be broken
> Formed thee for His own abode:
> On the Rock of Ages founded,
> What can shake thy sure repose?
> With salvation's walls surrounded,
> Thou mayst smile at all thy foes.
>
> See, the streams of living waters,
> Springing from eternal love,
> Well supply thy sons and daughters,
> And all fear of want remove:
> Who can faint while such a river
> Ever flows their thirst to assuage?
> Grace, which like the Lord, the Giver,
> Never fails from age to age.[2]

The sweet music of the organ, mingled with the melodious voices of the choir and congregation, brought these lyrics to life. Fragments lingered in my mind: "What can shake thy sure repose?" If God established a city that could not be shaken, surely God could/would establish me steadfastly in my faith. The "living waters" symbolized the Spirit of God, to which both the sons and daughters have access, and unfailing grace, sufficient to meet *all needs,* sufficient even to chase away the shadows of gloom and death. All needs? What about those rejected, despised, demeaned even here within the church?

After a call to worship, there was more singing, a medley of praise songs including "Bless the Lord, O My Soul" and "We Have Come Into His House and Gathered in His Name to Worship Him." These songs were followed by a pastoral prayer and the time to honor particular achievements within the church community. On this particular Sunday, our attention was given to the adults and children who participated in the children's church. Some thirty children of various ages participated in the children's church. Elementary school, high school, college, and seminary graduates, too, were complimented for the achievement of their dreams. In some instances, they were also given financial assistance to help further their education. Parents, grandparents, and guardians were called to stand with the children as they received their awards. The service continued with preaching, money collections for various needs, the recitation of the Apostles' Creed, hymn singing, and a benediction.

A critical analysis. Two questions guide my analysis of this service of worship: How does the style of leadership enable mutual ownership of the ritual? How does the liturgical experience honor women as embodiments of divine activity in our world?

The Reverend Terrence Hensford, pastor, is a dynamic worship leader who encourages the full involvement of the congregation. Many of the songs are congregational praise songs for everyone, designed to set the praise mode. Repeatedly during the service, Hensford urges, "Everybody sing!" The emphasis is on everyone praising God, unashamedly, with joy and thanksgiving, expressed through lively participation. As I observe the congregational response, it appears that they feel part of the worship.

The St. Mark children's church makes worship more meaningful for the children, thus spawning new leadership. As worship begins, the whole church is at worship together. Just before the sermon, the children are acknowledged by the pastor or another minister and then escorted to the lower level where a special service is held for them. The children's church not only provides materials for their particular age groups but allows greater participation and enables the children to understand early the responsibilities associated with religious life in the AMEC, as they learn important truths about God. They are not merely observers but active participants.

Like most African-American churches, St. Mark has more female members than male. However, unlike many African-American churches, it has three ordained women on its staff: Linda Smith, assistant pastor, and Alicia Cambridge and Weltha Morris, administrators. These women boldly represent that which is female in their sermons, insisting on the particular concerns of African-American women without neglecting the dreams of African-American men. Their presence in the work of worship honors women as embodiments of divine activity, but this alone is not enough. They join the male leadership in continuing to use language that perpetuates women's invisibility.

What message does the church send to women when its leaders (even women) stubbornly hold on to exclusively male imagery and language? What does this resistance to seeing the connection between language and their dreams of fulfillment imply? How do the christological views of the black church and the Bible reinforce male-centered images about God? How can present liturgical forms (songs, prayers, sermons, creeds, etc.) be transformed into liturgy that both praises God and affirms *all* worshipers? How can African-American women in leadership and nonleadership positions address the issue of inclusive language without being perceived as insubordinate to the pastor or other authority figures?

In considering these questions, I begin with my experience at the AMEC Christian Education Congress in Dover, Delaware, about two years ago. Many of the workshops were conducted by eminent AME denominational leaders. The women in attendance were noticeably visible. Yet male workshop leaders addressed the group as "brethren" and "mankind," and used "he" or "his" repeatedly when referring to God. The male workshop leaders were not unaware of the presence of women. They chose to speak in a way that deliberately ignored our presence.

The use of "he" and "his" exclusively when referring to God gives males identification with the Divine and eliminates women as sources for divine revelation and activity. This type of speech also reinforces oppressive notions about women preachers. Consider this incident:

> It was time for worship. The people were gathered; the worship leaders had taken their places. I was in the back preparing to enter when a young man came by, looked in, and saw that the preacher in the pulpit was female. He then loudly declared as he turned to leave, "A woman can't tell me nothing."

Where is the truth in that statement? Isn't the preacher merely a vessel or a messenger of God who proclaims what the Lord says? This young man meant one of two things: (1) *God* can't tell him anything, or (2) what male preachers have been telling us all these centuries have been *their* own thoughts in *their* own words for *their* own glorification. Could Mary Daly's analysis be true that if "God is male," then the "male is God"? Perhaps the young man was saying only a man can preach to him because the man is God; when man speaks, God speaks. Could this really be the implication of this kind of statement?[3]

When the church fails to acknowledge the presence of women, it treats women as if they are not full members of the church, as if their presence is meaningless and their voices insignificant. What purpose does using the "Old English" term "brethren" serve in a group of male and female believers except to alienate the women in the group? Is God a God of alienation or a God of unity?

The centrality of Jesus in worship in African-American churches is unmistakable, as is immediately apparent in the songs and prayers alluded to earlier in the Sunday worship at St. Mark AMEC. African-American believers, whose experience in America was marred by extraordinary suffering and pain, readily identify with the historical Jesus, holding that because Jesus, too, experienced extraordinary suffering as a human being, Jesus has the capacity to understand their pain (Heb. 2:18, NIV). The problem is that African-American believers still seem to think and speak of

Jesus as human only (i.e., Jesus' male humanity) rather than as a spiritual presence that nourishes and sustains our daily lives. Do we worship Jesus, the historical man, or the God revealed through belief in Jesus? Theologian Kelly Brown commented on the Christology of African-American churches:

> There are several instances that illustrate understandings of Jesus which are oppressive for black women. One such example is the equation often made in the black faith between Jesus and God. Black church people have consistently understood Jesus as God; they make little distinction between the two. Given Jesus' maleness, is such an equation evident when a black church woman says, "calling God 'she' just doesn't sound right"? Does a male Jesus imply to black women that God is also male? Does the lack of distinction between the male Jesus and God prevent black women from exclaiming, "I found God in myself and I loved her / I loved her fiercely"?[4]

Men have used Jesus' maleness as a basis for not ordaining women, arguing that women are not the embodiment of the image of Christ. Likewise, certain scriptures have been used to keep women voiceless (1 Cor. 14:33b–35; 1 Tim. 2:11–12) and submissive to their husbands (Col. 3:18; Eph. 5:22; 1 Peter 3:1). Such notions are still perpetuated uncritically in too many African-American churches and accepted by women as the "natural order of things," sanctified by the Bible as God's exclusive word.[5]

Many African-American women seem to think that the writers of the Bible wrote as if in a trance, in a mystical communion with God. So for them everything is "truly stated." These women feel they cannot interpret the scriptures for themselves (as Sojourner Truth did). Thus, instead of being freed by scripture they are bound by it. African-American women understand Paul's command to be submissive to their husbands as a scriptural mandate to stay in physically and emotionally abusive relationships in their own homes as well as outside them. They understand their plight as God's will. For example, a woman whose suspicions of infidelity were confirmed when her husband was diagnosed with a sexually transmitted disease felt compelled to remain in the marriage because of scriptural injunctions. Another woman and her preteenage daughter, though constantly harassed verbally and beaten, accepted perpetual abuse as God's will.

Where does the church begin the monumental task of transforming liturgical experiences that perpetuate such injustice? Oppressors will not take the initiative to set the oppressed free. Male pastors often are annoyed with what they deem unimportant. The language of worship and the sacred texts are the work of God. "This is the way God inspired men to write it and this is the way it should be." Change threatens their authority. So the transformation will require the collaboration of many.

Whereas a single woman seeking to initiate significant change may be perceived as insubordinate, a substantial number of women bonding together with a well-thought-out plan to help expedite their request will command more respect and attention and meet with greater success. First, they have to appreciate themselves as images of God, people called by God to embody the essence of God. This realization will lead them to learn about the tradition, to understand the misogynist interpretations handed down from generation to generation, and subsequently to resist them. They will be motivated to reword prayers to include female images (e.g., Mother God and Giver of Life), to study scripture and to use it more selectively (interpreting it against itself), to reword songs, and to discover new metaphors for sermons. Inclusive liturgical forms best reflect the nature of God, who loves and affirms all humanity and invites all to be partakers of salvation, regardless of race, gender, sexual orientation, class, age, or other differences.

Like African-American Protestantism as a whole, the AMEC must accept the challenge to "widen its margins."[6] African-American slaves were not averse to a critical examination of the scriptures, accepting those that were liberating and rejecting those that were intended to keep them enslaved.[7] Otherwise, they would not have resisted slavery. Can we, in good faith, be any less critical of scriptures used to keep women, the gay and lesbian community, and children on the fringes?

This critical work in no way diminishes our love for Jesus nor our devotion to God. Rather, it will help clarify our perspective and articulate what our church fathers and mothers have found to be true about God, about God's revelation in Jesus, about the Spirit and the tremendous effect it continues to have on African-American spirituality.

Can any attempt to honor women as the embodiment of divine activity be truly complete without regard to inclusive language? Most assuredly not! To say that women embody divine activity and then address them as other than what God created them to be is a contradiction. To assert that God is Spirit and speak of God anthropomorphically as male only attempts to cloud female qualities of the divine. Women have been taught to dishonor and exclude ourselves and each other through sexist language. Hence, as Brown noted in the passage cited earlier, we have difficulty perceiving the divine in other women or ourselves. Many women, like the young man in the story, say "A female preacher can't tell me nothing."

In the past, African-American brothers might have preached, taught, sung, and prayed using the sexist language of the Bible, unaware of the damage it did and does to women. However, this is no longer the case. Women have stated emphatically the kind of oppression associated with such practices. To persist in such behavior is to deliberately perpetuate sexist attitudes that lead to sexist praxis.

Using inclusive language about God in the AMEC is a lonely pursuit. Women and men who become adept at it in the seminary and academy often resort to old habits when they enter a church. Women are afraid because they will be perceived as troublemakers.

The Reverend Gloria Bennett exhorted the community of St. Mark to "hold on to your dream." Like the dreamers Bennett referred to in her sermon, I too have a dream, one that envisions African-American and other men and women of faith as not merely transformers of liturgical forms, but agents of God's liberating activity in every area of human life and work.

I dream of a church committed to the total well being of women, one that is unafraid to address the particular problems of women such as the prevalence of breast cancer, AIDS, sexually transmitted diseases, single parenting, and single and same-sex life-styles, as well as women's need to appreciate their own beauty, talents, and age.

I dream of a church where there will be no more tolerance of emotional abuse, where rape on any level (husbands, other men, clergy) will be named and declared evil, where incest (which often damages our male and female children for life) will be exposed and stopped. I dream of a time when there will be no need for women and men to repress pain over past hurts, when they can freely speak of their hurts and find healing in the church.

I dream of a church that speaks out about violence against women and children, one that does not encourage needless suffering, of a church that dares offer sanctuary (safe space). I dream of a church where all human sexuality is appreciated and affirmed, a church where lesbian and gay Christians find full acceptance and need not question the legitimacy of their existence. I dream of a church where distortions about women's sexuality as evil are corrected. I dream of a church where the humanity of Jesus is emphasized more than his gender, where the maleness of Jesus is not used to subordinate women or keep them from leadership roles in the church. I dream of a church that welcomes the poor and combines prayer with social and political action to eliminate poverty. I dream of a church where assaults on one's body, for example, AIDS, cancer, and other diseases, are not understood as an indication of God's wrath or will but as a consequence of conditions and circumstances that need to be addressed (stress, pollution, et cetera). I dream of a church where inclusive language about God is not considered too much to ask. I pray that others who share this dream will work together to make it a reality.

Notes

1. St. Mark's AMEC Bulletin, Sunday, June 28, 1992.

2. Words by John Newton. *AMEC Bicentennial Hymnal* (Nashville: AME Church, 1984).

3. Jacquelyn Grant, "An Epistle to the Black Church: What a Womanist Would Want to Say to the Black Church," *The AME Church Review*, vol. 106, no. 342 (Nashville, 1991), p. 54.

4. Kelly Brown, "God Is as Christ Does," *Journal of Religious Thought,* vol. 46, no. 1 (Howard University School of Divinity, Summer–Fall 1989), p. 14. Brown quotes Ntozake Shange, *For Colored Girls Who Have Considered Suicide When the Rainbow Is Enuf* (New York: Macmillan, 1975).

5. Ibid., p. 15.

6. Clarice Martin uses this phrase in "The Brief Statement" in *To Confess the Faith Today,* ed. Jack L. Stotts and Jane Dempsey Douglass (Louisville, Ky.: Westminster/John Knox Press, 1990), p. 107.

7. Clarice Martin, "The Haustafeln (Household Codes) in African American Biblical Interpretation: 'Free Slaves' and 'Subordinate Women,' " in *Stony the Road We Trod,* ed. Cain Hope Felder (Minneapolis: Fortress Press, 1991), p. 213.

4

Sin, Grace, and Gender in Free-Church Protestant Worship

Ruth Duck

Consider this typical prayer of confession, not unlike many prayed in free churches across the country on any Sunday morning: "O God, we confess that we think of ourselves more highly than we ought. Forgive us our pride and teach us humility." Such confessions of sin are a normal part of free-church Protestant worship. But what assumptions about the meaning of sin and the needs of women in the congregation lie beneath such prayers? How are women, who normally struggle daily with self-esteem, sexism, and violence, going to hear such prayers?

Sin in Christian Worship

Christian theology argues that sin is a concrete reality of human existence. Sin can be individual—as when one person hurts another needlessly through thoughtless speech. Sin can be social—as when unjust structures give people unequal access to what they need to live. Individual and social sin may be mixed—as when assumptions based on social injustice cause one person to ridicule or violate another. In worship, Christians are able to face the wrong they do and the unjust structures in which they participate, knowing that God's love and the community's support can help them in the process of turning from sin and learning to live in love, kindness, and justice.

Western Christian worship, Roman Catholic and Protestant, has been preoccupied with sin and forgiveness. For example, sacramental orders have emphasized these themes and excluded other scriptural and theological themes. Approaches to baptism and communion emphasizing sin and redemption have eclipsed those emphasizing new life in community with the risen Christ. While Protestant Reformers emphasized grace, not works, as means of forgiveness, they continued liturgical emphasis on sin; later Protestants often lost the emphasis on grace. Western Christians were ready for the renewed sacramental theology produced by Vatican II or recommended by the Faith and Order Commission of the World Council of Churches. Biblical themes such as dying and rising with Christ, the gift of the Spirit, and renewed life in community were recovered. Recent Roman Catholic, Anglican, and Lutheran liturgies address sin and grace as part of a fuller range of concerns.

Changes have come more slowly in the free churches of North America, churches which have local freedom in creating liturgy (such as the United Church of Christ, of which I am a member, and the United Methodist Church, in which I am a teacher). Revivalistic frontier religion continues to influence the way these churches approach sin and grace in worship. Revivals sought to evoke conviction of sin, repentance, and conversion to faith. They began with singing to warm the heart, continued with preaching directed toward conversion, and culminated in the "altar call," an invitation to dedicate oneself to Jesus Christ.[1] As free churches move away from frontier religion due to theological and social changes, their worship typically still reflects the revival structure. Preliminaries, including an act of confession, have replaced gospel singing. The sermon remains central and is perhaps more legalistic than before—often railing at individual or social sins, without emphasizing divine grace. The altar call is gone, rarely replaced by significant opportunities to respond to scripture and sermon. Congregations are sent out with a song and a blessing. From the opening prayer to the closing hymn, the service often refers continually to human sin, without a word of grace.

Free-church denominations such as the United Methodist Church and the United Church of Christ have offered alternatives in their worship books and hymnals.[2] Both have encouraged churches to place the act of confession after the sermon, so that it responds to a specific scripture and sermon. Many are coming to understand that sermons should bring the good news of grace, as well as confront people with their sin. Denominationally developed prayers tend to avoid many pitfalls, but local churches that follow frontier patterns of worship and create prayers locally often demonstrate the problems I am outlining in this article.

A Feminist Critique of Sin

Sin has been defined in the Western liturgical tradition, including free-church Prestantism, from the perspective of privileged males. Contemporary feminist theologians have offered a critique of this dominant interpretation of sin and grace. Valerie Saiving's historic 1960 article "Androcentrism in Religious Studies"[3] critiqued modern theologians such as Reinhold Niebuhr and Anders Nygren, who defined sin as pride and self-assertion, calling for selfless, self-sacrificing love instead. Saiving argued that society expects women to be self-giving in child care and household maintenance. Women are less likely to be overly proud and self-assertive than to lack self-identity, leading to another constellation of sins:

> triviality, distractibility, and diffuseness; lack of an organizing center or focus; dependence on others for one's self-definition; tolerance at the expense of standards of excellence; inability to respect the boundaries of privacy; sentimentality, gossipy sociability, and mistrust of reason—in short, underdevelopment or negation of the self.[4]

Accompanying the problem of the definition of sin is the definition of love that extols *lack* of self-esteem and self-identity: "Love, according to these theologians, is completely self-giving, taking no thought for its own interests but seeking only the good of the other."[5] This definition matches what patriarchal society expects of women and others in servant roles.

Saiving assumed (falsely, I believe) that biological differences, not socially defined gender roles, cause differences between men and women. However, her basic point—that definitions of sin that emphasize pride and self-assertion do not speak adequately to women's situation—started an important discussion, which Judith Plaskow continued in *Sex, Sin, and Grace*.[6] Plaskow analyzes Reinhold Niebuhr's and Paul Tillich's understandings of sin and grace. For Niebuhr, sin centers on pride as rebellion against God and refusal to accept human limits; grace shatters the prideful self so that the sinner may depend upon God. Tillich stresses the sin of pride, though naming failure to be a self as sin; Plaskow believes his emphasis on participation in the divine life discourages healthy self-development. She argues that culture shapes differences between men and women, that it calls women to sacrifice themselves for others, and that "the language of self-sacrifice conflicts with personhood and becomes destructive when it suggests that the struggle to become a centered self, to achieve full independent selfhood, is sinful."[7] Ideals of self-sacrifice reinforce women's roles of servitude and passivity; they discourage women from taking responsibility for their own lives. Self-giving without self-nurture and without limits depletes the human personality, as Plaskow observes: "Sacrifice, not balanced by self-consolidation and creation, can drain selves to the point where they are incapable of entering into genuine relationships with themselves or others."[8] Further, the expectation that some will adapt themselves to the needs and desires of others—husbands, fathers, children, and employers—keeps persons from adequately developing selves.[9] Thus the cultural expectation that women or others (male clergy, for example) practice total self-giving is not a fulfillment but a distortion of love.

Rosemary Radford Ruether has furthered the discussion. She agrees that both pride and lack of self-development are dimensions of human sin but denies that these characteristics fall neatly along gender lines. For example, privileged women can be prideful. Though they may accept the feminine "virtue" of passivity and subordination to men, "they also exist within class and race hierarchies" where they may exploit persons under their power.[10]

Women and less privileged men may also use power manipulatively "to control those whom they cannot dominate directly."[11] Moreover, male pride is not all that it appears; it often masks insecurity, vulnerability, and fear of the mother:

> The more insecure his "manhood," the more the male in patriarchal society needs to aggressively put down his wife and other women in order to emancipate himself from his mother. Thus the need for secure, dominating power at the heart of egoistic aggression is an unending cycle, feeding on the unsatiated void of the insecure, ungrounded self, with its unresolved fears of vulnerability and dependency.[12]

Both women and men are influenced by gender stereotypes, yet along with exploitative, sinful patterns, we also find men and women whose behavior challenges those stereotypes. Ruether's discussion reveals the complex sensitivity needed in dealing with sin in worship.

Selfishness and Self-giving

I once attended a church that used gender-inclusive language but whose emphasis on and understanding of sin seemed to work against my own growth as a woman and a Christian. Prayers, hymns, and sermons constantly referred to individual and social sin, often without also affirming grace. We were encouraged to give more and more of ourselves, to stop protecting our personal boundaries, and to give up self-concern. Urgent appeals to attend more meetings and demonstrations than anyone's calendar could hold contributed further to a sense of inadequacy. I went away burdened with guilt and undermined in my growth toward learning self-care as well as self-giving and toward setting realistic limits. I felt overwhelmed, rather than empowered, even for self-giving.

Prayers of confession, hymns, and sermons in free churches often identify selfishness as sin, while praising self-giving. Often confessions of selfishness are placed in the context of prayers related to social sin. Such prayers may be valid in some congregations in the United States, whose people consume much more than their share of the world's resources. Even so, constant confession of selfishness undermines women and others who need to grow in self-nurture and self-esteem. The prayers of confession in Lavon Bayler's three recently published books of worship resources include numerous references to self-interest, self-concern, and self-ishness. One prayer that is striking in this respect reads:

> Sovereign God, just when we think we have buried our wickedness from everyone's view, you expose it and call us to deal with it openly and courageously. We have not treated others with the sympathy and kindness you expect. Instead, we have used them for our own ends. We have been selfish, conceited, and arrogant, putting our own interests first. We play God as we grasp and manipulate things and people. O God, turn us inside out, and replace the demons inside us with your own loving spirit. We pray in Jesus' name.[13]

What would it mean for a woman whose life is constantly given over to the needs and desires of others to pray this prayer? Would she "tune out" the prayer, or would she be discouraged from healthy self-assertion and development? The problem is not one such prayer but an unbalanced diet of similar prayers. Bayler provides balance in particular prayers, such as one which confesses both arrogance and timidity.[14] Other prayers confess lack of self-nurture[15] or lack of self-esteem.[16] Balance is needed, since both selfishness and self-giving are found in congregations and individuals, and in some contexts both can be either sin or virtue.

Prayers of confession often subtly discourage self-nurture. One summer I was recovering from pneumonia. The doctor prescribed rest, but resting was difficult for me. I felt I was wasting time when I should be working, and felt guilty lying around reading novels. Then I went to church and had the eerie experience of being undermined in self-nurture by listening to a prayer that I had written several years earlier:

> O most gracious God, we confess that we spend much of our lives on that which does not satisfy. We do not always count our time and resources as precious gifts, but squander them in meaningless activities and seemingly urgent needs. Look kindly upon us, for the

temptation to waste is overwhelming in the world. Enable us to understand what is important, and to use the gifts of life responsibly, for we want to be your people in word and deed.[17]

I have learned since writing this prayer how important it can be to "waste" time—watching a sunset, walking with a loved one, or reading a novel. The prayer is likely to evoke certain cultural assumptions about time ("time is money" or "time is productivity") that are not helpful in developing genuinely Christian life-styles.

Self-giving without self-nurture can lead to sin. Personal needs are rarely suppressed entirely; they emerge in disguised and perhaps destructive ways. Those who sacrifice themselves for others may be "helpful" in ways that subvert others' growth. A life-style of self-sacrifice without self-nurture creates tired, distracted people who may lack good judgment about ethics or make mistakes that endanger human lives. Further, when self-sacrifice is expected of some social groups and not others, injustice and abuse are supported.

The hymn text "Awake, Awake to Love and Work" is dangerous to persons who do not limit their self-giving. It begins:

> To give and give, and give again
> What God hath given thee;
> To spend thyself nor count the cost;
> To serve right gloriously . . . [18]

This text glorifies unlimited self-giving. Although God is stated as the primary receiver, is it implied that God supports all giving we may do, even in a context of injustice or abuse? Isn't it important to count the cost? This text may encourage church workers (particularly women) to neglect relationships without counting the cost to themselves and others.

A recent hymn text by Fred Kaan says that as we "leave the shell of worship" we are "called to the risk of unprotected living." It ends with the request that God "give us the nerve to lose our life to others."[19] While the text rightly calls the church to go beyond institutional self-maintenance, it will be heard differently by persons in different social locations. What does "the risk of unprotected living" mean to a woman who is trying to decide how to protect herself from her battering husband? And what does it mean for a woman without much sense of self to "lose [one's] life to others"? We must avoid one-sided glorification of self-giving in worship.

Women, Pride, and Social Location

Another issue related to confession of sin in worship concerns whether social location influences what one ought to confess. Feminist theological discussion has particularly critiqued the theological traditions that focus on pride and selfishness as central human sins.

Pride could be defined as arrogance, or in Paul's words, as thinking "of yourself more highly than you ought to think" (Rom. 12:3, NRSV). Pride is putting oneself or one's group in the place of God/ess and refusing to acknowledge any limits to one's knowledge or power. Pride is the refusal to be vulnerable, when vulnerability (in admitting guilt or need) could build bridges between humans or between humans and the divine. Patriarchal society encourages pride in all these senses in members of privileged groups. Pride—as assumed superiority—justifies greater access to power, resources, and self-determination; thus, pride among dominant groups keeps unjust systems intact.

Women—and all in less privileged groups—are discouraged from pride in patriarchal society and are expected always to be vulnerable. A woman who dares to express confidence in herself will receive many signals that she is not behaving appropriately. All women in our society learn to be ashamed of their bodies and to distrust their perceptions of reality and their ability to affect the world around them. Mary Field Belenky and others, for example, have shown that women who grow up in abusive families lose a sense of self and voice, and can only see themselves through the distorted view of others.[20] The English language uses male terms for God and has a broad range of derogatory terms for women, often (to give one example), portraying a negative view of their sexuality and sexual ethics. Thus, the language itself identifies men with God and women with sin.[21] The need, then, for women and others in socially subordinate groups, is not so much to overcome arrogance as to develop healthy self-affirmation.

Violence Against Women and
Prayers of Confession

In our churches are many survivors and perpetrators of patriarchal violence and abuse. Joanne Carlson Brown and Rebecca Parker have written: "Only if the church is the place where cycles of abuse are named, condemned, and broken can it be a haven of blessing and peace for women."[22] The importance of naming, condemning, and breaking abuse has direct implications for the church's approach to sin and grace in its worship.

The development of a centered self with clear but flexible boundaries is particularly important for those who have experienced physical or sexual abuse as children. Such abuse involves violation of the personal and bodily integrity of a child by a powerful adult. People who were abused as children often struggle to develop an adequate sense of their personal boundaries, in some cases, they need more awareness of others' boundaries, as well. Healing occurs, in part, through development of boundaries to protect the self from violence and violation. Hymns, prayers, and sermons that discourage boundaries or limits to self-giving are counterproductive for these persons' growth toward wholeness.

To minister to survivors, the church must be aware of its use of language about sin and redemption. Sheila Redmond observes that victims of abuse can develop "a sense of guilt disproportionate to their actions" and the "focus on the need for redemption creates a sense of unworthiness and, eventually, guilt."[23] Indeed, since society projects its sin and evil onto women, many women report feeling a generalized sense of guilt simply because they are women. The doctrine of original sin contributes to this generalized sense of guilt, since supposedly Eve's choice condemned the whole human race. It is much more helpful to consider sin in a historical and relational way; if it is true that we all sin, "sin" is not (contra Tillich et al.) a generalized condition, but a specific thing we do that harms our relationship with ourselves or other people or undermines peace and justice in the world. Concern with sin in this sense has a place in liturgy, but not as the whole focus. It is important that worship be a place where Christians enact new reality—in

a ministry of healing and inclusive love. Overemphasis on generalized sin and the need for redemption contributes to women's generalized sense of guilt, and it hampers our ability to enact new
reality in worship.

When we consider our ministry to church members who are
perpetrators of abuse (whether we know it or not), enacting new
reality is key. Here also we need relational understandings of sin,
knowing that reconciliation between exploiter and exploited is
impossible until the unjust and hurtful behavior ceases.[24] Corporate confession sometimes focuses so much on human relationship with the divine (and salvation of the soul) that a short act of
confession appears to be a substitute for changed human actions
and relationships. St. Paul's African Methodist Episcopal Church
in Cambridge, Massachusetts, has a yearly service of reconciliation
in which members move around in the sanctuary and reconcile
with one another. They may restore a relationship broken in conflict, or admit to a harmful word or deed. However, reconciliation
between abused and abuser is much more complicated, and an act
of confession, however heartfelt at the time, is an inadequate substitute for changed behavior.

It seems clear that ministry to the abused and to the abuser puts
different requirements on corporate confession. For the abused,
and for all who are genuinely seeking to live in new ways, the
word of grace must be strong to overcome self-doubt, preoccupa-
tion with the past, and generalized cultural self-blame. For the
abuser, and for all who are unwilling to change the ways they hurt
themselves and others, the word of grace must include admonition to change their hurtful actions and the expectation that they
be able to demonstrate that they have changed. Thus, grace is
conditional. Though extended to all people, it becomes a reality
only to those who are open to being transformed by divine love.

Proposals

Sin as a reality of human existence is a proper concern for
Christian liturgy. The question is, since people in different situations experience sin and grace in different ways, how can free-

church worship leaders address these themes effectively? And in particular, how can sin and grace be addressed in worship in ways that take account of women's daily struggles and needs? My constructive proposals fall into three categories: content, leadership, and context.

The content of corporate prayers of confession needs reform in free churches. Truly general prayers of confession may allow people in many different situations to pray honestly. Worship leaders who compose prayers of confession might learn from general prayers confessing that "we have left undone those things which we ought to have done, and we have done those things which we ought not to have done."[25] If worship leaders feel that such prayers fail to name the real sins and wounds of worshipers, they can provide opportunities to confess lack of self-development and nurture as well as pride and selfishness, as this prayer by Maren Tirabassi does:

> Gracious God, we confess that we have not loved you with all our heart, our soul, our strength, our mind. We have not loved our neighbors with a deep and abiding compassion. And we have not loved ourselves and cared for our own truest needs. Transform our shallowness, enliven our deadness, heal our broken, wounded places, and so fill us with your spirit that we can be forgiven, even as we forgive ourselves and others. For we pray in the name of Jesus Christ who brings love that has no end.[26]

More general or balanced prayers of corporate confession can address social differences and individual complexities.

The way prayers are led bears thought. Body language can help to communicate grace; words of assurance should be proclaimed confidently with good eye contact. A former parishioner told me that she first came to realize God's love for her while I was proclaiming God's forgiveness after a prayer of confession. Though I am a manuscript preacher, I never read assurances of pardon, lest I seem to lack conviction. Gracious leadership is an embodied witness to transforming grace.

Who leads corporate confession also bears thought. Acts of confession should model clergy-lay mutuality; they should not reflect traditional dominant-subordinate relationships. When only clergy proclaim forgiveness, it appears that they are more powerful or holy. On the other hand, at the church I currently attend, the only part laity lead in worship is the act of confession; they begin by sharing an aspect of their own failure to live faithfully. One jester called the lay leader the "sinner of the week"! Clergy and laity should share in leading the prayer of confession and assurance of forgiveness.

Mutuality between leaders and congregation is also modeled in liturgies in which the worship leader says, "In the name of Jesus Christ, you are forgiven," and the congregation responds, "In the name of Jesus Christ, you are forgiven."[27] This replaces the idea that only clergy can proclaim forgiveness with the awareness that we all may receive and proclaim grace.

Both the content and leadership of corporate confession can benefit from reconstruction, in many free-church congregations, but perhaps confession could better take place in other contexts than as a brief part of public worship. Liturgical scholar James F. White suggests that services of reconciliation might be more helpful:

> Quarterly services of reconciliation . . . could confront us with God's word, engage us in introspective examination of conscience, lead us to confess our sin, and give assurance of God's will to forgive. Such services would allow the eucharist to be more frequent and free it from its penitential baggage.[28]

Such quarterly corporate services of reconciliation, which might or might not include individual confession of specific sin, could replace weekly confession of sin.

The context of a whole worship service matters, too. Worship leaders should place confession of sin together with confident proclamation of God's grace to forgive and free us from our sin.[29] In free-church worship, confession often slips into the opening prayer and the pastoral prayer—leading to an overemphasis on sin in the service, often without any corresponding emphasis on grace.

Another way to change the context of confession would be to place it in small groups, replacing or complementing corporate confession in entire worship communities. Roman Catholic theologian

Monika Hellwig has argued that in one-to-one dialogue or peer groups, one can engage in honest self-exploration about one's life as a whole, including places where one needs to grow in love of God or neighbor. Spiritual direction relationships, twelve-step groups, and retreats can encourage growing self-awareness and witness to God's grace at work in life.[30] Twelve-step groups emphasize making amends to any person one may have wronged—creating the possibility of changed human relationships. Another alternative is groups of parents who abuse children or men who abuse women, which provide a supportive and honest environment that can empower change.

Hellwig calls "kitchen table confession" a particular part of women's experience.[31] When women share their struggles to be whole and loving persons over a cup of coffee, reconciliation is often taking place. Many people turn at times to a woman who is a gifted kitchen table confessor, known by her hospitality, graciousness, and listening rather than by official designation as a minister of reconciliation. Hellwig's discussion of kitchen table confessors is reminiscent of Plaskow's discussion of consciousness-raising groups.[32] In these groups, women "become aware of both the social context of sin and their own collusion with it, and the possibilities for new individual and communal life."[33] They name the social expectations that have constricted them and take responsibility for their own lives, freely sharing their stories, their anger, and their pain. The group members hear one another into speech (to use Nelle Morton's term) and support each other in living in new ways individually and in community.

Addressing sin and grace in small-group settings, as in "kitchen table confession" or consciousness-raising groups, would give free-church Protestants the opportunity to address women's experience of sin and brokenness in ways that are neither harmful nor defined by dominant social groups.

If the free churches are to deal constructively and honestly with sin and grace, it is necessary to begin to hear women's voices and to examine the content of prayers, sermons, and hymns. Only by means of such self-examination can the church become a place where reconciliation truly takes place.

Notes

1. James F. White, *Protestant Worship: Traditions in Transition* (Louisville, Ky.: Westminster/John Knox Press, 1989), p. 177.

2. United Church of Christ Office for Church Life and Leadership, *Book of Worship: United Church of Christ* (New York: United Church of Christ Office for Church Life and Leadership, 1986); *United Methodist Hymnal* (Nashville: United Methodist Church, 1989).

3. Valerie Saiving, "Androcentrism in Religious Studies," *Journal of Religion*, April 1960. Reprinted in *Womanspirit Rising* (see n. 4).

4. Valerie Saiving, "The Human Situation: A Feminine View," in *Womanspirit Rising*, ed. Carol P. Christ and Judith Plaskow, (San Francisco: Harper & Row, 1979), pp. 25–42, esp. p. 37. [Written in 1960 and retitled and reprinted in this volume.]

5. Ibid., p. 26.

6. Judith Plaskow, *Sex, Sin, and Grace: Women's Experience and the Theologies of Reinhold Niebuhr and Paul Tillich* (Lanham, Md.: University Press of America, 1980).

7. Ibid., p. 87.

8. Ibid., p. 166.

9. Ibid., p. 67.

10. Rosemary Radford Ruether, "Feminist Metanoia and Soul-Making," 1991. Manuscript, p. 5.

11. Ibid., p. 5.

12. Rosemary Radford Ruether, "Dualism and the Nature of Evil in Feminist Theology," 1991. Manuscript of a lecture delivered at Garrett-Evangelical Theological Seminary, December 5, p. 21.

13. Lavon Bayler, *Fresh Winds of the Spirit: Liturgical Resources for Year A* (New York: Pilgrim Press, 1986), p. 115.

14. Lavon Bayler, *Refreshing Rains of the Living Word: Liturgical Resources for Year C* (New York: Pilgrim Press, 1988), p. 3.

15. Ibid., p. 100.

16. Bayler, *Fresh Winds*, p. 99.

17. Ruth C. Duck, ed., *Bread for the Journey* (New York: Pilgrim Press, 1981), p. 59.

18. Congregational Christian Church, *Pilgrim Hymnal* (Boston: Pilgrim Press, 1958), number 34.

19. Fred Kaan, *The Hymn Texts of Fred Kaan* (London: Stainer & Bell, and Carol Stream, Ill.: Hope Publishing Co., 1985), p. 74.

20. Mary Field Belenky, Blythe McVicker Clinch, Nancy Rule Goldenberger, and Jill Mattuck Tarule, *Women's Ways of Knowing* (New York: Basic Books, 1986).

21. Ruth C. Duck, *Gender and the Name of God: The Trinitarian Baptismal Formula* (New York: Pilgrim Press, 1991), pp. 32–40.

22. Joanne Carlson Brown and Rebecca Parker, "For God So Loved the World?" in *Christianity, Patriarchy, and Abuse*, ed. Joanne Carlson Brown and Carole R. Bohn (New York: Pilgrim Press, 1989), p. 4.

23. Sheila Redmond, "Christian 'Virtues' and Recovery from Child Sexual Abuse," in *Christianity, Patriarchy, and Abuse*, ed. Joanne Carlson Brown and Carole R. Bohn (New York: Pilgrim Press, 1989), p. 77.

24. See James Cone, *God of the Oppressed* (New York: Seabury Press, 1975), pp. 226–46.

25. The Episcopal Church, *Book of Common Prayer* (New York: Church Hymnal Corporation, 1977), p. 79.

26. Maren C. Tirabassi, "Prayer of Confession for the Twenty-fourth Sunday After Pentecost," in *Touch Holiness*, ed. Ruth C. Duck and Maren C. Tirabassi (New York: Pilgrim Press, 1990), p. 115.

27. *United Methodist Hymnal*, 1989, p. 8.

28. James F. White, *Sacraments as God's Self-Giving* (Nashville: Abingdon Press, 1983), p. 133.

29. Theodore W. Jennings, *The Liturgy of Liberation* (Nashville: Abingdon Press, 1988), pp. 118–41.

30. Edward C. Sellner, "What Alcoholics Anonymous Can Teach Us About Reconciliation," *Worship* 64/4 (July 1990), pp. 331–48.

31. Monika K. Hellwig, *Sign of Reconciliation and Conversion* (Wilmington, Del.: Michael Glazier, 1982), p. 112.

32. Plaskow, *Sex, Sin, and Grace*, pp. 170–75.

33. Ibid., p. 170.

5

"Remember the Good, Forget the Bad": Denial and Family Violence in a Christian Worship Service

Sheila Redmond

> When you are knee deep in crocodiles, it's hard to remember your intention was to drain the swamp.

Violence against women and children is now an acknowledged social problem. Domestic violence in Christian families includes both physical and sexual assault, and it is being addressed slowly but surely among some Christian denominations. The workshops being offered by Marie Fortune of the Center for the Prevention of Domestic Violence and Sexual Assault have been instrumental in making Christians and in particular the clergy aware of the problem in their midst and in offering strategies for solving the problem.[1] Many denominations have published handbooks and pamphlets and have held workshops to heighten awareness of violence against women, specifically in the domestic sphere. But we are far from eradicating the problem within the church. Women are still battered and abused with impunity and children are raised believing that violence is part of interpersonal relationships. Solving the problems that have created a society where violence against women and children is endemic requires that all sectors of society make serious efforts at analyzing their own complicity,

71

passive or active, in the structures that allow such violence. Christianity, in any of its many forms, must scrutinize itself unflinchingly. For almost two thousand years it has been the backbone of Western civilization, and the roots of our present difficulties can be found in its history, its reform movements, its documents, its confrontations with and accommodations to its environment, its prayers, and its liturgies.

Many Christians are survivors of physical, sexual, and psychological abuse. Their methods of survival, such as defensiveness, secretiveness, belligerence, and aloofness, sometimes become so destructive to themselves that their ability to generate sympathy from those around them becomes restricted. When the truth about their abuse comes out, the ease with which those who should be supportive of the victim, but who spring instead to the abuser's defense, is phenomenal, and this is no less true of Christians and Christian institutions than it is of the world at large. Introducing the problem of violence against women and children into the structure of a Sunday service is a difficult issue. However, if violence is to be eradicated within the Christian environment, it is crucial that Christians understand both the specifics and the subtle pervasiveness of interpersonal violence.

To look at the more subtle aspects of family violence, I will consider a Mother's Day service held in 1990. Issues relevant to family violence were underlying the sermon, which focused on a generational story of the survival of women in the face of desertion. Unlike some Mother's Day observances, the service did not focus on the value of the nuclear family as an ideal, or tell women to keep their heads covered and be silent in church, but like many such services, it placed mothers on a pedestal while denying much of the reality of motherhood for many women.

The Mother's Day Sermon

The sermon is the centerpiece of the service in this church. The sermon for this Sunday was concerned with the minister's own personal experience of family turmoil and his family's ability to survive. He focused on the value of unconditional love, illustrated with stories from his own childhood. We were given some of his family background. His maternal grandmother had been unhappy about the need to leave Scotland, but in the end, she remembered the story of Ruth and followed her husband. His paternal Dutch grandfather had abandoned his wife and six children after she refused to go with him and leave their children behind. Later the paternal grandmother had immigrated to Canada on her own, temporarily leaving two children in an orphanage, sending for them two years later. The minister's own father had abandoned his family when the minister was six. While preparing this sermon, the minister called his mother to get some of the details. She told him that the important thing for him was to "remember the good and forget the bad." This then became the focal point of the sermon.

Commentary. This story could have made an excellent basis for the discussion of the problem of the self-centered, irresponsible, and potentially battering male in family structures. This is really a story of survival amid abandonment. The women in this sermon are the ones who are the examples of unconditional love. All the men are either demanding or abandoning, or both. Unconditional love for one's children was presented as the exclusive sphere of the mothers.

What we did not hear in this story was the minister's feelings of abandonment and how they affected his life and his belief in a male God. Did an abandoning father make his relationship with the god-father forever problematic? Or did the god-father become idealized and incapable of mistakes and change, making it impossible to achieve a form of reconciliation with the abandoning biological father?

I had a few moments of discussion with the minister about the problem of the congregation and family violence issues. He felt that the worship service is not the place to bring up this problem and that it is better left for group work.[2] Furthermore, he asked, if the congregation gets up and walks out when you talk about family violence issues, how much good can you do? This brings up another set of questions. How intransigent are the present constructions and conceptions of God to those creating liturgies and to the congregation that participates in them? What about the widespread human tendency to resist change? How quickly can changes in conceptions of God and attitudes toward biblical authority, for example, be introduced to people? Issues of violence against women—from sexual harassment to rape—and violence against children—physical, emotional, and sexual—are a reality, now and for the foreseeable future. Therefore it is imperative that these issues be raised within the worship service.

Is it realistic to fear that if the issue of corporate responsibility for violence against women is introduced, the congregation will walk out? Does this fear become a justification for keeping all the issues raised by Christian feminists in the closet or at least isolated in small working groups? In fact, the witness of ministers who bring issues of wife assault and child abuse into the forefront of their ministry, into their worship services, indicates that parishioners come to them seeking help and bring their individual stories of pain and suffering. Perhaps this is exactly what some ministers fear, since most are unprepared by their seminary training to deal with such issues.

Finding, creating, and using new symbols and rituals that can be broad in application and still address the difficult, uncomfortable issues can be daunting. However, to replace God the father with God the mother, for example, may only exacerbate a problem, since mothers too may be abusers or may defend the abuser or deny the abuse. The destructiveness of the present Christian "god the father" image on the functioning of humans is well documented in the works of James Jones, Philip Greving, and James Poling.[3] Deification of parents is dangerous. Using parents as models or symbols of God creates a burden and responsibility for the parents that can only induce guilt or denial and self-doubt when they fail to meet the standards set by a human conception of God. Whenever we create new symbols or models for God, we always run the risk of doing harm, even though it is not our intent.[4]

The church has in general adhered to the admonition of the minister's mother to remember the good and forget the bad. Part of the problem is found in denial: denial of our own personal unreconciled anger with the past, anger at our parents, and even more scary, anger at God. Perhaps the fear of not knowing what to do when confronted with the abused woman or child in the congregation is one of the fears that keeps the mouths of many ministers, pastors, and priests shut. Facing the pain and suffering of widespread abuse and the questions that arise from counseling victims can cause a crisis of faith in the pastoral counselor.[5] The understanding of the Christian message that many victims have can cause one to question the necessity of the cross, thus questioning the very foundations of the Christian belief system. Better to deny the possibility that our basic theological presuppositions are a problem than to wrestle with the disturbing questions that arise.[6] Better to keep a god who is in total control of the world and blame ourselves for messing up than to contemplate a world with a limited god.

One issue that is of crucial importance in restructuring worship services is that each participant in the pews comes to the service with all of her or his own personal life story. It is through these unique experiences that the message is filtered and interpreted. This in itself makes any attempt at change, the analyzing of the impact of any given service, a task of monumental proportions. The love of tradition and the forms of one's life make it hard to change the basic structures of church life.[7] Over and above everything else, a worship service is supposed to be about communication and community, and how that community relates with its God, within itself and with the rest of society. Consensus building is needed to change community structure. And to change structure, one must give reasons for the need to change.

I sometimes feel like Marjorie Procter-Smith, who claims that "it is necessary [to use the imaginative enterprise] because the past and the present offer so little evidence of hope, such limited possibilities for survival and change."[8] History tells us that revolutions drag along with them all the presuppositions of the past, often disguised in new language, but nevertheless still there. Christianity in its earliest forms may have been revolutionary in its attitudes toward social construction. But these forms of Christianity were as much bound by the past, by Jewish, Roman, Greek, and personal history, as we are by ours. Change is a slow-moving, burdensome beast, but change will come and it will be based on our interpretation of the past. The one reality that relates to liturgical change is the fact that human beings have a difficult time changing and accepting a new reality, especially if that new reality causes personal discomfort and suffering.

In order to effect real change and through the imaginative enterprise to dream of new possibilities for interpersonal relationships, those who want the change must question every one of their own presuppositions and truths about themselves, their beliefs, and their society, and confront every possibility, no matter how painful, when trying to search out the roots of a social ill such as the violence we perpetrate and allow to be perpetrated on others. In that search there can be no sacred cows. One of those sacred cows seems to be that there is a truth that cannot be tampered with at the core of Christianity and therefore must be the foundation for Christian worship. What one may find is that there are truths that must be worked with and that are malleable. The ability to compromise, to move slowly through life's quagmire and to remain hopeful of a better tomorrow is hard won and seems at times to lead to chaos. It is often easier to see and explain what one does not believe than to find out what one does believe. To keep a faith in humanity and the deity, to believe that things are changing for the better, that apparent defeats can bring about renewed faith in living is hard enough on a personal level, let alone on a societal level.

Feminist Liturgy

As feminists, it is easy for us to forget that there are many people who share neither our knowledge nor our personal experience of the pain and suffering that exist in the lives of the abused. One of the methods through which we can impart the insights gained is in the worship service, through its hymns, its prayers, and the sermon and liturgies. But there are questions we must ask ourselves as we look for ways to share our knowledge. First, who makes up our community? As feminists, are we committed to lightening the suffering of one person by creating issue-specific liturgies, sermons, and worship services? Can an issue-specific Christianity begin to resolve the problem of violence against women on a societal level? For example, on a theoretical level, it would be better, in my opinion, if we completely did away with the use of parental images for God. However, on a practical level, we have to compromise that position, since it is very difficult to talk about God without using some concrete image, and familial images have certain advantages. Despite the fact that there are many abusive parents, the possible nurturing aspects of parental images make them both comforting and useful. While this means that one has to compromise one's ideal position, perhaps a moderate approach will help more people come to a new understanding of their relationship with God and thus will have a broader impact on society. Thus, we have to ask ourselves the following questions: Are we trying to address a broader societal agenda when we reform, revolutionize, or dismiss traditional forms of liturgy? Do we understand that the needs of an individual worshiper may not be addressed when we focus on a larger perspective? What, quite simply, do we believe to be the relationship between liturgical change and social change?

The creation of feminist liturgy requires an understanding of contextuality, a commitment to an ongoing process, a willingness to experiment, an explicit rejection of hierarchical forms of liturgical leadership, and a corresponding commitment to shared leadership, pluralism, and ecumenicity.[9] A major problem for Christian feminists is the integration of these values into mainstream liturgies. Our perspective of wholeness, the idea that personal stories tell us something about spirituality on a broader level, is a positive value that must be shared. But care must nonetheless be taken. As was discussed above, a personal story can be used yet contribute nothing toward forwarding change; it can, in fact, have the opposite effect.[10] It is the interpretation that is placed on the personal stories and new theological concepts that is the crux of the whole issue of what we can expect from liturgical change. Pastoral counseling with battered women and abused children becomes an exercise in practical theology, as James Poling notes. However, some writers, offering support and help to Christian battered women, have used Valerie Saiving's classic article "The Human Situation: A Feminine View" to argue that women are guilty of the sin of silence.[11] Refusing to let go of the notion that Jesus died on the cross for human sin, means, in this case, that even though abused, women must still be guilty of something. Articulated theologically, it means that women's sin becomes the sin of silence. If liturgy is the practical side of Christian feminist theology, what kind of liturgies will this theological interpretation of Christian teaching and Jesus' mission produce and how helpful will they really be to the abused?

In a courtyard outside Emmanuel College, the United Church seminary in Toronto, there is a statue of the Crucified Woman, the Christa. During a weekend think tank on how Christian denominations can help to eradicate family violence, a liturgy was created focusing on this symbol and its relationship to the suffering Jesus/God/Servant by using a slide presentation of the statue from various angles.[12] It sent shivers down my spine. It is not enough that women are battered, bruised, raped, and otherwise denied a reality, it must now be glorified as suffering for the greater good. For many people, this statue of the Christa has been seen as revolutionary and liberating, but I can only see the healing offered as a temporary respite and not destined to be a part of the equation for solving systemic violence. A focus on a dying god rather than the possibilities of the empty cross has far greater potential for continuing suffering and abuse than for healing the world's wounds.[13]

Another example of the problem of interpretation and personal life histories can be found in the use of the spider's web as a metaphor describing the interconnectedness of life and a new way of focusing on spirituality. The spider's web is gossamer and temporary. It often needs to be rebuilt if it is to function. However, spider's webs are also traps used to entice other creatures to their destruction. Spiders even eat their own young and the black widow eats her mate. One writer in an as yet unpublished manuscript wrote a devastating poem about her experiences of child sexual assault couched in the metaphor of the spider's web. The spider became the most terrifying of creatures; the spider's web, a nightmare from which she could not awake. Any use of this or any other symbolic structure must keep in mind the multiple meanings that all symbols inherently bear.

Suggestions for Ministers

Over the years, it has become very clear to me that a commit-ment to change and a social agenda is very much dependent on a minister who can guide the members of a congregation into new paths of relating to God and to one another. Commitment to process must also mean commitment to learning about abuse is-sues, learning how difficult it is for women who have been abused to change, and why. It is not enough that individual women be helped. Economic issues, for example, play a large role in the maintenance of family violence. This too must be understood. It is incumbent on the leadership of the Christian communities to face up to the systemic issues of family violence and child abuse. A congregation depends on its minister for leadership. But where does the minister go to find alternatives for liturgies, for bringing her or his congregation, individually and corporately, to an un-derstanding of the pain in peoples' lives and the understanding necessary for change? The place to begin is within and by carefully listening to women telling of pain and suffering and children's voices as they articulate their understanding of the gospel.[14]

And so I suggest to ministers: Think about every prayer, sermon, scripture. Put yourself in the shoes of a battered woman and try to understand through her experience. Remember what it was like to be a child, and experience through a child's eyes and ears what you are going to say. This is not an easy exercise. If your own life expe-rience includes episodes of abuse, they may surface for the first time or resurface with a new face. If this makes you feel uncomfortable, sit it out, work it through, be open about the questions that are raised. Pastors and counselors are not gods. However, they are the ones who have to be committed to cooperative ministry, to the continuing search for the messages that are coming from those around them, and to the realization that there are no easy answers.

If you have trouble coming to terms with the past and respecting the reality of your past pain and suffering, you will have a difficult time respecting that of others. Rather than offering easy solutions, try sharing the pain instead of burying it behind the fear that re-venge and anger will be uncontrollable. You cannot expect others to respect the pain of those battered women and children if you don't respect it by accepting its reality. The problem must be eradicated, not hidden in the blood of Christ.

It is argued that worship, ritual, and liturgies precede theology, and this is true during the early development of a religious system. But Christianity is no longer without well-developed theologies. Often the changes to the outward parts of the Sunday service—the dress, the placement of the minister and altar, the inclusion of the laity in service—look as if they make a difference. But it is the words and the day-to-day relationships of the leadership and the congregation that end up telling the real story of how a message of caring and love is being presented. However, it is also true that if the theology doesn't change, nothing will change in any major sense. The possibilities for disaster, a return to the old message, will always remain. Theology must also change and its consequences must be understood if we expect worship and liturgies to aid in the task of making the world safer for all human beings to live in.

When you are responsible for the worship service, watch your congregation. Look for those people who are uncomfortable, who are sad, who may be hiding behind the mask of sacrifice. They are there, and they may not often come forward. The open mind and the open heart will bring forth stories that can be devastating to listen to. But the stories must be heard and the tellers must be helped if we ever hope to end the violence that plagues our society.

Conclusion

Boxed in white chalk in the middle of the blackboard in my office I have written a statement attributed to Thomas Hardy:

> If a way to the better there be,
> It exacts a full look at the worst.

Whenever we fail to take a full look at the worst, whenever we deny the imperfections of our belief system, whenever we deny the evils our theologies have created and perpetuated, whenever we deny the abuse we have ourselves suffered from and caused in the name of our

Christian beliefs, we risk, at the least, perpetuating the present violence and at the worst, causing even more harm, however inadvertently. Most of the time, I feel "knee deep in crocodiles." For those who work with abused women and battered and sexually assaulted children every day, there is barely enough time to keep up with the caseload, let alone to try to fathom what causes the swamp. They are thus often dependent on those who have the time to reflect on the whole swamp. The worship service is an important place, a place where we can begin to change attitudes and make the world a safer place for women and children. This is not an easy task and demands commitment to change and a belief that our God supports that change—wherever it may lead.

Notes

1. Marie Fortune, *Violence in the Family: A Workshop Curriculum for Clergy and Other Helpers* (Cleveland: Pilgrim Press, 1991) and *Keeping the Faith: Questions and Answers for the Abused Woman* (San Francisco: Harper & Row, 1987). See also Gail Golding et al., *Hands to End Violence Against Women* (Toronto: Women's Inter-Church Council of Canada, 1988).

2. While I did not ask about how much group work actually occurs in this congregation, talks with various members of the congregation led me to the conclusion that there was none.

3. Philip Greving, *Spare the Child: The Religious Roots of Punishment and the Psychological Impact of Physical Abuse* (New York: Alfred A. Knopf, 1991); James M. Jones, *Contemporary Psychoanalysis and Religion: Transference and Transcendence* (New Haven, Conn. and London: Yale University Press, 1991); James Poling, *The Abuse of Power: A Theological Problem* (Nashville: Abingdon Press, 1991).

4. See Sheila Redmond, "The Father God and Traditional Christian Interpretation of Suffering, Guilt, Anger, and Forgiveness as Impediments to Recovery from Father-Daughter Incest," dissertation, University of Ottawa, 1993.

5. See Poling, *Abuse of Power.*

6. See Poling, *Abuse of Power,* and Joanne Carlson Brown and

Carole Bohn, eds., *Christianity, Patriarchy, and Abuse: A Feminist Critique* (New York: Pilgrim Press, 1989).

7. See John M. Hull, *What Prevents Christian Adults from Learning?* (Philadelphia: Trinity Press International, 1991 [1985]).

8. Marjorie Procter-Smith, *In Her Own Rite: Constructing Feminist Liturgical Tradition* (Nashville: Abingdon Press, 1990), p. 56.

9. Ibid., pp. 13–35.

10. Personal stories or testimonies, as they are called, have always played a large role in Christian fundamentalist worship. Yet as a group, fundamentalists have more than their share of physical and sexual assault on children and wife assault. See Grant Martin, *Counseling for Family Violence and Abuse* (Waco, Tex.: Word Books Publisher, 1987).

11. Valerie Saiving, "The Human Situation: A Feminine View," in *Womanspirit Rising: A Feminist Reader in Religion*, ed. Carol P. Christ and Judith Plaskow (San Francisco: Harper & Row, 1979), pp. 25–42. While there is certainly a move away from Saiving's work among some recent feminist theologians, her ideas have taken hold among many of the Christian writers dealing with the problem of wife assault.

12. See *Family Violence in a Patriarchal Society: A Challenge to Our Way of Living* (Ottawa: Church Council on Justice and Corrections and the Canadian Council on Social Development with financial assistance from Health and Welfare Canada, 1988), pp. 95–99. This section contains commentary on the statue, plus views both pro and con on its effectiveness.

13. Has anyone noticed how anorexic this statue is? It has been suggested that perhaps a sign of change will be when we see a risen Christa. But given the dangers inherent in any anthropomorphic representation of God, I'm not sure how much further ahead this would make us.

14. See Andrew Lester, *Pastoral Care with Children in Crisis* (Philadelphia: Westminster Press, 1985), and his edited volume, *When Children Suffer: A Sourcebook for Ministry with Children in Crisis* (Philadelphia: Westminster Press, 1987).

6

The Easter Vigil:
A Theological and
Liturgical Critique

Ann Patrick Ware

In the Christian calendar, Easter, as the celebration of the resurrection of Jesus, is the greatest of feasts. The liturgy that initiates the celebration of this central event is the most elaborate of the year in those churches which call themselves catholic. Here we will examine in detail the Easter Vigil of the Roman Catholic Church.

This celebration is viewed best as the culmination of the liturgies of Holy Thursday and Good Friday. Known as the Sacred Triduum, these three days commemorate in turn, the institution of the Eucharist (and some say the Christian priesthood), the recollection of the details of the passion and the veneration of the cross, and the entry with Christ into new and changed life.

The Easter Vigil is divided into four parts: a service of light; the Liturgy of the Word: scripture readings that relate God's wonderful acts for the people; the blessing of water and baptism of catechumens (persons learning about the Christian faith and preparing for baptism); the Liturgy of the Eucharist, that is, the Easter Mass.

The Service of Light: Blessing of the Fire and Lighting of the Easter Candle

Ideally this part of the liturgy begins at night, an hour or two before midnight. A large fire is prepared, generally outside, in a place large enough to accommodate the number of people present. Each person is given a small candle. The priest and his ministers, one of whom is carrying the Easter candle,[1] enter. The priest reminds the people through a series of prayers and actions (the blessing of the new fire and lighting of the Easter candle) of this night's meaning. It is the passover of the Lord. It is the night when the Christian community remembers Christ's victory over death. Then the priest or deacon takes the Easter candle, lifts it high, and sings, "Christ our light." The assembly sings, "Thanks be to God."

Now the procession starts, led off by an acolyte swinging a thurible from which clouds of incense rise. All move toward the darkened church. At the entrance the minister lifts the candle high and sings a second time, "Christ our Light," with the people giving their response. Those nearest the Easter candle light their candles from its flame and pass that light on to others while the procession moves forward. When the minister arrives at the altar, he faces the people and sings the refrain a third time. All the lights in the church are turned on, and the people take their places. The priest installs himself in the presider's chair, the deacon places the Easter candle on its stand.

Now the Easter proclamation, the Exsultet (so called from its first word in Latin), is sung, while all stand with lighted candles in their hands. This may be sung by one of the ministers or by a lay person. Because the Exsultet is regarded as one of the church's most beautiful hymns and expresses Easter's predominant theological themes, I give the text in full:

> Rejoice, heavenly powers! Sing, choirs of angels!
> Exult, all creation around God's throne!
> Jesus Christ, our King, is risen!
> Sound the trumpet of salvation!
>
> Rejoice, O earth, in shining splendor,
> radiant in the brightness of your King!

Christ has conquered! Glory fills you!
Darkness vanishes for ever!

Rejoice, O Mother Church! Exult in glory!
The risen Savior shines upon you!
Let this place resound with joy,
echoing the mighty song of all God's people!

It is truly right
that with full hearts and minds and voices
we should praise the unseen God, the all-powerful Father,
and his only Son, our Lord Jesus Christ.
For Christ has ransomed us with his blood,
and paid for us the price of Adam's sin
to our eternal Father!

This is our passover feast,
when Christ, the true Lamb, is slain,
whose blood consecrates the homes of all believers.

This is the night when first you saved our fathers:
you freed the people of Israel from their slavery
and led them dry-shod through the sea.

This is the night when the pillar of fire
destroyed the darkness of sin!

This is the night when Christians everywhere,
washed clean of sin and freed from all defilement,
are restored to grace and grow together in holiness.

This is the night when Jesus Christ
broke the chains of death
and rose triumphant from the grave.

What good would life have been to us,
had Christ not come as our redeemer?

Father, how wonderful your care for us!
How boundless your merciful love!
To ransom a slave
you gave away your Son!

O happy fault, O necessary sin of Adam,
which gained for us so great a Redeemer!

Most blessed of all nights, chosen by God
to see Christ rising from the dead!

Of this night scripture says:
"The night will be as clear as day:
it will become my light, my joy."

The power of this holy night
dispels all evil, washes guilt away,
restores lost innocence, brings mourners joy;
it casts out hatred, brings us peace, and humbles
    earthly pride.

Night truly blessed when heaven is wedded to earth
and man is reconciled with God! Therefore, heavenly
    Father, in the joy of this night,
receive our evening sacrifice of praise,
your Church's solemn offering.

Accept this Easter candle,
a flame divided but undimmed,
a pillar of fire that glows to the honor of God.

Let it mingle with the lights of heaven
and continue bravely burning to dispel the darkness of
    this night!

May the Morning Star which never sets find this flame
    still burning:
Christ, that Morning Star, who came back from the
    dead,
and shed his peaceful light on all mankind,
your Son who lives and reigns for ever and ever.[2]

After this proclamation, all extinguish their candles and are
seated.

Critique. The Service of Light is profoundly reminiscent of Jewish Passover themes: the saving blood of the paschal lamb, the crossing over from slavery into freedom, the Israelites going dryshod through the sea, the pillar of fire. And, like many other instances in Christian liturgy and theology, this service relies on "displacement theology," that is, whatever there was in Judaism that was salvific has now been replaced by Jesus, the Christ. (See discussion in critique of "The Liturgy of the Word," below.) Thus it is Christ (instead of Moses) who leads the people; Christ's blood (instead of the lamb's) that causes death to pass by; Christ's light—or, indeed, Christ the Light—(instead of the pillar of fire) that leads to salvation. The service also relies heavily on the dichotomy of good and evil with metaphors of light, grace, holiness, glory, radiance, splendor, joy, salvation, merciful love, innocence, peace, and the Morning Star set over against darkness, sin, death, slavery, defilement, chains, guilt, hatred, and earthly pride.

Women have learned that dichotomies do not serve them well. We are all too familiar with those philosophical separations of form and matter, soul and body, reason and emotion, light and darkness, through which women are related to the less significant in the pairing: disposable matter rather than essential form, mortal body rather than the immortal soul, erratic emotion rather than logical reason, unpredictable darkness rather than the clarity of light. The words of the Exsultet assure us that these dichotomies are overcome, for it is Christ who has wedded heaven and earth, who has reconciled God and humankind (Christians), and who has made night as clear as day. With this women are to be satisfied.

Symbols. The symbolism of this part of the Easter Vigil is rich and varied. There is, first of all, the great Easter candle, large enough to burn for the forty days until Ascension Thursday, big enough to be seen by all as it is elevated for the procession into the darkened church. Clearly a phallic symbol, it represents Christ leading the people, enlightening the world. Its form carries the message that a man, Christ, leads, and women are expected to follow. As the lighting of the smaller tapers indicates, it is from this Light that all other light proceeds.

There is the cross with arms embracing the world from east to west, pointing to the four corners of the earth. It stands even with no further adornment as a symbol of Christ. It also stands for suffering and death, the great price paid for our redemption.[3]

However, the most obvious symbol of the Service of Light is the male and clerical dominance, shown in all the priests and deacons and other even the acolytes on the liturgical scene and in the man-centered language of the ritual.

The language, except for one use of "friends" and one of "God's people," is unremittingly masculine and triumphalistic. The language is found not only in reference to Christ, the post-resurrection appellation of the historic male Jesus of Nazareth, but also in a long recitation of masculine terms: Lord, King, Son, Father, all-powerful Father, his only Son, Eternal Father, our fathers, heavenly Father, man, and mankind. Other terms, in themselves genderless, become masculine by association with Christ: lamb, redeemer, Morning Star. On the other hand, women may marvel that the sin which cost such a price is twice referred to as "Adam's sin," not Eve's! One may rightly wonder whether this is a theological attribution of blame where blame should fall or whether the introduction of Eve might introduce a discordant note into the masculine litany.

The one feminine note occurs in the use of "Holy Mother Church," who is called upon to rejoice. But there is cold comfort here, since there are too many images crowding into our female psyches of the subordinate relationship of Church to Christ (woman to man; human to divine). Thus, the words "Holy Mother Church" end up marginalizing women, because the term in fact is a patriarchal construct that systematically oppresses women.

The Liturgy of the Word: Readings from the Hebrew Scriptures, the Gloria, Epistle and Gospel

This section consists of readings, from as few as two to as many as seven (at the will of the presiding priest), with the proviso that the reading from Exodus 14 must always be read. The pattern is this: a reading, a response sung or recited (or a period of silence), a prayer said by the priest. The readings include the Creation account

(Gen. 1:1–2:2); the sacrifice of Isaac (Gen. 22:1–18); the flight from Egypt (Ex. 14:15–15:1); God's fidelity (Isa. 54:5–14); God's bounty (Isa. 55:1–11); paean to wisdom (Bar. 3:9–15, 32–4:4); renewal of the promise to Israel (Ezek. 36:16–28).

Responses to these readings are hymns of praise and thanksgiving, taken from Psalms (104, 33, 16, 30, 19, 42, 43, 51), from Isaiah (12), and from the song of the Israelites (Exodus 15), which is also the song of Miriam, but no mention is made of her in the text as assigned. Each of the prayers offered by the priest begins by recalling one of God's wondrous deeds or promises and concludes with a petition for the grace to be properly thankful and virtuous.

After the last reading with its response and prayer, the acolytes light the candles on the altar, the priest intones the *Gloria in Excelsis,* which the congregation takes up, and church bells are rung.

The service now proceeds as at Mass with an opening prayer by the priest, a reading from Romans 6:3–11, Alleluia and response (Psalm 118), and an account of the resurrection from one of the synoptic Gospels. A homily by the presider concludes this part of the Vigil.

Critique. The readings have been carefully selected to give a basic outline of salvation history: God's omnipotence and promises of unfailing love and care toward creation, human failure, God's merciful rescue of a floundering people through Moses, then Christ. Originally they were designed to present a summary instruction for those who are to be baptized, but they also remind the already baptized of God's continuing largesse. Unfortunately, to the sensitive ear the readings give the impression that this fidelity and largesse extend only to men. One hears an endless repetition of "man," "mankind," "he," "his creation," "his Son," "his redemption," "Lord," "father," "him who sows," "him who eats," "Son of Man." References are to Moses, Abraham, Isaac—even the animal is male, a ram!—pharaoh, officers, army, Jacob his [God's] servant, Israel his [God's] son. Likewise in the responsorial hymns and in the Gloria, God is indubitably male: "the Lord is a warrior, Lord is his name"; "the Lord . . . covered himself in glory"; "the God of my father, I extol him"; "Lord God, heavenly King, almighty God and Father."

In the prayers there is similar emphasis on God's maleness and God's predilection for maleness: "God and father of all who believe in you, you promised Abraham . . ."; "Lord God, the creation of man was a wonderful work"; "may the peoples of the world become true sons of Abraham"; "the spirit of sonship." And the Gloria, a climactic moment in this part of the service and regularly sung (or recited) on most Sundays of the year, hails God three times as "Father" as well as King, Lord almighty, and Most High. Such terms reinforce popular notions of fathers as having ultimate control.

Several passages deserve special scrutiny. To give credit where credit is due, the creation account is that of Genesis 1, where man and woman are created together, rather than the second account, which tells of Adam created first and given the power to name (and thus to have control over) every living creature, including the woman.

The passage from Isaiah (54:5–14) is especially problematic for women. The image of Israel as a wife, "forsaken and grieved in spirit," "a wife married in youth and then cast off," is reminiscent of the thousands of older women whose philandering spouses have found younger, prettier partners. To make God into a husband who casts off his wife but who now in pity and forgiveness "calls her back" reinforces the notion that whatever has gone wrong in this marriage is the woman's fault. There is no way that image can sit well with today's woman.

One reading that uses female imagery in a positive sense is the passage from Baruch[4] (3:9–15, 32–4:4). This little-known and little-used instruction eulogizes wisdom and deserves to be quoted in part:

> Hear, O Israel, the commandments of life:
> listen, and know prudence!
> . . . .
> You have forsaken the fountain of wisdom!
> . . . .
> Learn where prudence is,
> where strength, where understanding;
> . . . .
> Who has found the place of wisdom,
> who has entered into her treasuries?

He who knows all things knows her;
 he has probed her by his knowledge—
. . . .

He has traced out all the way of understanding,
 and has given her to Jacob, his servant,
 to Israel, his beloved son.
Since then she has appeared on earth,
 and moved among men.
She is the book of the precepts of God,
 the law that endures forever;
All who cling to her will live,
 but those will die who forsake her.
Turn, O Jacob, and receive her:
 walk by her light toward splendor.

(NAB)

Refreshing as it is to female ears to hear a "she" and a "her" now and then, we must note that, since the full complement of readings is seldom included because of the length of the service, this is one which generally falls by the wayside. Also, one cannot help but note that the beneficiaries of wisdom are all men: "He" has given her to "Jacob, his servant," and to "Israel, his beloved son," and she, having now appeared on earth, moves "among men." Still, it is gratifying to have a vibrant female image—those who cling to her will live and those who forsake her will die—even if the poet speaks here not of a real woman but of an abstraction.

Whatever positive image may be given in Baruch's use of wisdom as female is quickly undone by Ezekiel's reference to the uncleanliness of all women (36:16–28): "Thus the word of the Lord came to me: Son of man, when the house of Israel lived in their land, they defiled it by their conduct and deeds; in my sight their conduct was like the defilement of a menstruous woman."[5] There are occasional places where—we may hope by design and not by mere coincidence—inclusive words occur where one might have expected masculine ones: descendants, God's people, friends (as a term of address to the congregation). Also, there are some stunning scriptural images, mainly in the responsorial psalms, which bring a lift to the hearer: gathering the waters of the sea as in a flask; in cellars confining the deep; planted on the mountain of inheritance; weeping entering in at nightfall but with the dawn, rejoicing; drawing water (traditionally the work of women) at the fountain of salvation; ordinances more precious than a heap of purest gold; [ordinances] sweeter than syrup or honey from the comb.

The Isaiah 54 passage stirs the imagination with pictures of pavements in carnelians, foundations in sapphires, battlements of rubies, gates of carbuncles, and walls of precious stones. Further, Isaiah issues the classic invitation, "All you who are thirsty, come to the water! You who have no money, come, receive grain and eat; come, without paying and without cost, drink wine and milk!" (Isa. 55:1). But these words are cold comfort in our crumbling cities, where long lines form in front of soup kitchens and where, despite eucharistic overtones that many see in Isaiah 55, even in Christian churches the "table" is not open to all.

All this might be more bearable if the prayers that follow the readings took some note of the situation around us, but instead they continue to deal in generalities that leave grim realities unrecognized and most of us untouched: "May the goodness you now show us confirm our hope in your future mercy"; "Help us to be your faithful people for it is by your inspiration alone that we can grow in goodness"; "May we see in the Church the fulfillment of your promise."

Moreover, despite the fact that it is mainly passages from the Hebrew scriptures that are used, everything surrounding the texts indicates that the religious insights that produced these writings were incomplete and now have met their fulfillment in Christ. The church is the new chosen people, Christ is the new Moses, a new and natural heart will now replace the stony hearts of faithless Israel, the old is made new, the Eucharist is now the new passover mystery. Still, older Catholics can recall that not many years before, they were praying on Good Friday that God would take away the veil from the hearts of the Jews that they too might recognize "Our Lord Jesus Christ," and that God would listen to "our prayers for these unseeing people, that they may perceive the light of your truth, which is Christ himself, and so be brought out of their darkness." New understandings do break through, but the underlying premise that Christianity completes Judaism needs to be examined. Not to be offensive is only a first step; the ones that follow are just as necessary. Can we not understand Jesus the Jew who acts within his own tradition without our making Judaism effete? Must all Christology be "displacement" or "fulfillment" theology?

Finally, at the very end of this long series of readings, written by men for men and about men, comes the reading of the Gospel, and that reading, whether from Matthew, Mark, or Luke, is about women. It is about the women who go early to the tomb to anoint the dead body of Jesus, who meet an angel (Matthew), or two men in bright clothes (Luke), or a young man in a white robe (Mark), and are commissioned to spread the good news that Jesus has been raised from the dead. True, they are pictured as bewildered, trembling, and in great fear (Mark), and the apostles thought what they said was nonsense and did not believe them (Luke), but they are the ones to whom the message is given and thus can be called "apostles" in their own right. It is ironic now that the same church that celebrates this Easter reading, highlighting it by carrying the book in a procession with candles and incense, has managed to ignore God's choice of women to tell the Good News: official church teaching continues to declare women unfit for preaching or even for reading the Gospel at Mass.

The Blessing of Water, Sacraments of Initiation, Renewal of Baptismal Promises

This part of the Easter Vigil varies greatly depending upon the local situation: whether there are any people to be baptized; whether they are adults (in which case they may also receive the Sacrament of Confirmation if there is a bishop present or a priest authorized to administer this sacrament); whether the baptismal font is to be used (if it is visible to the congregation or if there is a procession to the baptistery) or whether some smaller vessel of water will be brought to the sanctuary; whether, if there is no one to be baptized, the celebrant still wishes to bless the water with which he will sprinkle the whole congregation as they recall their baptism.

If there are candidates to be baptized, the priest now calls them forth with their godparents, and the congregation joins with the cantor in the singing of the Litany of the Saints. If there is to be a procession, the Easter candle is carried first, followed by those to be baptized, their godparents, and the priest and his ministers, while the litany is being sung.

The Litany of the Saints is now much shorter than its earlier form, which invoked all three Persons of the Trinity, Mary under three of her titles, several angels, twelve categories of saints (for example, "all you holy monks and hermits," "all you holy maidens and widows," thus including them all) and twenty-one saints specifically named. The present litany calls upon Christ (Lord), Mary, and the angels, and then invokes twenty-five saints by name, six of whom are women, concluding with a petition to "all holy men and women" to pray for us. This litany is one of the few places in the whole liturgical corpus, outside of minimal references in the Gospels, where women are now named or, in fact, where any reference is made to them.[6]

The priest now addresses the congregation as "dear friends in Christ" (a recent improvement over the earlier unfailing use of "brethren") and asks either that all help with their prayers the "brothers and sisters [who] approach the waters of rebirth" (in the event there are candidates for baptism) or (if there is no one to be baptized) that God "bless this font where your children will be reborn."

Now follows a blessing (recited or sung) of the water, in which God's many uses of this element are celebrated: the Spirit breathing on the water in creation; the waters of the great flood; the delivery of Israel from slavery through the waters of the Red Sea; the baptism of Jesus by John in the waters of the Jordan; the effusion of blood and water from Jesus' pierced side; Jesus' command to his disciples to baptize all nations. The prayer now links this water to the waters of birth, saying, "Give to this water the grace of your Son, so that . . . all those whom you have created in your likeness may . . . rise to a new birth of innocence by water and the Holy Spirit." Here the priest is given an option: he may touch the water with his right hand, or he may lower the paschal candle into the water one or three times and hold it there as he prays that all who are buried with Christ in the death of baptism may rise with him to newness of life.

The manifestly sexual implications of this ritual were even clearer before the changes of 1973.[7] This blessing of the water contained such phrases as "Make this a life-giving water . . . that sons [sic] of Heaven may be conceived here in holiness, and emerge from the spotless womb of this divine font reborn, a new creation."[8] Rubrics ordered the priest to "plunge" the foot of the paschal candle into the water, chanting, "May the power of the Holy Spirit come down into this font and all it holds," and then to repeat the action and the words twice, "each time plunging the candle lower" and finally holding the candle in the water while he said, "Charge this water through and through with the power to give new life."[9]

If the priest has chosen to hold the Easter candle in the water, he now raises it, and the people sing some suitable acclamation. "Springs of water, bless the Lord" is suggested.

The baptism now proceeds, followed by confirmation, if appropriate, and the ritual of clothing the newly baptized person in a white garment.

After the celebration of baptism all present, standing and holding lighted candles, renew their baptismal promises. Then the priest, making his way through the aisles of the church, sprinkles the whole congregation with the newly blessed water while the choir or the whole assembly sings a suitable song. A final prayer by the presider concludes this portion of the Vigil.

Critique. Just as the first part of the Vigil service celebrates fire and light, common necessities of human living, so this part celebrates water. But the liturgy fails to note the scarcity of water in many countries and the facts that women across the world walk miles to carry water to their families, that drought and famine are interconnected, and that acid rain and toxic pollution of the world's water supply make fresh and life-giving water one of our most precious commodities. If the liturgy can be criticized for anything, it is for this utter disregard of contemporary realities. One cannot expect the modern situation to be reflected in ancient texts, but surely such reference is not too much to expect in prayers addressed to God, prayers that the congregation is expected to affirm with an "Amen."

The symbolism of the baptismal font as womb in which new Christians are conceived and from which they emerge as children of God is once again problematic for many women. While it is a relief to have a symbol with which most women can identify, for others it is yet another assertion that the special role—indeed, the only worthwhile role—of women is to bear children.

One must applaud the new recognition in language that everyone baptized is not male. "Brothers and sisters" are invited to the baptismal font whence they emerge as "sons and daughters." But then those baptized are anointed so that they may be a member of one who is Priest (male) and King (male). Thus what is given with one hand is taken away with the other. Can Christ not also be described in more inclusive terms, like friend, healer, lover, neighbor?

The Liturgy of the Eucharist

The rest of the Easter Vigil follows the regular pattern of the Catholic Mass, beginning with the presentation of the gifts, bread and wine. The prayers said over these elements are reminiscent of the Jewish *berakhot* ("Blessed are you, Lord our God, King of the Universe"). They give thanks to God for these gifts of the earth and of human hands, and recall the memory of Jesus at the Last Supper, celebrating the Passover with his disciples. Addressing the congregation, the priest says: "Pray, brethren, that our sacrifice may be acceptable to God, the almighty Father." To this, all reply: "May the Lord accept the sacrifice at your hands for the praise and glory of his name, for our good, and the good of all his Church." A final prayer, before moving on to the Preface of the Mass, asks God's help that this Easter mystery of our redemption may bring to perfection the saving work that God has begun.

A dialogue (generally sung) now ensues between priest and people. Then follows one of several prayers (prefaces), sung or said by the priest, elaborating why it is right to give God thanks and praise, for example: He sent his beloved Son to redeem us; he created all things and filled his creatures with every blessing.

Every preface concludes with ". . . we say: Holy, holy, holy Lord, God of power and might. Heaven and earth are full of your glory. Hosanna in the highest! Blessed is he who comes in the name of the Lord. Hosanna in the highest!" Because every mass, according to Catholic doctrine, makes present in a sacramental way the passion and death of Jesus and also commemorates the resurrection, this acclamation recalls Jesus' triumphal entry into Jerusalem, which this congregation will have celebrated only a week before on Palm Sunday.

Now comes one of four eucharistic prayers, which the priest is at liberty to choose. Each of them contains the words of institution:

[Over the bread] Take this, all of you, and eat it: this is my body which will be given up for you.

[Over the cup] Take this, all of you, and drink from it: this is the cup of my blood, the blood of the new and everlasting covenant. It will be shed for you and for all so that sins may be forgiven. Do this in memory of me.

Each of them also contains specific prayers for the present pope, for the bishop of the diocese, mentioned by his first name; for all other bishops; for the clergy; and for the rest of the people.

Below are two of the eucharistic prayers, selected because to many women they represent the best (II) and the worst (IV):

II

Lord, you are holy indeed,
the fountain of all holiness.
Let your Spirit come upon these gifts to make them holy,
so that they may become for us
the body and blood of our Lord, Jesus Christ.

Before he was given up to death,
a death he freely accepted,

he took bread and gave you thanks.
He broke the bread,
gave it to his disciples, and said:
[words of institution as above].

When supper was ended, he took the cup.
Again he gave you thanks and praise,
gave the cup to his disciples, and said:
[words of institution as above].

Let us proclaim the mystery of faith:
[All recite one of four acclamations, proclaiming that
Jesus will come again in glory and that he is the Savior
of the world.]

In memory of his death and resurrection,
we offer you, Father, this life-giving bread,
this saving cup.

We thank you for counting us worthy
to stand in your presence and serve you.
May all of us who share in the body and blood of Christ
be brought together in unity by the Holy Spirit.

Lord, remember your Church throughout the world;
make us grow in love,
together with John Paul our Pope,
[Name] our bishop, and all the clergy.

Remember our brothers and sisters
who have gone to their rest
in the hope of rising again;
bring them and all the departed
into the light of your presence.
Have mercy on us all;
make us worthy to share eternal life
with Mary, the virgin Mother of God,
with the apostles, and with all the saints
who have done your will throughout the ages.

May we praise you in union with them,
and give you glory
through your Son, Jesus Christ.

IV

[Bold print is mine]

Father, we acknowledge your greatness:
all your actions show your wisdom and love.
You formed **man** in your own likeness
and set **him** over the whole world
to serve you, **his** creator,
and to rule over all creatures.
Even when **he** disobeyed you and lost your friendship
you did not abandon **him** to the power of death,
but helped all **men** to seek and find you.
Again and again you offered a covenant to **man,**
and through the prophets taught **him** to hope for salvation.
Father, you so loved the world
that in the fullness of time you sent your only **Son** to be
    our Savior.
He was conceived through the power of the Holy Spirit,
and born of the Virgin Mary,
a **man** like us **in all things** but sin.
To the poor he proclaimed the good news of salvation,
to prisoners, freedom,
and to those in sorrow, joy.
In fulfillment of your will
he gave himself up to death;
but by rising from the dead,
he destroyed death and restored life.
And that we might live no longer for ourselves but for him,
he sent the Holy Spirit from you, **Father,**
as his first gift to those who believe,
to complete his work on earth
and bring us the fullness of grace.
Father, may this Holy Spirit sanctify these offerings.

Let them become the body and blood of Jesus Christ our Lord
as we celebrate the great mystery
which he left us as an everlasting covenant.
He always loved those who were his own in the world.
When the time came for him to be glorified by you,
    his heavenly **Father**,
he showed the depth of his love.

While they were at supper,
he took bread, said the blessing, broke the bread,
and gave it to his disciples, saying:
[words of institution].

In the same way, he took the cup, filled with wine.
He gave you thanks, and giving the cup to his disciples,
    said: [words of institution].
Let us proclaim the mystery of faith:
[All sing or recite acclamation.]

Father, we now celebrate this memorial of our redemption.

We recall Christ's death, his descent among the dead,
his resurrection, and his ascension to your right hand;
and, looking forward to his coming in glory,
we offer you his body and blood,
the acceptable sacrifice
which brings salvation to the whole world.
Lord, look upon this sacrifice which you have given
    to your Church;
and by your Holy Spirit, gather all who share this one
    bread and one cup
into the one body of Christ, a living sacrifice of praise.

Lord, remember those for whom we offer this sacrifice,
especially **John Paul our Pope**,
[Name] our bishop, and **bishops** and **clergy** everywhere.

Remember those who take part in this offering,
those here present and all your people,
and all who seek you with a sincere heart.

Remember those who have died in the peace of Christ and
all the dead whose faith is known to you alone.
Father, in your mercy grant also to us, your children,
to enter into our heavenly inheritance
in the company of the Virgin Mary, the Mother of God,
and your **apostles** and saints.
Then, in your **kingdom,** freed from the corruption of sin
and death,
we shall sing your glory with every creature
through Christ our Lord,
through whom you give us everything that is good.

At the conclusion of this prayer the congregation sings the
Great Amen.

The Communion rite now begins with the saying (or singing)
of the Lord's Prayer, followed by the sign of peace. The priest, recalling the greeting of Jesus to his followers after the resurrection,
"Peace be with you,"[10] asks God for peace and unity and bids the
congregation to give one another "the sign of peace" (usually a
handclasp but in some settings an embrace). A triple invocation is
sung to the Lamb of God to have mercy and to grant peace. Then,
holding up the consecrated host for all to see, the priest says:
"This is the Lamb of God who takes away the sins of the world.
Happy are those who are called to his supper." All respond:
"Lord, I am not worthy to receive you, but only say the word and
I shall be healed." The celebrant invites those present who are
Catholic to receive Communion with these words: "Christ has
become our paschal sacrifice; let us feast with the unleavened bread
of sincerity and truth." Those who wish now file up to where ministers of Communion are stationed and receive the sacrament. In
some instances, women may serve as eucharistic ministers. After
Communion there is a period of silence or a hymn of praise. The
service, which up to this point may have lasted as long as two hours,
comes quickly to an end. The priest offers a last prayer, asking God
once again for unity in peace and love through the Spirit. Then he,
or a deacon, dismisses the assembly, singing "Go in the peace of
Christ, alleluia, alleluia," to which all respond (also singing),
"Thanks be to God, alleluia, alleluia."

Critique. Catholics until only recently[11] commonly referred to Mass as the Sacrifice of the Mass, and the texts, besides explicit references to "sacrifice" and to "death freely accepted," make frequent use of the concept of Jesus as the paschal lamb (whose blood marked the doorposts of the Hebrews in Egypt and saved them[12]).

The notion of sacrifice is an ambivalent one for many women. On the one hand, some feel deep gratitude for the love of Christ, which went to such lengths to save them. On the other, some feel that they have been unfairly singled out as the ones especially called to imitate Christ in sacrifice. They often hear from their male advisers, clerics as well as others, that they should sacrifice their aspirations for a career in favor of supporting their husbands, sacrifice their safety when their mates abuse them, sacrifice themselves for their children. Women do not understand why their blood, shed in a menstrual flow as part of the life process (a process that can even leave them dead in giving birth), should make them "unclean," while Christ's shedding of blood is salvific.[13]

The two eucharistic prayers illustrate how (in prayer II) it is possible to use some other form of address than "Father" (although "Lord" is not much of an improvement), and how a text may relieve in part the oppressively masculine nature of the language with a reference to the Spirit, to God as "fountain of holiness," and to "brothers and sisters."

Eucharistic prayer IV makes no attempt at all to use inclusive terms. In fact, the authors seem to have gone out of their way to exemplify the so-called "generic use of man." Women, sitting in their pews, are all too likely to agree that, yes, God did set *man* over the whole world—and there he sits in business, in government, in the home, and especially in the church. It is insulting for women to be told by this church, in the heart of its liturgy, that Jesus "is a man *like us* in all things but sin," and to be told by that same church that they are not possible candidates for ordination because they are not male. And what is to be said of the narcissism evident in the priestly caste's assumption that pope, bishops, and other clergy should be the main object of the people's prayers for their loved ones?

This portion of the Easter Vigil caters to almost total passivity on the part of the congregation. The priest does it all: offers the prayers, does lengthy reading, consecrates the bread and wine, displays them to the people, invites to Communion, dispenses Communion (which people "receive"), and dismisses the congregation. Having an occasional woman eucharistic minister positioned here and there is no countervalent. It is this dominance of the priest which makes many doubt whether the unrelieved hierarchy of the situation would be improved if women were to be ordained.

Conclusion

The Easter Vigil presents liturgy in its most dramatic and colorful form, using familiar objects and situations—darkness and light, incense, water, candles, oil, bread, wine, bells, colors, parades, words and song—to portray God's grace in human life: birth and death, slavery and freedom, love, forgiveness, and deliverance from evil. Hearing the church bells ring out on Holy Saturday night at the singing of the Gloria and experiencing the festive chant of the Alleluia, which has been suppressed throughout the forty days of Lent, can be moments of true spiritual joy.

But if the Easter Vigil does not enchant all of its participants today as it once did, it may be because of these reasons:

First, women with a new-found consciousness find themselves aliens in the rituals of the Roman Catholic Church. The sexist language makes it impossible for them to overlook the fact that they are excluded even verbally from those rituals. They do not recognize themselves—nor are they willing to any longer—as sons, brothers, men, mankind, priests, prophets, kings.

Second, women, seeking feminine dimension in God that might allow them, too, to believe that they are made in God's image, reject the traditional God-language of the liturgy: Father, Son, Lord, Almighty, Most High, Judge. They find Christocentric rituals painful and disturbing—controlled, presented, and interpreted as they are by men and men alone. There may also be here a crisis of faith: Can it really be God's plan that everything having to do with our redemption is the work of one man, holy as he is? Doesn't the incarnation symbolize God's partnership with all humanity, each person embodying aspects of divinity. If this is a real question for some, then the insistence that the symbolic reenactment in the sanctuary, which also demands the presence of at least one properly ordained man through whom the paschal mysteries are accomplished, is likewise questionable.[14]

Third, Catholics who are deeply engaged in the agonies of contemporary society squirm when they hear liturgical language that is timeless, addressing a vacuum in which there is no homelessness, addiction, grinding poverty, squalor, AIDS, or a host of other ills. It is not enough to lump all of these under the category of "evil" and to proceed blithely with the assertion that "Christ has conquered sin and death." To these Catholics, such liturgy is a luxury, which might be excused for its disdain of temporalities if it offered comfort to its hearers, but they (we) are not comforted by it. We are more likely to be scandalized.

It would be possible to have women, even under the strict present rubrics, take visible roles in the Vigil. There is no reason why a woman cannot sing the Exsultet or why women should not serve as lectors in all the readings of the Liturgy of the Word. In fact, in one religious community of women, the whole Liturgy of the Word is presided over by a woman, who also says the prayers ordinarily offered by the priest. All eucharistic ministers could be women. But all this is at the sufferance of the pastor, and even with these changes it is not clear that women would be present and active except as "friendly helpers"—a subordinate role that duplicates women's traditional roles in society and family.

Finally, this ritual (and all the others of the Catholic Church) could be enriched by a deliberate search for new descriptive names for God instead of the overworked "Father." How refreshing it would be to hear God addressed as "God, arrayed in justice," "God of all generations," "God of light and sun," "Heart's delight," "Inspiration to goodness," "Searcher of hearts."[15] May this God assist us in our search.

Notes

1. The Easter candle is specially designed. It is of pure wax, some three feet or so in length and two inches or so in diameter.

2. This text and all the following ones not noted otherwise are from *Today's Missal: Holy Week Triduum* March 24–April 6, 1991 (Portland, Ore.: Oregon Catholic Press, 1991). The Bible translations are from the *New American Bible*.

3. Editor's Note: For some women the primacy of the cross and Jesus' death on it are profoundly disturbing. Womanist theologian Delores Williams says that all too often, the action of Jesus seen as submitting voluntarily to the will of God for the sake of sinful humankind conveys the message that surrogacy is a sacred act. For black women especially, whose history is marked significantly with surrogacy roles (as mammies, or as "masculine" women whose bodies were so strong they could sustain more pain than white women), a surrogate Jesus can continue to reinforce their own exploitation. Thus, Williams asks, "If black women accept the image of redemption, can they not also passively accept the exploitation surrogacy brings?" Does the message of the cross legitimate destructive self-sacrifice? See Delores S. Williams, "Black Women's Surrogacy Experience and the Christian Notion of Redemption," in *After Patriarchy*, ed. Paula M. Cooey, William R. Eakin, and Jay B. McDaniel (Maryknoll, N.Y.: Orbis Books, 1991), pp. 1–14.

4. Baruch is a book that Protestants consider apocryphal but that Catholics have included in the canon of the Old Testament since the Council of Trent (1546).

5. Some "missalettes" (booklets that enable Catholics to follow the service) omit this reference (Ezek. 36:17b) without giving any hint that a portion of the text is missing. However, the full text is included in the lectionary. This suggests that this demeaning verse is read in many churches and may well be contained in missalettes from publishers other than the one from which I have quoted.

6. Editor's Note: It is notable that in the Roman Canon (Eucharistic Prayer) used in the church for fifteen hundred years, the names of women were listed. With the recent revisions, such inclusions are optional.

7. The last revision of the Missal of the Roman Rite was published in 1973.

8. *Layman's Daily Missal: Prayer Book and Ritual* (Baltimore: Helicon Press, 1962), p. 532.

9. Ibid., p. 533.

10. Matt. 28:9; Luke 24:36; John 20:21, 7.

11. In the changes that followed Vatican II, effort was made to incorporate more emphasis on the joyous character of the rite and on communion. (Jesus is, after all, not dead but alive!) "Celebrating the Eucharist" became the new term for "saying Mass" or "going to Mass." The "altar" became the "table," but Jesus' death on the cross is still a basic reality.

12. Ex. 12:7, 23.

13. See Janet Walton's "The Missing Element of Women's Experience," in *The Changing Face of Jewish and Christian Worship,* ed. Paul F. Bradshaw and Lawrence A. Hoffman (Notre Dame, Ind.: University of Notre Dame Press, 1991), pp. 199–217.

14. For more on this point, see Daphne Hampson, *Theology and Feminism* (Cambridge, Mass.: Basil Blackwell, 1990), especially her section on "Feminist Christologies," pp. 59–66.

15. These titles are taken from an unpublished list, "Non-Sexist Names, Titles and Phrases Applied to God," compiled by a group of Jewish women and distributed by the late Annette Daum.

PART 3

Building Anew:
Critique and Commentary
on Emerging Feminist Ritual

The women's movement, reinitiated vigorously in the late sixties, called women to take responsibility for their own lives. In that pursuit women recognized the power of ritual to sustain the struggle, to offer insight, and not insignificantly, to provide pleasure. "Yes it is bread we fight for but we fight for roses, too." Not finding what they needed in many institutional settings, women shaped their own forms, some with tangential connections to the traditions of which they were a part, others with more dependence on ancient sources and/or newly articulated concerns. Most of the essays in this section are descriptions of such gatherings. Since ongoing evaluation is an essential part of this work, each chapter includes a critical review of the ritual activity as well.

Sue Levi Elwell surveys the development of Rosh Hodesh (new moon) celebrations by a feminist group over a period of a year and a half. By placing this process in the context of the traditional Jewish prohibitions against women's speaking, Elwell interprets the development of these rituals as Jewish women's search for their own words, their own language. But, she asks, what is the relationship of this ritual language, growing out of women's culture and experience, to Judaism? How are the oral traditions developed for Rosh Hodesh in this community related to the text-centered traditions of Judaism?

Irene Monroe is a member of the Aché Sisters, a worshiping group of Zamis, Christian and post-Christian women presently or formerly members of African-American churches, who want to claim their homosexual, homoerotic, and homospiritual identity in their ritual experiences. With courage and passion, Monroe tells their story.

Wendy Hunter Roberts is a Neo-Pagan. Her ritual work is based on collective resources from a synthesis of traditions, ancient and modern, as well as the intuitive movements among the men and women who gather. It is an intriguing example of the relationships between the rich symbols of nature and the emerging insights of contemporary life. An especially helpful critique illumines the ongoing discussions about claiming these ancient traditions.

Diann Neu describes a Pentecost liturgy developed for an international gathering of Christian women. The liturgy begins with the traditional Christian festival of Pentecost but pushes that tradition to locate women's issues and justice issues at the center. Neu's concern that feminism be engaged in the struggle for justice on a large scale as well as small is seen in her interests in documenting and publishing feminist liturgies and in her insistence on the need for feminist liturgy groups to retain a connection with established churches. It differs from the commitment to oral feminist tradition found in other settings and groups.

Patricia Malarcher writes from her experience as a member of a women's liturgy group, primarily Roman Catholic, that has gathered monthly since 1981. These women, dissatisfied with the painfully slow recognition of women's gifts in their churches, committed themselves to work together to discover what ritual would look like if it took women's experiences seriously. Malarcher describes a particular celebration for one of its members.

Ada María Isasi-Díaz describes a liturgy used at a conference of an organization of Hispanic Catholic women, LAS HERMANAS. Like Neu's Pentecost liturgy, this mujerista liturgy intentionally connects the participants with their Hispanic Catholic liturgical tradition while at the same time moving them beyond it to claim their power as liberated Hispanic women.

7

Reclaiming Jewish Women's Oral Tradition? An Analysis of Rosh Hodesh

Sue Levi Elwell

What are the words
we want to sing talk scream whisper together?
what are the days we want to gather in new spirit?
what are the seasons of earth and life we want to
celebrate lament remember create together?
what is the dance
or stillness
of this cycle?

—from "A Guide to Celebration,"
by Rabbi Lynn Gottlieb

For Jewish women, these are new questions.[1] For five thousand years, Jewish women have been told what words to say and when to say them, or, more often, when *not* to say them. *Kol isha erva*, the rabbinic dictum that a woman's voice is potentially sexually provocative and should therefore not be heard in public, has kept many women in silence. Too many of the words that *have* been spoken and sung by Jewish women have not been heard. Words of praise and petition, words of thanks and of pain, words of joy and of sadness have remained stifled in the mouths and hearts of Jewish women through the centuries.[2] Jewish women are now in the process of establishing a new claim to language that is our birthright. As this century draws to a close, Jewish women are reclaiming our mother tongue as our own. Jewish women are in search of a few good words.[3]

Because Judaism is a text-centered tradition, finding words to tell women's stories is an urgent task. Without women's words, the ancient scrolls are incomplete and wanting.[4] Without women's stories, the pageants and recitations that are so central to Jewish life portray half-truths. When women begin to look for words, they set in motion a process of transformation that can restore and heal our rich and ancient tradition.

Jewish women have begun the process of recovering language by speaking to one another. Following Nelle Morton's direction to "hear one another into speech,"[5] we have gathered in small circles to pray and sing and share our stories. The task of recovery is an arduous one, but we have begun with ourselves, unrolling the texts of our own lives. In communities of trust, we have listened to one another and begun to see the emergence of patterns of strength and of hurt, of vision and of failure, of courage and of struggle. We have begun to acknowledge the depth of our disempowerment by a tradition that has celebrated the lives and achievements and words of men, a tradition that has relegated women to the back, or the balcony, of the synagogue. We now see what it has cost for women to have been barred from creating and studying the texts that are at the heart of Judaism. When we begin, haltingly, to tell our stories, we find that we can recover our ancient language. As we tell the texts of our lives, slowly we find that our stories are resonant of a legacy that stretches back to the beginning of time.

The process of reclaiming our mother tongue, the language of Judaism, as our own, has led to the creation of a rich harvest of rituals and ceremonies. Most of the early rituals were compensatory attempts to establish women as equals of men in a traditional context: baby naming for girls, bat mitzvah, egalitarian *ketubot* (marriage contracts), and adaptations of traditional divorce decrees that fully acknowledge both spouses. More recently, women have developed rituals to acknowledge rites of passage connected with biological experience: weaning rituals, rituals for a first menstruation, ceremonies for pregnancy loss and abortion, rites to acknowledge hysterectomy or the removal of a cancerous breast. Twenty years after Jews first created ceremonies to welcome girls into the covenant, Jewish women are asking profound questions about the nature of Jewish women's spiritual experience. How can we acknowledge not only biological passages but other points of transition in Jewish women's lives in a way that is authentically Jewish, in a way that resonates with this ancient tradition? And, on the other hand, can the tradition expand sufficiently to accommodate, acknowledge, and celebrate the rich variety of Jewish women's lives and life passages?[6]

The Rosh Hodesh Ritual:
Examination and Critique

For the last twenty years, Jewish women across the country have been coming together in small groups to celebrate Rosh Hodesh, welcoming the first day of every new Hebrew month. Rosh Hodesh, the celebration of the new moon, has been linked with the natural cycle of women's lives since ancient times.[7] The Babylonian Talmud, the second-century compilation of Jewish legal discussions, discusses women's exemption from work on this day. Other rabbinic sources explain this exemption as a reward to women for their refusal to contribute their jewelry to the construction of the Golden Calf.[8] By linking Rosh Hodesh to the Golden Calf incident, the rabbis historicize ancient lunar celebrations and claim them as their own. While this was a common practice among the ancient framers of Israelite religion,[9] the establishment of a Jewish historical context for this distinctly female celebration claims it as a celebration for all Jews, rejecting the false dichotomy that identifies men with culture and women with nature.[10]

The Talmud mentions that Rosh Hodesh is called a Day of Good Beginnings, and it was considered to be "an appropriate day for . . . housewarmings, dedications, . . . wearing new clothes and shoes, for [blessing] newly ripened fruit, and for beginning a new

book in school."[11] While synagogue liturgy is enhanced to acknowledge the special status of the day, the holiday readings and
songs of the synagogue service do not acknowledge the connection of women with the New Moon.[12] Contemporary Jewish
women have reclaimed the day and developed a range of ritual
observances.

Some orthodox women come together monthly to pray in an
all-women's minyan. The form may be absolutely traditional, but
the very existence of an all-women's prayer quorum where
women take all the leadership roles directly challenges traditional
norms. Another important Rosh Hodesh innovation was established by Women at the Wall, a group of women who pray together at the Western Wall of Solomon's Temple in Jerusalem. In
December, 1988, as part of an international conference on Jewish
women, a group of delegates decided to pray together at this historic holy site. No group of women had ever prayed at the wall *as
a group* with a Torah scroll, and traditionalists objected by hurling
obscenities and then, several days later, chairs. Several women
were injured, and the police finally dispersed the crowd with tear
gas. An international support group was formed, and a class-action
suit was brought against the Israeli government for denying access
to a holy site. The case is still under consideration by the Israeli
Supreme Court. Undaunted, the Women at the Wall continue to
gather in the early hours of each new moon to pray together.

When the Los Angeles Jewish Feminist Center opened in the
fall of 1990, we decided to celebrate the birth of the center with a
Rosh Hodesh ceremony. We wanted to make a strong statement
that the center is both a Jewish and a feminist organization, dedicated to teaching about Judaism while simultaneously challenging
its androcentric assumptions and patriarchal past. With its ancient
roots as a women's holiday, but without any strictures for observance, Rosh Hodesh seemed an ideal entry into the world of ex-
perimental feminist ritual.

At that time, there were only a very few women in the Los Angeles area observing Rosh Hodesh. The Rosh Hodesh groups that
existed met monthly in member's homes, like similar groups in
other parts of the country. These groups were participant-led,

loosely structured, and focused on sharing experience. For those who participated, these monthly gatherings provided a welcome alternative to public, liturgically bound synagogue services. In the hopes of seeding other such groups, we wanted to create a public ceremony that would model how a smaller group could work.

What and for Whom? Initial Assumptions

Some of the planners, all feminists and liberal Jews, began with an unexamined assumption that the rituals would reflect a cultural feminist or essentialist understanding, that women share a biology, a history, and a culture. While this may seem to be a radical departure from a traditional Jewish worldview, apologists for traditional Judaism are quick to point out that Judaism has always acknowledged women's particular spiritual needs, and indeed, the strict separation of sexes in Judaism enables the creation of a woman-centered culture.[13] However, this distinction assumes a concept of women's complementarity with men and is the creation of an androcentric, not a gynocentric, worldview.

By welcoming men to the Rosh Hodesh ceremonies, the planners challenged the traditional separation of the sexes that restrict women's activities to women (men participate only in leadership roles), and men's activities (i.e., all normative prayer) to groups made up exclusively of men. By fashioning an event that was imagined as a reflection and an expansion of an essentialist women's culture, the planners created a ritual that would, finally, find little or no resonance in mainstream Jewish practice.[14]

By creating woman-centered ritual, the planners claimed that they hoped to challenge and change normative Jewish practice by integrating women's experience into Jewish prayer and Jewish praxis. However, the celebration of women's experience as particular and unique challenges the rabbinic historicization of Rosh Hodesh. Thus the rituals were *not* created as a first step toward an integrated celebration for all Jews.

A third assumption was that those who participated in the ritual would share the needs, visions, and expectations of the planners. The planners wanted to create a ritual that, while welcoming the new month, was actually a ritual that welcomed Jews back to Judaism. We wanted to weave together words and symbols that were comforting in their familiarity and simultaneously challenging in their newness. We wanted participants to experience a sense of connectedness to one another and to the tradition that would be both unexpected and compelling.

The Celebration Evolves

Over the next year and a half, a fairly standard Rosh Hodesh ritual developed. Each ceremony began with music, usually led by a trained leader (always a woman). The opening singing was followed by invocations of the matriarchs, introductions of participants to one another, and readings about the new month. The central focus of the celebration was usually text study, most often in groups. Sometimes the groups used assigned leaders, most of whom were women, and many of whom were clergy and other recognized community teachers. The study often culminated in some kind of group project: writing a *midrash*, an interpretation or explanation of the biblical text; creating a dramatic presentation; composing a holiday song; retelling an ancient story with contemporary words. Each celebration ended with song, dance, and always with food. The themes of each celebration reflected the cycle of the Jewish year, contemporary world events, and events within the local community.

The celebrations, which were open to the public, attracted a very wide range of participants: from feminists with a keen understanding of sociopolitical issues who were doubtful that Jewish study or practice could be reclaimed, to Jews who were skeptical that anything "feminist" could also be authentically Jewish. Most of those who were most conversant with feminist issues had very little formal Jewish education, and thus they had few tools for entering into informed conversations with traditional Jewish texts. Conversely, those who were most comfortable with Jewish texts were the least familiar with basic feminist ideology.

The initial celebrations seemed to offer something to everyone. While the opening welcome was patterned on a circle casting common to many Goddess rituals, it was reframed as an invocation of the four biblical matriarchs. This had the effect of mirroring what some would consider to be an essential feminist ritual while restoring the matriarchs to a place of honor.[15] The words to the songs that began and concluded each program were provided in English, in Hebrew, and in transliteration, so that none were at a disadvantage. All study materials were introduced in an inclusive manner, and all texts were distributed in English as well as Hebrew. The emphasis was on celebration and inclusion, on bringing participants into the tradition and providing a forum for women's voices.

Response and Analysis

For some, participation in the Rosh Hodesh ceremonies was a step toward increased comfort in Judaism and the Jewish community. Participants were welcomed into a Jewish space that both acknowledged and celebrated women's experience. Each Rosh Hodesh was held in a synagogue, and the simple act of coming to a synagogue for an explicitly feminist event had a profound impact on some of those who attended. Participants' introductions, by their own names followed by their mother's names, enabled women to place themselves in the chain of Jewish tradition in a way that has been traditionally reserved for men.[16] Participants were further empowered by having access to the translations and transliteration of Hebrew prayers and songs, and by repetition of the songs that have become a basic Jewish feminist repertoire. As the months passed, some who felt profoundly disconnected from the cycle of Jewish time realized that they can begin to synchronize their lives with the rich and ancient cycle of the Jewish year.

Each of the rituals was planned by a committee of lay women and clergy, and some who participated in these planning sessions very consciously used the rituals to apply feminist theory, or to experiment with new or reclaimed symbols and signs. Others used the opportunity to deepen their own familiarity with a particular text, and then to teach that text.

Attendance at the rituals varied between thirty and one hundred participants, with an average of sixty people at each gathering.

Several people attended regularly, but many more came once or twice. The community that was created was a community of the moment, a community for an evening. And while many people who missed a ritual expressed to one or another of the leaders that they wished they could have attended, it was clear that no one felt a sense of obligation or responsibility either to other individuals or to the group to attend. While this may reflect the culture of Los Angeles, it may also reflect the participants' attitudes toward this alternative, clearly optional ritual observance.

Some rituals were more "successful" than others. Music, the connective tissue of most powerful rituals, was an essential ingredient of each ritual. More important than the choice of songs or their placement in the program was the energy of the song leader. The rituals that most deeply touched the participants were led by women with a charismatic, but not overpowering presence, and a strong, clear voice. Music is the most immediate means for moving people into sacred space, for it moves beyond potentially leaden words and directly addresses the hunger of the seeker.

Another yardstick for measuring the success of the ritual was the amount of prayer in the celebration. Less was clearly more. The early rituals included only two short prayers: a blessing for study and a blessing over the food. Both were written in Hebrew in unconventional prayer formulas, but their "success" was clearly their brevity, not the alternative to traditional liturgy that they represented.[17] When leaders tried to incorporate longer Hebrew blessings, there was very little response from the participants.[18] Hebrew continued to be seen as the province of an elite, even if that elite included some women.

One of the rituals that "worked" most effectively was Rosh Hodesh Sivan, the month in which *Shavuot*, the holiday of the giving of the law is celebrated. Working with the theme of "Standing Again at Sinai," borrowing both the title and the intention of Judith Plaskow's book-length study of Jewish feminist theology,[19] participants broke into small groups and were challenged to choose a woman from Jewish history and to recover *her* response to being present at the revelation at Sinai. After about twenty minutes of intense discussion, group members presented moving portraits of women from several centuries of Jewish life, each claiming her place in a sacred history that teaches "You are standing here this day, all of you, before your God. . . . Not with you only do I make this covenant, but with each one that stands here with us this day . . . and also with each one that is not here with us this day" (Deut. 29:9–14, Tanakh). By conjuring the voices of historical women, each celebrant claimed the possibility of standing at Sinai herself.[20]

A more problematic ritual was the celebration for Rosh Hodesh Av, the month in which Jews commemorate Tisha B'Av, the destruction of the ancient temple. When we arrived at Av, we had been celebrating together for nearly one year. The study texts for the evening included biblical materials from the book of Kings that describe in great detail the ancient temple and its contents. After these texts had been studied in small groups, the leader created a guided meditation that led participants into the ancient sanctuary and asked them to claim it as their own. Several participants reacted very angrily to the premise of the evening, claiming that the ancient temple was a physical monument whose express purpose was to centralize worship and to destroy a rich goddess culture that sustained many of the people of the land. "How can you ask us to imagine a sacred space that forbids any representation of the Goddess who has been wrenched from our midst and from our hearts?" they asked. "As Jewish women reclaiming our roots, why aren't we exploring Goddess worship?"

The boldness of this articulation, the first in a Rosh Hodesh setting, helped some of the participants see the universality of women's anger. Those who spoke out were clearly among the most "radical" in attendance, but their passion was shared by others who had simply been unable to find any way "into" the texts of the evening. For some, the implicit conflict in using traditional, patriarchal texts as the basis for our Rosh Hodesh study was made explicit by this challenge.

Those leading the discussion felt unable to answer the questions of the angry few, and turned to two "experts" who were present, teachers of Jewish studies. The teachers acknowledged that the texts are clearly sexist and that they exclude women.

They went on to explain that the goddess traditions, while wide-spread in the Ancient Near East, were never formally integrated into ancient Jewish practice, and that both biblical and subsequent rabbinic literature clearly *reject* both the idea and the practice of god-dess worship. They agreed that the invisibility of Jewish women, not the invisibility of goddesses, was the essential source of pain when confronting these texts. For the first time in a Rosh Hodesh ceremony, a commitment to reclaiming Judaism came face to face with a commitment to claiming women's culture.

Some departed with a deep sense of discontent and anger at having been led in what seemed to be an exercise that reinforced women's deep sense of alienation from the tradition. Instead of finding sacred space, some participants keenly felt their sense of spiritual homelessness. While the evening provided an excellent opportunity to discuss the development of monotheism as a reli-gious ideology, it also illuminated the shared and the divergent norms and values of the emerging Rosh Hodesh group culture. The evening also led at least one of the angriest protesters to con-tinue her own study; she registered for a text class and began He-brew study within two months of the Rosh Hodesh celebration. Most left asking new questions about what it means to be a Jew and to be a woman.[21]

Many of those who came together for the Rosh Hodesh cele-bration were looking for a balm for a wound. Some could name their pain as the sexism endemic in American society, the injury of invisibility sustained by those who live in a society that still considers male experience as the norm. Others had identified their pain at being rejected as persons by their Judaism. Others were in recovery from other kinds of abuse and neglect. For those women, Rosh Hodesh became a haven, a kind of halfway house.

A halfway house that fulfills its mandate welcomes in wander-ers from the cold, and after a period of intensive care, offers them the skills to go forth into the world. But a halfway house provides real help only if two conditions for change exist. First of all, those who enter the facility must come not only for succor but also with a willingness to master the tools and learn the language of the world beyond. Second, there must be places on the "other side" in the "wider world" in which the traveler can ultimately make a home. If Rosh Hodesh is indeed a temporary dwelling, it "fails" when those who enter its welcoming doors are unwilling to leave or when the Jewish world is too narrow to integrate these *Ivriot*, these wandering Jewish women. Then Rosh Hodesh becomes a final destination, and a dead end.

This use of Rosh Hodesh raises serious questions about the distinctions between ritual and therapy. Ritual seeks to provide a spiritual context for one's experience of the world. The Rosh Hodesh ritual was intended to bring women back into Judaism, a Judaism that the planners saw as sufficiently expansive to respond to the challenge of feminism. Rosh Hodesh should be about healing, but in a communal, rather than an individual context. Rosh Hodesh may indeed be a halfway house, but those who pass through its doors must see it as a way station on a journey toward greater involvement and investment in a tradition that, if it is to survive, will celebrate women's lives.

The halfway house metaphor enables us to ask whether women-only rituals, or celebrations where women play all the primary roles and men are welcomed but remain peripheral guests, are the ultimate expression of Jewish feminist spirituality? Women who are empowered only in the presence of other Jewish women, women who reclaim only this single celebration, which is not yet a part of the cycle of Jewish ritual life, may remain cut off from much of normative Jewish religious life and ritual. While an individual woman's alienation from Judaism may be diminished, her reentry into mainstream Jewish life is incomplete.

Rosh Hodesh and Women's Oral Tradition

The initial Rosh Hodesh rituals achieved many of the goals of those who initiated the celebrations. The celebrations brought Jewish women together as Jews, welcoming them into an ancient tradition that continues to be vibrant and responsive after five millennia. The gatherings opened the world of traditional Jewish text study to women, and many have been in an environment, for the first time in their lives, where women study text together, both under the watchful eye of a woman guide and with peers. Some of the women in attendance have discovered the possibility of connection where there was only alienation and anger.

Given the centrality of structure and predictable prayer language in all normative Jewish celebrations, it is striking that the Rosh Hodesh celebrations continue to operate with a very loose structure and only a negligible liturgy. While the welcoming ritual of self-naming has been a staple of almost every ritual, the invocation of the matriarchs has not. The attempt to incorporate an adaptation of the traditional synagogue prayer for the new month failed. Certainly, the creation of new liturgy is a complex process, and few are able to write new formulations that are neither archaic nor colloquial, neither stilted nor quotidian.[22]

One attempt to create replicable liturgy was on Rosh Hodesh Elul, the last Rosh Hodesh before the Days of Awe. In preparation for the soul searching of the season, participants were asked to consider what might be "sins" or failings particular to women. In groups, participants compiled a list of "sins" that resonated with their experience as women in the world, and then, at the end of the evening, the lists were chanted in liturgical style. However, no plans were made to either replicate the lists nor to use them again in a more formal prayer setting.[23]

Other liturgical pieces that were created and then not repeated were songs composed for Rosh Hodesh Kislev (the month in which Chanukah begins) and Rosh Hodesh Adar (the month in which the lighthearted holiday of Purim occurs). In both cases, neither planning group for the second year's celebration chose to utilize the work of the previous planners. Does Rosh Hodesh, then, provide a vehicle only for the *temporary* reclamation of women's voices, while in fact perpetuating their emphemerality? In the course of the rituals, women have indeed shared their stories, but the word remains spoken and has been neither saved nor savored. Each ritual has been written down, but the interactions between the participants, the life stories, the historical vignettes, the poems and insights shared in the course of the evening have been treated as oral tradition: treasured and repeated, but not written down.[24]

Perhaps the sociocultural conditioning that has traditionally kept Jewish women outside of the walls of the academy while permitting them to become conversant in the language of the home and the marketplace has underscored the dual message that women's wisdom remains in the vibrant realm of oral tradition, while men's insights have ossified on the page. The perpetuation of women's oral tradition in the modern context of Rosh Hodesh rituals may reflect the tension between the individual and the community that exists in any group that comes together to share a ritual experience. Words penned by an individual may seem inadequate when repeated in the collective, communal setting, while liturgies composed by committee are clumsy and feel inauthentic. So the extemporaneous, the spontaneous, and the well-turned phrase of the moment become the liturgy, not the carefully turned phrase of the poet or liturgist.

Rosh Hodesh ceremonies enable some Jews to make a connection between Judaism and their own lives. For some, Rosh Hodesh forms a bridge to a previously obscured past. Rosh Hodesh welcomes women into a safe place to explore the possibility of Jewish expression in the present. And Rosh Hodesh also opens the door to a future of greater comfort and familiarity with the language, the liturgy, and the community of Jews.

The development of Jewish women's rituals in the last quarter of the twentieth century reflects the unrolling of the "unwritten scrolls" of Jewish women's lives through the ages, and our first attempts to read those scrolls, piecing together the oral traditions much as our ancestors compiled what we now call the Torah.[25] Our experience with Rosh Hodesh suggests that the arduous process of finding the words, and locating the language, will enable Jewish women to share their truths with one another and, finally, with the world. Rosh Hodesh may be the first step toward reclaiming our mother tongue, an oral tradition of women that will soon take its place alongside the written tradition that has so dominated Jewish life and Jewish scholarship throughout the generations.

Rosh Hodesh is one step toward community and away from the silent loneliness that isolated Jewish women from one another and from Judaism. Our words, spoken or sung, are indeed the beginning of a new language.[26]

The words that we are learning to speak may feel awkward at first, but soon we recognize them as our own, our birthright. When we reclaim our songs, we discover ourselves. And slowly, we create rituals that celebrate both our lives and the tradition that must recognize that without women's voices, a Judaism of integrity has neither past nor future.

Notes

1. I am grateful for Rachel Adler's keen understanding of the issues explored in this chapter and for Lisa Edwards's comments on an earlier draft.

2. The biblical figure of Hannah has, for too long, symbolized the Jewish woman: filled with anguish and longing for a sign that she is a part of the continuity of her people, she turns to God in prayer. Yet her silent petition is misunderstood and ridiculed by the mortal who observes her at prayer (1 Samuel 1:3–18).

3. In her poem "Transcendental Etude," Adrienne Rich writes: "Birth stripped our birthright from us, / tore us from a woman, from women, from ourselves" (*The Fact of a Doorframe: Poems Selected and New 1950–1984* [New York: W. W. Norton & Co., 1984]). Etty Hillesum wrote in her diary on October 20, 1941, "I am always in search of a few words" (*An Interrupted Life: The Diaries of Etty Hillesum 1941–43* [New York: Washington Square Press, 1981], p. 45).

4. In 1979, Cynthia Ozick wrote,

> It is not a fantasy or an imagining to say that Torah is silent, offers no principle of justice in relation to women, no timeless precept of injustice-contradiction, and in general consorts with the world at large. . . . Torah—one's heart stops in one's mouth as one dares to say these words—Torah is in this respect frayed.

("Notes Towards Finding the Right Question," reprinted in *On Being a Jewish Feminist,* ed. Susannah Heschel [New York: Schocken Books, 1983]).

5. Nelle Morton, "Hearing to Speech," in *The Journey Is Home* (Boston: Beacon Press, 1985), p. 202.

6. Rebecca Alpert's comprehensive and incisive essay on this topic is required reading: "Our Lives *Are* the Text: Exploring Jewish Women's Rituals," *Bridges* 2:1 (Spring 1991/5751).

7. Arlene Agus's pioneering essay "This Month Is for You: Observing Rosh Hodesh as a Woman's Holiday" in *The Jewish Woman: New Perspectives* (New York: Schocken Books, 1976) remains the essential introduction to Rosh Hodesh celebrations.

8. *Pirke de Rabbi Eliezer,* ch. 45, cited by Agus in "This Month Is for You," p. 86.

9. See studies such as *Festivals of the Jewish Year,* by Theodor H. Gaster (New York: William Sloan Associates, 1953).

10. See Sherry B. Ortner's "Is Female to Male as Nature Is to Culture?" in *Women, Culture and Society,* ed. Michelle C. Rosaldo and Louise Lamphere (Stanford, Calif.: Stanford University Press, 1974), and Susan Griffin, *Woman and Nature: The Roaring Inside Her* (New York: Harper & Row, 1976).

11. Taanit 15b, cited by Agus, in "This Month Is for You," p. 88.

12. One line in *Kiddush Levana,* a blessing said when the new moon is sighted for the first time, reads: "May the light of the moon be like the light of the sun." Traditional interpretations suggest that Israel (the moon) will not be diminished when redemption comes. Some women have used this sentence in Rosh Hodesh rituals with a different interpretation in mind.

13. See Tamar Frankiel, *The Voice of Sarah: Feminine Spirituality and Traditional Judaism* (San Francisco: HarperCollins, 1990).

14. See Linda Alcott's "Cultural Feminism Versus Post-Structuralism: The Identity Crisis in Feminist Theory," *Signs: Journal of Women in Culture and Society* 13:3 (Spring 1988), p. 421. Thanks to Rachel Adler for bringing this article to my attention.

15. The traditional *Amida,* called "*the* prayer," stands at the center of a Jew's daily prayers, and begins: "Our God and God of our Fathers, God of Abraham, God of Isaac, God of Jacob . . .' Liberal Jews now add the names of the matriarchs to this prayer. Invoking them in the Rosh Hodesh celebration corrects this historic omission.

16. When Jews are called to the Torah in a traditional synagogue

service, they are called by their name and the name of their father (Joseph ben [son of] Jacob). Many liberal Jews now call women as well as men to the Torah, and call men and women by their names, followed by the names of both of their parents (Leah bat [daughter of] Joseph and Rachel, or Joseph ben [son of] Jacob and Rachel).

17. We used Marcia Falk's blessing over bread, *N'varech et mayan hehayim ha motzia min ha aretz* (We bless the Source of Life who brings forth bread from the earth), and a blessing for study that I composed from two biblical sources: *Hochmot banta veita; bo-ou sha'areyha b'todah, hatzroteha bit'heela* (Wisdom has built her house; let us enter her gates with thanks, her courts with praise). See Marcia Falk, "Notes on Composing New Blessings: Toward a Feminist-Jewish Reconstruction of Prayer," in *Weaving the Visions: New Patterns in Feminist Spirituality,* ed. Judith Plaskow and Carol Christ (San Francisco: Harper & Row, 1989).

18. Rachel Adler composed a Rosh Hodesh *kiddush* for Rosh Hodesh Elul 5751, and Naomi Levy reintroduced *kiddush halevana* for Rosh Hodesh Kislev 5752.

19. Judith Plaskow, *Standing Again at Sinai: Judaism from a Feminist Perspective* (San Francisco: HarperCollins, 1990.)

20. Rosh Hodesh Sivan 5751 (13 May 1991), created by Donna Malamud and Lisa Rauschwerger.

21. Rosh Hodesh Av 5751 (11 July 1991), created by Sharon Kushner.

22. See Riv-Ellen Prell's insightful analysis of the difficulty that modern Jews have with prayer and prayer language, *Prayer and Community: The Havurah in American Judaism* (Detroit: Wayne State University Press, 1989), pp. 204–11.

23. Rosh Hodesh Elul 5752 was created by Rachel Adler and Donna Malamud.

24. Greater attention is now being paid to the systematic documentation of the rituals, through photography, videotape, and audiotape.

25. "Illuminating the Unwritten Scroll" was the title of a conference on Jewish women held in January 1985 in Los Angeles, organized by Rabbis Laura Geller and Patricia Karlin-Neuman.

26. See Rich's "Transcendental Etude."

8

The Aché Sisters:
Discovering the Power
of the Erotic in Ritual

Irene Monroe

> We have attempted to separate the spiritual and the
> erotic, thereby reducing the spiritual to a world of
> flattened affect, a world of the ascetic who aspires to
> feeling nothing.
>
> *Audre Lorde,*
> *Sister Outsider*

We convene tonight, and each of us will bring food to the Welcoming Table. Tonight, for most of us, is that one precious moment during our week when we can truly come as we are.
Tonight we do not have to be cloaked or closeted in the world.
Tonight we do not have to conceal our pain, our faces, or our
lovers. Tonight we do not have to watch our pronouns, our spontaneity, or our backs. Tonight we heal! We actualize our power of
the erotic! We celebrate our spirituality before our ancestors,
God/Goddess, and the divine ourselves.

We call ourselves the Aché Sisters. *Aché* is a Yoruban word that
denotes the power to make things happen, the breath that gives
life. It is the personal and the divine power with which we are all
born. It "is not power over or domination."[1] Aché is power that
"passes through us, is used by us, and must be replenished by us."[2]

As Aché Sisters, we are empowered by the erotic released in us, in nature, mother earth, and our ancestors. We embody and reclaim our African-American Christian foresisters' spiritual history, especially their use of the erotic to "make a way out of no way."

Because the term "lesbian" often projects Euro-American women's history, movement, and politics, we refer to ourselves as "Zamis." The word identifies one of the most marginalized and oftentimes invisible groups within the African-American church community: the homospiritual lesbians. The name "Zami," like "womanist," is an Afrocentric term, indigenous to African diaspora women's culture. It mirrors the ethos and essence of the term "womanist"; however, it brings to the fore, without ambiguity, the homosexual, homoerotic, and homospiritual identity of this group of African-American women. We appropriated the name from Audre Lorde's autobiography, *Zami: A New Spelling of My Name*. Zami was a Carriacou name for African diaspora women who once inhabited the isle of Carriacou, near Grenada, where these women worked together as lovers and friends. Lorde describes Zamis as "women who survived the absence of their sea-faring men easily, because they came to love each other, past the men's returning. Madivine. Friending. Zami. How Carriacou women love each other is legend in Grenada, and so is their strength and their beauty."[3]

We are a spiritual support group of practicing Christian and post-Christian Zamis. As practicing Christian Zamis, we admit to either compromising or closeting ourselves in order to remain in the black church. As post-Christian Zamis, we are willfully or forcefully exiled from the black church. We are and were Christian spiritual African-American women from predominantly Afro-Baptist, Afro-Pentecostal, and A.M.E. traditions. Some of us are compromised or closeted seminarians and ministers in these churches today. Some of us have had to leave our beloved denominations to join others, such as Unitarian Universalist, Metropolitan Community Church, and the United Church of Christ, that would permit us to come fully out of the closet and through their doors. We see ourselves not as victims of the black church but instead as continued survivors of it whether we are practicing or exiled Zamis.

As a church that is born out of struggle, we indict the black church for spiritually abusing its own people in the face of its God. The black church propagates a Christian ritualization of black male supremacy, expressed in its theology, ordination process, and worship, as well as its gender-role-designated positions and job duties. Black male power and control are preached as the will of God and considered to be the primary resource for the survival of the black church, black family, and black traditions. Such a self-righteous attitude (and learned behavior) perpetuates itself generationally, from minister to lay person, from male to female. It promotes a literalist, restricted reading of the Bible for women and homosexuals, in contrast to a liberal and liberationist reading for men. It discourages supportive female and homosexual images during worship.

The origin of the Aché Sisters as a worshiping group was five years ago when six Zamis got together to discuss the spiritually abusive aspects of black church worship. We recognize that black church worship was once (some would argue that the same still holds true today) the central locus for black male spiritual development and articulation. We do not want to obliterate or mar this valuable history and continued development. However, we do want the history to be corrected by the recognition of African-American women's contributions to the spiritual development of the black church, and that includes *all* us women, of *all* sexual orientations. We want to be allowed our full spiritual development. We want to articulate truth as we know it in worship undefiled by sexist and heterosexist interpretations.

Many of our African-American sisters in the church agree with our challenge to the black church, although most will not join us in the struggle. They are prevented from doing so by many factors: their own homophobia, their own fear of reprisals, such as not being ordained or hired, or being fired or silenced. What also separates us from our heterosexual sisters is our claim as Zamis that the erotic is a component of full spiritual growth and an important part of our worship.

As Zamis we regularly explore the relationship between the body and the power of the erotic as one way to dismantle the patriarchal and hierarchical structures embedded in black church worship. By erotic we mean "a resource within each of us that lies in a deeply female and spiritual plane."[4] The erotic is an untapped, innate power and informational source, especially in women; it provides us with an energy for motion, action, self-empowerment, and change. Because it is an energy that moves in nonrational, nonlinear ways, this resource is often misconstrued as sexual exploitation and seen as extremely dangerous by the leadership of the black church. We realize that our speaking about the erotic in connection to religion is risky and some might say heretical. However, we believe that the erotic belongs in religion, and especially in worship. As Audre Lorde states, too often "we are taught to separate the erotic demand from the most vital areas of our lives other than sex."[5]

As Zamis, we claim that the freedom to explore the power of the erotic allows us to tap into our own personal divine powers; to appreciate all bodies, male and female, as temples of God, and as vessels to do good works; to accept sex as a divine power for responsible coprocreation and cocreation by choice. We accept all sexual orientations as part of the human continuum, seeing such as the varied images of God living cocreatively in the world.

We believe that in order for the male/female, heterosexual/homosexual, soul/body splits to cease to exist in our worship, we must begin, as frightening as it seems, to look at those ways in which black church worship is presently neither a safe, sacred, nor liberating expression of the divine, but is a ritual expression of the larger society's racism, sexism, classism, and homophobia. The black church, a church born out of struggle, which asserts that God is on its side, the side of the oppressed, has become the oppressor. It is upholding patriarchy in a black face. By persisting with its patriarchal paradigms, the black church is against all women and gay men, anti-children, anti-family, and anti-God. Its worship then becomes merely the ritualization of black male supremacy modeled after, and in competition with, white male supremacy.

Our spiritual support group of Zamis was formed in response to this acute resistance on the part of the black church. We seek to evoke the power of the erotic in ritual, to replenish and recycle its energy for spiritual healing and affirmation; to rid ourselves of the isolation and alienation we experience at home, at work, and in church; to celebrate our bodies and our sexual orientation; to love, to value, and to embrace ourselves; to become agents for ecclesiastical changes in our churches. In other words, to be for one another what the black church and the world is not. We are aware of the physical and emotional risk of being Zamis in a racist and heterosexist world. We Aché Sisters do not chide those sisters who are closeted, nor cheer those sisters who are out. Our night of ritual is to affirm one another wherever we are in our processes of liberation and affirmation. For practicing Christian Zamis, church worship on Sundays is devoid of affirming images of women and homosexuals, so our spiritual support group serves as a vital supplement. For those post-Christian Zamis who no longer attend the black church, our support group is the only time they can safely return to their religious traditions. It becomes church for them.

Our ritual at each gathering begins around the Welcoming Table. In the basement of a Zami's home, the space consists of two large rooms partitioned by two wooden doors—one room used for dining, the other, "the altar room," for meditation and group prayer. At any given meeting there are about thirty women, with openings for newcomers and our friends and lovers.

Each Zami comes with a dish or a drink to share. One volunteers to bake the bread and another to bring the wine. Before the meal we gather in the living room upstairs, exchanging hellos and hugs and chatting about our day. When the triangle is struck the first time, we process downstairs to the basement and sit down at a central table in the middle of which is always a chalice of red wine, a loaf of freshly baked bread, and a vase of flowers. The table is set with purple plastic picnic wear (a color claimed by lesbians to express their identification and solidarity), and on each plate, face down, is an index card of one of four colors. Each card contains a quotation from an African-American sister, some famous, some unknown. A white card bears a quotation from a sister in religion; blue, from a sister in law, government, or politics; yellow, from a sister in literature, journalism, or TV broadcasting; and pale green, from a sister in the arts—theater, music, dancing, or painting. The cards invite conversation around the table before we start dinner.

When the triangle is struck the second time there is silence. A Zami stands up from the table to give the blessing. After the blessing she takes the chalice from the table and pours libation for our ancestors, passes it to all of us, and recites our rewriting of a Yoruban proverb: "We stand tall and proud and in reverence, because we stand on the shoulders of our many ancestors who have come and gone before us, but still remain and watch over us." We then name our ancestors: we call them out in no particular order, just as a spontaneous litany.

When we have quieted down, the Zami returns the chalice to the middle of the table and picks up the bread. She breaks off a piece and passes it to the Zami beside her, who does likewise. When we all have a piece of bread, she lifts up her arm and says, "Let us all eat!" We do. She then holds up the remaining bread loaf and says, "We have all broken and eaten bread together at this Welcoming Table as a family. The bread that remains with us is a sign to feed and to welcome many more." When she sits down we all say amen and begin to eat the food we brought with us. The discussion around the table is often about the black church. Some examples are: the black church and its need for an AIDS ministry; the black church in the postmodern era; the black church and its relationship to homeless people, women, addicts, and homosexual people.

After dinner, some of us stroll into the altar room for quiet meditation. We listen to music, always something from Sweet Honey in the Rock. We smell sage burning as a purifier and garlic hung outside the door as a reminder to bad spirits that they are not welcome inside. The room is lit with a candle and the seats are arranged in a circle with the altar in the middle. On the altar are symbols of the four elements and a mineral. To represent the earth we use a rock, for fire, a burning incense candle, for air, two lavender balloons on each side, and for water, a small earthenware bowl filled with spring water. The mineral is a quartz crystal.

On the three walls of the altar room hang pictures of African diaspora women of history. Among them are pictures of two Christian women. On the left side wall is a reproduction of a sixteenth-century picture of the black Madonna and the baby Jesus, and beneath it sits an upright piano. On the right side wall is a picture of Rev. Barbara Harris, an African-American who was the first woman to be ordained bishop in the Massachusetts diocese of the Episcopal church. On the front wall, high above the altar, hangs a large image of Isis with her arms raised toward the sky in prayer.

Our main group service begins fifteen minutes after this time of quiet meditation. The triangle is struck loudly, in rapid succession, to call those Zamis who have spent their quiet time upstairs in the living room, or out in front of the house. This portion of our service always begins with gospel music. Our pianist calls for requests. When the requests are for upbeat tunes we sing, clap, and wave our hands, and the volume heightens to a crescendo. Zamis shout, speak in tongues, or are carried out of the altar room because they have passed out in excitement. Other times the requests are for songs that are slow, heavy with the language and mood of pain. During these songs Zamis weep and are patted on their back, kissed on the cheek, or embraced by their lovers and friends. In both instances we feel relieved, quieted, and at peace.

A homily follows this singing. It may be based on a text traditionally called sacred, such as the Jewish Torah, Christian scripture, the Muslim Koran, and the Hindu Bhagavadgītā, or other texts, such as modern poetry and song. Some examples include Maya Angelou's poem "And I Still Rise," Audre Lorde's "A Litany for Survival," the words of Diana Ross's songs "Reach Out and Touch Somebody's Hand" and "I'm Coming Out." The homily (about twenty minutes long) is prepared by the leader and may be spoken, silent (printed for people to read), or danced. At the end of this segment of the worship we share personal stories that relate to the homily. Then we read the meditation that has been placed on our seats. We conclude our worship with the sounds of drums. Three Zamis play for about thirty minutes. We fold up our chairs and dance to the beat.

Why does this form of worship meet our needs?

This group began because of a collective dissatisfaction with the African-American churches of which we are, or in some cases were, a part. The primary problem was our homosexuality. The very heart of our human expression was not accepted, much less honored or celebrated. Since homophobia is pervasive and rarely mentioned in African-American churches, it was necessary to locate a safe place for ourselves where we could develop rather than deny what we are. As we began planning our worship we recognized other characteristics of the black church that we found inadequate: its unbending format, the exclusive use of the Bible for reading and preaching, and the resistance of the black church to expression of the erotic. The worship was static and the control of it so determined by patriarchal rules that our Zami voices were not heard. Our developing expression honors mutuality, change, spontaneity, the erotic, and the stories of women's lives.

What have we learned?

In five years of worshiping together, the prevalent thread has been the willingness to change. Needs vary. It is critical to adjust our plans to meet what emerges. For example, at times, especially around major Christian feasts, anything "Christian" (songs, symbols, biblical text) is oppressive and alienating. At the Christmas season, we avoid the story of the virgin birth of Jesus because this retelling reminds some women that rape can be glorified. So for a number of weeks our leaders avoid any Christian sources or references. At other times, very little devotional time, drumming, or words are needed. Rather what is called for is space for silence, for grieving, moaning, lamenting, for body language rather than oral language. When the message is flat for any reason and nothing seems to move we try a different approach the next time.

What are our dreams?

Our alienation from the African-American church is painful. We look forward to the day when what we see or know and have learned will be welcomed in the mainstream church. We imagine a community that will be a resource for universal as well as particular empowerment, one that respects the widest spectrum of human experiences—that expects divine energy and revelation to be felt and known in both predictable and surprising ways, and thus is reluctant to quickly dismiss or judge what challenges traditional thought or modes of action.

Notes

1. Luish Teish, *Jambalaya: The Natural Woman's Book* (San Francisco: Harper & Row, 1985), p. xvi.

2. Ibid., p. xvi.

3. Audre Lorde, *Zami: A New Spelling of My Name* (Trumansburg, N.Y.: The Crossing Press Feminist Series, 1983), p. 14.

4. Audre Lorde, *Sister Outsider* (Trumansburg, N.Y.: Crossing Press, 1984), p. 53.

5. Ibid., p. 55.

9

In Her Name:
Toward a Feminist Thealogy
of Pagan Ritual

Wendy Hunter Roberts

It is the first weekend in November, time once again to enter the ancient, sacred circles of death and rebirth. I feel I have entered this circle (for every circle is the same circle) thousands of times past. My genes remember. My bones remember. As I robe (warmly, for we shall be outside for the night), I have a sense of timelessness, of deep connection to my ancestral roots. For did not our ancestors—native people of Europe, Africa, the Americas, the Fertile Crescent of the Middle East, and Asia—gather in circle to mark the passages in their lives and in the earth's cycles, for thousands of years before the coming of the missionaries and invaders?[1]

Archeological evidence indicates that masked, feathered priest-esses danced funereal rites around the interred bones of their dead in circle, at Catal Huyuk, a Neolithic village in what is now Eastern Turkey, nine thousand years ago.[2] Thousands of years and miles away, pre-Celtic peoples circled their observances of sun and earth cycles by the mysterious stones of Stonehenge and Avebury in Neolithic Britain.[3] Moreover we know that indigenous peoples still do so, hidden from the eyes of official religion, on the mountain peaks of Peru and the islands of the South Seas.[4] So we too gather to honor our passage through the wheel of the year, in the manner of our ancestors. My body remembers this.

For nearly a decade now I have circled with this motley tribe of Goddess worshipers at least twice every year—in the spring and in the fall—to mark through ritual the passing of the seasons, to reaffirm our connection to the divine and the connection of our own lives to the cycles of nature.

We are women and men together in this circle. We are predominantly white heterosexual and bisexual adults between the ages of thirty-five and fifty-five. We are writers, welfare mothers, teachers, therapists, poets, students, computer programmers, healers, professionals, paraprofessionals, environmental activists, clerical workers, small-business owners, musicians, crafts people, and scientists. We are rural and urban dwellers.

We of the elder generation were raised in a variety of traditions and none at all. We are former Roman Catholics, born-again Christians, mainline Protestants, Christian Scientists, Jews, Mormons, and humanists. Some of us rebelled against the religions of our childhood as the result of deep wounding. Others of us simply moved on, out of a longing that was not being satisfied, or out of irreconcilable thealogical[5] or political differences with our childhood faiths.

Some of our members have been worshiping together for as many as twenty-five years, and the ritual style that has evolved over that time derives from a highly creative synthesis of Native American spirituality, Wicca, psychedelic experience, science fantasy, ancient texts and myths, feminist spirituality, deep ecology work, naturalism, humanistic psychology, the new physics, Western esoteric occultism, and Eastern mystical traditions, as well as our own deep longings and intuitions of the divine.

We refer to ourselves as Neo-Pagans, after the term *paganus* ("peasant" or country dweller), originally used to describe the rural people who continued to worship the old nature deities long after most Roman subjects had been converted to Christianity.[6] We are Neo-Pagans in that we realize full well that we neither can nor wish to re-create whole the Paganism of the past. Rather, we weave ourselves into its living tradition, as we augment, re-create, reinterpret ancient patterns in the light of today's world, through our own needs and imaginations. Currently we are estimated to be the fastest growing religion in America, our numbers having increased from an estimated one hundred thousand in 1985,[7] to as many as half a million at the time of this writing.[8]

Because we are a nature-based religion, most of our rituals take place out of doors, in nature. From Halloween until May Day we emphasize and celebrate winter's darkness by holding our rituals at night around a fire. In the warmer weather we can be found dancing our circle in a garden, a meadow, or at water's edge, glorifying the sun's warmth and light. Our major celebrations usually last all or most of the night, and sometimes into the next day, with between thirty and one hundred people in the circle.

A woman and a man are chosen each season by the clergy to be the worship designers and leaders, or priestess and priest for that season's ritual. If they are not themselves ordained clergy, they are supervised by ordained clergy.[9] This is our way of trying to walk the fine line between our basic commitment to the notion of a nonhierarchical priesthood of all believers on the one hand, and quality control on the other. These two people engage the active participation of the general congregation in a variety of ways, often with additional people selected in advance to lead particular segments of the ritual.

Because of the vast amount of planning and work involved in developing an original ritual of this size and scope, leadership tends to rotate. This allows for a wide range of liturgical styles to coexist, some more formal, some more spontaneous, some more verbal, and others more kinesthetic or auditory. A. J., for example, uses harps, flutes, choreographed movement, and rhyming couplets in rituals often based on esoteric systems describing and/or intervening in cosmic patterns. R. D. H. favors few words and lots of hypnotic chanting and drumming. Storytelling and songs prevail at O. S.'s rituals, while O. Z. and M. G. love to reenact myth in an ancient form called the mystery play. I myself tend to focus on global concerns with a prophetic tone and a rock and roll beat, while D. J.'s style is more pastoral, focusing on issues of personal transformation. We have no "one, true, and only way."

Our major symbols include: the ever-turning wheel of the seasons of the year, the four directions (north, south, east, and west) with their corresponding four elements (earth, air, fire, and water), the marriage of God and Goddess, the dying and reborn God (dying in the fall to be reborn in the returning light with the new greenery), and the Triple Goddess (Maiden, Mother, and Crone). Our basic ritual structure includes: casting a circle, calling on the four directions and elements, invoking Goddess and God, raising power, grounding the power, communion, announcements and sharing, thanking God and Goddess, dismissing the four elements and directions, opening the circle.

Our most important celebrations are seasonal, commemorating not one-time events, but our place in the spiral of time and space that is ever turning, and the phases ever repeating themselves within that spiral. By focusing on seasonal spirals rather than on historical events, we are locating divinity primarily in nature's processes and cycles rather than exclusively in human history. Our liturgy reflects our place in nature, rather than placing ourselves and our god(s) outside of, or above, nature. This creates problems for some feminists, who, having reified nature, have internalized a nature/culture polarity. They identify nature as the source of woman's subordination, and culture as her liberator.[10] We, on the other hand, see the proprietorship of woman and of nature by the patriarchy as having gone, and continuing to go, hand in hand.[11] We do not identify or romanticize woman as being in any way "closer to nature" than man in her basic makeup or essence.

We meet in a circle, symbol of the wheel of the year and leveler of hierarchy and difference. There is no face-off of clergy and laity here; we are celebrants together. When we enter the circle, it is said that we enter a "world between the worlds," a sacred, liminal space where it is possible to enter into communion with the divine, step into the mythic, and actually alter the fabric of reality, if we enter it with perfect love and perfect trust. A song we frequently sing asserts, "We are a circle within a circle with no beginning and never ending."[12]

Our circle has four orientation points describing its circumference: north, south, east, and west, usually with an altar placed at each point. We begin by invoking the four elements into our circle, identifying and situating each element in its particular, appropriate geographical direction, depending on our locale. Because my community lives in Northern California, we identify the element of water with the Pacific Ocean, and so place water in the west. We call forth fire from the warmer south, air from the east, bastion of airy intellect. We situate earth in the cold, rocky north, according to Celtic tradition. (Were we in Maine or in New York, this would all be different, of course, because we would have a large body of water to our east.)

There is one more piece of liturgical business that must be completed before moving to the substance of the particular celebration that has brought us together: that of calling forth and recognizing the presence and assistance of deity: invoking. In our tradition, that means invoking or evoking the female, biological life-giving force we call the Goddess. Anything that can reproduce itself is, by biological definition, female. Let me be perfectly clear about this: the Goddess is primary in our thealogy. She is the sine qua non of biological existence on this planet, and our thealogy and liturgy first and foremost honor and celebrate physical, biological life on this earth.

This is not to say anything about superiority or inferiority. This is simply to say that there is no life on earth without reproduction and birth. There is no reproduction and birth without the female. Since we primarily honor deity as creator and devourer immanent in nature, in other words as that mysterious regenerative process known as evolution by which life creates and re-creates itself, we primarily honor the Goddess as our deity.

With the introduction of external genetic material come death and difference. This is the biological contribution of the male to evolution. Therefore secondarily but equally we honor the God, the Goddess's counterpart and equal, as embodiment and sire of that force and process. It is usual, therefore, to recognize and call both Goddess and God into our circle. But it is imperative to call the Goddess. The following excerpts of invocations, written in the aftermath of the Gulf War in the spring of 1991, reflect this bio-thealogical distinction.

Invocation of the Goddess

(W.H.R., R.D.H. April, 1991)

Canto (spoken by the priest):
She is the Mother
She is the Lover
She is the Dancer . . .
And . . .
She is the Devourer

Through her body all things are made new

Response:
Oh Lady, give us new Life!

Canto:
She gives—
And She taketh away

She is the storehouse laden with grain,
She is the famine-ridden land,
And She is the rain.
She flows in mountain streams and rivers,
Her heart beats in the primordial seas' ebb and flow,
She is the sandy river bottom blown away on
Summer's wind
And the starry skies spinning constellations
and swallowing them whole,

Through Her body all things are made new.

Response:
Oh Lady, give us new Life!

Invocation of the Wounded God
(Spoken by the priestess)

Oh wounded God, come home.
How much longer must you wander in your fear and pride?
Don't you know that you are part of me?

You are my wildest dream and my worst nightmare.
You are difference, my ecstatic whim.
Wounded God, come to me,
Be my sweetness and surprise.

Take me where I would never venture alone.
Touch me.
Change me.

There are many ways of doing these basic liturgical steps. There is not a single set of words we mouth each time we cast a circle or call an element. Often our invocations are inspirations of the moment, but equally often they are written by a group member, a favorite author, or taken from an ancient text. We might choose to invoke without words at all, by making an auditory circle with the sound of a Tibetan singing bowl or an aboriginal bull-roarer, for example. And there is no such thing as a generic invocation of an element; the flames of transformation and the warm glow of the hearth are very different kinds of fire, and a worship leader is well advised to consider which kind she wants invoked in her circle.

Likewise, the Goddess has many faces, and we consider it prudent to choose or be chosen by some particular aspect of Her nature to predominate in a given ritual, depending on the season and the nature of the occasion. Remember, the Goddess is the body and soul of nature in the changing year. As a rule, therefore, in the spring we would honor a maiden goddess by some name: Persephone or Artemis, for example. In the summer and at harvest time, we would celebrate the Goddess in the full bloom of maturity, perhaps calling on Demeter or Asherah. In the late fall and mid-winter we would honor the death crone and wise woman, asking Hekate, Cerridwen, or Nekhbet to help us reconcile the need for death in life. None of this is absolute, however. A priestess might, on rare occasion, have good cause for invoking Kali, Hindu devouring mother, on the night of madness preceding a spring fertility celebration. In May of 1991, for example, there had been such rampant death and destruction the preceding winter that it had to be honored, mourned, and offered, before truly celebrating new life at the maypole. All good worship in any tradition begins with deep truthfulness.

The ritual I am choosing to examine here is one my congregation performed last November for our internal Samhain celebration. I believe it to be more or less typical of our ritual style, in its strengths and weaknesses.

Samhain ("Summer's end") is the Celtic name for the holy day honoring the year's entrance into the winter cycle of death and darkness, leading to spring's rebirth. In the secular culture of the United States, we know this time as Halloween, from the British All Hallows' Eve. The Mexican people celebrate it as Día de los Muertos, or "Day of the Dead." The Anglican and Roman Catholic churches call it "All Souls' Day." According to all these traditions, this is the time, when the year is dying, when the veil between the worlds is thinnest, the time when we honor and communicate with our dead. Samhain is our most solemn sabbath, and our most intimate. It is our new year, the time when trees drop their seeds before the winter frost, to wait in darkness for germination. Therefore it is the time we lay down the seeds of what we wish to see taking root in the coming year. This ritual is a recognition of the core bio-thealogical principle that light and life emerge from death and darkness.

We begin after dark, with half an hour of silence. Then thirty of us (all adults except for three adolescents who have completed their rites of passage, and one insistent girl of eleven, with her mother) process single file across the rickety, wooden bridge under the big tree, into a circle that is sheltered from wind by a tall fence. The circle is cast by the priestess who walks around the circumference chanting

> *Magic, magic everywhere, in the earth and in the air,*
> *How to hold the magic here?*
> *How raise it up and bring it down?*

She returns to the north altar and seals the circle with the vow of perfect love and perfect trust. "By the earth that is Her body," she declares, holding up a rock. Then she raises her chalice of water and spills some upon the ground, saying, "By the water that is Her womb and Her flowing blood." She lights a candle so that it flares, and vows, "By the fire that is Her quickening spirit," and, finally, fanning the air broadly and spinning with a bird's wing, "By the air that is Her sacred breath," she declares our circle cast.

The elements of air, fire, water, and earth are called by members of the congregation. Then the priest steps forward and invokes the Goddess as wise woman/crone in the priestess. The priestess is well chosen. She is a gray-haired woman, recently croned, having lost her mother and begun her menopause. She is a psychotherapist by profession. She removes her ritual cloak to reveal a purple running suit beneath it. She comments humorously on the pleasures of being a modern crone, dressed for comfort and ready for action. She is obviously comfortable in her body. Her voice is clear and natural, easy to listen to.

The priestess then evokes the Lord of the Underworld into a priest, who is, appropriately enough, a geologist by profession. He is beseeched to overcome his shyness, to remove his helmet of invisibility and preside over our ceremonies as he presides over his own realm of departed souls. The congregation follows the invocations with a chant that invites the dark lord to guide us "Down in the darkness, where we go alone . . . where we cry our tears . . . where we face our fears."

Another priestess takes the circle now, one who is experienced in such matters, to lead the next section of the rites: welcoming the beloved dead. She invites us one by one to call out the names of those we would have with us, telling us to leave behind good Aunt Elsie if she would be uncomfortable at such an event. The litany begins: Gene Roddenbury, Bill Graham, Dr. Suess, Miles Davis, friends and relatives lost to AIDS and other illness, Iraqi children and marine life, plants and wildlife as well as human life lost in the Oakland Hills fire, all dead this year; then those friends, lovers, teachers, and family members we still remember and mourn, including Gwydion, whose ashes are spread on this land he left us seven years ago. We add the names of those long dead whose inspiration we seek in these times: Martin Luther King Jr., Gandhi, Crooked Fox Woman, Elizabeth Cady Stanton, Margaret Sanger, Chief Seattle, Emma Goldman, Enheduanna, and Hypatia, librarian of Alexandria. These are hard times and we need a lot of inspiration. We call on our foremothers and guides. At last, after nearly half an hour of naming, the priestess rings a bell, inviting those named to break bread with us in silence. As we pass around specially prepared food, we feel a sense of communion with those named. This completes the first section of the ritual.

There is quite a lot here worthy of examination from a feminist perspective. In several obvious ways our liturgical style and tradition are deeply feminist and are empowering to women. The basic equality of female and male is explicit and built in at ground level, as shown by the equal roles of priestess and priest,[13] and the invocations of Goddess and God. Women carry a strong liturgical role, as priestesses of the Goddess. This should not be underrated in its importance. Being able to see oneself and one's religious leaders as a reflection and embodiment of the divine is inestimable in its value to women's self-image.[14] It is very different in its impact from having a neuter soul in a body of "otherness."[15] Our deity is embodied, hence our bodies are divine in all their phases and forms. In this case there is a strongly feminist affirmation of the Goddess embodied in aging women, not just in nubile maidens or nurturers, but in a strong, active, mature, independent person. The gray-haired priestess of our Samhain circle is her own woman and w/holy. Our Goddess is powerful in all of Her changes.

Still, contradictions do exist and sometimes even flourish in an atmosphere in which we easily become complacent about the subtleties of sexism in language and practice. These are more quickly noticed by more vigilant feminists in a more traditionally patriarchal environment, such as the Roman Catholic Church. Sexism can slip by in Pagan groups. And there are other "-isms" that grow in an all-too-often self-congratulatory atmosphere.

Let us take, for example, the location of our retreat center. It is important to us to worship in as wild and private a place as possible, especially for our highest holidays. We are fortunate to have inherited a fifty-five-acre land trust in the hills of Mendocino, a few hours' drive from San Francisco, where we can meet, frolic, and worship undisturbed among the trees and deer. We have loved, planted, and circled on this land since it became ours in the mid-1970s. We are, after all, nature worshipers.

The down side is that this site is remote and difficult to reach without four-wheel drive. It would be extremely difficult for a person in a wheelchair or with physical disabilities to negotiate its rugged terrain. Its primitive facilities can support only a limited number of worshipers without taxing the land we are committed to healing. These factors mean we cannot be as inclusive as some of us might like to be, which becomes more of a problem as we grow. Of course it is not only the land that limits our numbers. There is also the concern about the quality of participation and whether a sense of closeness and safety will be possible if the group is allowed to become too large.

These same questions plagued the early women's consciousness-raising movement: How do you maintain group integrity, intimacy, and safety while building a broad-based, inclusive movement? How do you stand for equality while maintaining an in-group and an out-group? How do you maintain your core ideological/thealogical/aesthetic identity while allowing others full participation? We attempt the same solutions as did the women's groups: we create spin-offs. We have held open rituals in accessible locations on the prior weekend. Attendance at the closed ritual depends on membership, length of involvement, depth of commitment, and promptness of registration. We try to be fair, but for the most part it is a core group of initiates, those who have been around for years, who are permitted to enter the "holy of holies," our sacred land at this most sacred time of year. This creates another, even more disturbing problem: those of us who have been around for years are all able-bodied Caucasian heterosexuals and bisexuals. As both cause and effect of this, our symbol system and mythology is predominantly heterosexual, our deities predominantly European. Of course it is theoretically possible for a literate person of any race or sexual preference to move progressively through the church hierarchy into the in-group, and it does happen occasionally, but as we have no affirmative action program, we are likely to remain largely homogeneous.

Another problem is that as we expand to let new people into the "inner circle," I notice a subtly New Age, antihistorical, antifeminist (so-called "postfeminist") bias creeping in, couching itself in therapeutic jargon and the language of the men's movement, advocating "men's liberation," which usually means a self-justifying refusal to deal with feminist issues or critique.[16]

One of the limitations of our highly participatory ritual style is that, because there is no sermonic form, there is no prophetic voice within our liturgy. There is no place within a worship context for our clergy to call us to accountability for racism, sexism, hypocrisy, or the just plain pettiness to which all churches, including this one, seem to fall prey. Should anyone choose to take that prophetic role, he or she will likely be accused of being anti-male, judgmental, laying a guilt trip, or, Goddess forbid, preaching. Thus we disempower our implicitly feminist moral imperative by not allowing it to be made explicit in sacred space. The voice of clergy is confined to the priestly and pastoral modes. Without a scripture and prophetic voice holding us accountable to our thealogy, it is easy for us to fall into mushy moral relativism, and for our diversity to disintegrate into mere individualism.

The question of children's attendance at rituals must also be broached. Reasons given for their exclusion include their being a distraction (especially to their parents), legal concerns about our sexually explicit symbol system, the ofttimes late hour of our celebrations, and their possible boredom. I suspect Pagan antichild bias can also be attributed to the tradition of secrecy in our Wiccan roots. If one's way of worship is outlawed, one is certainly hesitant to pass it on to one's children, however innocent one's practice may be in reality. Lives have been lost for less.

The tendency to exclude children from worship may also be traceable to our feminist roots and women's need to experience themselves and their spirituality outside of their identities as mothers, lovers, or wives. Many of us are still trying to heal ourselves spiritually and emotionally from the wounds of our own childhood, and often there seems to be no emotional room in this for real children. Certainly it would be nearly impossible to participate in shamanic trance work, for example, with a small child pulling at your sleeve. It is true that we need sacred space apart from children.

As a whole, we do not take our responsibilities to the next generation seriously enough. In part this may be because we are only beginning as a movement to fully recognize our values and practices as a religion to be passed on, rather than merely as a personal pastime or spiritual path to be enjoyed in our leisure. In part it may also be that we, especially those of us from the "me generation," have taken on the rampant narcissism of our society and are busy "spending our children's inheritance," spiritually speaking, and simply don't want to be bothered.

Withal the above concerns raised, however, the single most important thing from a feminist perspective about this ritual, and the thing that distinguishes it from any patriarchal liturgy, is its thealogical purpose. We are ritualizing and honoring the difficult and troublesome entry into the dark time of the year, and with it, into the dark parts of ourselves. It is fundamental to feminist thealogy and liturgy that we honor darkness and death, alongside light and birth, as intrinsic to the regenerative process.[17] We do not light a candle against the darkness. We enter with fear and trepidation, for we cannot see our way, but we enter, because it is the only way to transformation and rebirth. We know this from our own bodies. This is women's way—and nature's way—of creation. This is our act of supreme faith in the regenerative power of our Goddess.

This does not mean we are entering the realm of evil. Darkness has taken on a sinister, as well as a racist, meaning in the last several millennia. It was not always so. Archeologist Marija Gimbutas tells us that in the gynocentric religion of Paleolithic and Neolithic Old Europe, black was the color of fertility, like the earth, while the white of bleaching bones signified death. It was at the time of the Indo-European invasions, during the fifth and fourth millennia B.C.E., that (male) deity began to be identified almost entirely with light. At that point the artifacts and images representing deity show a startling transition from predominantly female embodied images to male warriors holding thunderbolts. This was the beginning of the worship of the god of light, who claims to create by word, or idea, alone.[18] Through the mythology and artifacts of numerous ancient cultures, it is possible to follow the banishment of the Great Goddess of All That Is first to the underworld and eventually into oblivion, being gradually replaced in the heavens by gods of thunder and light. Simultaneous with the subordination of the Goddess and of women was the systematic profanation of all the fleshy processes that happen in the dark.[19]

Good and evil reside in both darkness and light. When we say we enter the darkness, we do not refer to the demonic or inverted; we refer to the place where the old, worn-out forms break down in decay, making rich compost for the fertile womb of the earth to renew life. We refer to the restful darkness in which the inchoate gestates until it is ready to take form. This is an intrinsic part of a feminist view of creation.

The circle casting is worth noticing in this regard. It is clear from the first spoken words of this ceremony that we hold all of life as sacred. "Magic, magic everywhere, in the earth and in the air." We are not trying to get someplace else. It is clear that deity is here, embodied in air and rocks, water and fire, in female and male persons. Our priestess and priest are easy in their roles. It is all very human. We are sanctifying our life on earth, not in order to gain some reward elsewhere, but for the purpose of aligning ourselves with that magic, putting ourselves and our lives in the flow of divine will. Tears and laughter have a place in our liturgy. We do not fear the expression of feeling. Our practice is fleshy. We celebrate the privilege of being alive and embodied.

The next section of the ritual is this year's version of a fine old Samhain tradition: letting go of the old to make room for the growth of the new. Upon our return to the circle, we find Hekate sitting in its center, her features shrouded by a dark shroud and cloak, stirring a cauldron on her lap. Though we know this person as our friend and priestess, for us in this moment she is Hekate, the ancient Crone Goddess, reclaimer of lost and broken souls. She is the wise woman, able to see into all our dark secrets. She is kind. There is no need for harshness. There is nothing to hide. She is introduced with "The Crone Song," sung by its author, accompanying herself on guitar:

> *Mother Hekate, She stands at the crossroads*
> *Waiting to see which way you will turn*
> *She guides you along in her infinite wisdom*
> *But Her lessons of death are not easy to learn*
> *And you trust in your heart that She will safely lead you on*
> *Through the night's cold dark, into the dawn where*
> *Waiting alone, your dreams have shone*
> *The Ancient Crone.*[20]

She is here. Hekate takes the circle. She tells us what she has come for, what she can offer us: "Now is the sacrifice of souls, now is the giving up, the stripping down to the bone. The time of bones is the time of no compromise.

Throw it all into Hekate's soup, let Her stir it up and we shall see what will be born anew. Come," she invites us, indicating her cauldron, "throw it in. This is the womb of rebirth, the cup of immortality. Give yourselves freely. Do not hold back. This is the moment, I can use it all. Oh! What a spicy soup this will be!"

Last year's May King begins by offering his crown as symbolic sacrifice for all the life that comes to an end in the winter, that it might in exchange be reborn in the spring. One by one we step forward and place ourselves before Hekate, addressing Her for all to hear. By our own volition, we offer dysfunctional and worn-out parts of ourselves and our lives to be composted in Hekate's cauldron of rebirth. We feel the weight of old habits and attitudes dropping from our shoulders. What a relief that she will take them! We offer self-doubts and self-hatreds, addictions, self-deceptions and self-sabotage, fears, prides, shames, all into the soup. A welfare mother says she wants to give up poverty. A child gives up the pretense of perfection. A timid young woman throws in her fear of saying what she thinks. I feel the girdle around my soul growing tighter. I walk toward the cauldron, unsure of exactly what I will say. "I have grown so small and tight," I begin, "I have become so negative, so bitter, I hardly recognize myself." She beckons me forward. "I want to give you my rage, my suspiciousness, I find I am looking at everybody with suspicion, I have built a shell around myself, and I can't even laugh or love freely anymore." I place my head on her lap and begin to sob. "Yes, that's it," she assures me gently. She strokes my hair and invites me to place my head over the cauldron and put it all in. A roar forms in my belly, catches in my throat, then tears its way out through my vocal cords. I feel the tightness leaving me. The bitterness so long with me begins to evaporate. I feel able to breathe for the first time in years. I am released. "Thank you, Grandmother," I whisper, before returning to my spot in the circle.

The letting go continues at its own pace, peppered with wise comments form Hekate about nature's ways of breaking down even the most stubborn of substances. It is all grist for Her mill, food for Her worms. This is not the tragedy of life, but part of its mystery. We take our time. We have all night.

The natural cycle of life (decomposition, conception, gestation, birth, growth, reproduction, maturation, decomposition) provides a language and paradigm that lend depth to our liturgy, when used well, as occurred in the section of Hekate's cauldron, where we were dealing with predominantly personal material. In a nature-centered paradigm, rather than confessing to a transcendent god, then being granted absolution through penance or grace, we shed parts of ourselves and our lives to be decomposed and recomposed. Nothing is ever lost to the Goddess. It is important to realize, however, that this ritual moment is part of a longer spiritual process. It is effective in the transformation of sin and/or suffering only if it takes place in the context of genuine repentance, in its original meaning: To turn around and walk the other way. The cauldron can only transform what we genuinely release to it.

When all who wish to have added their ingredients to Hekate's soup, it is time for us to personally enter the underworld. This is the night of all the year when we can best complete old business, reclaim lost memories or exiled parts of ourselves. Hades, our priest, induces a trance state, and takes those of us who wish to follow down past layers of humus, rock, molten lava, down a dark narrow corridor, into our own unconscious. We find ourselves in a setting our conscious minds may have long forgotten, if indeed they ever knew it. It is a fragile moment. Suddenly a song begins, jolting me out of my reverie. It is a song of which I am very fond, appropriate for the season, but the timing is wrong. Rather than "taking me down" as the song requests, it yanks me out of my most private inner world, leaving me feeling violated. The process is not completed in any effective way, and I feel frightened of being left in the underworld, just as I was approaching an image I since have forgotten.

This has happened before with delicately induced trance states in other rituals, I recall. I feel angry about insensitivity of timing, with people in such vulnerable states. My background as a psychotherapist makes me aware that this sort of interruption can be more than annoying: it can be dangerous, leaving people unable to integrate the material that has been elicited. In our rush toward egalitarianism, we too frequently violate the trust of the congregation by allowing amateur psychotherapists to lead complex processes without adequate knowledge or training. As we learned painfully in the early feminist movement, equality does not mean we all have the same level of skill or expertise in all areas. Unfortunately our rituals sometimes suffer from our reticence to admit that.

Somehow we move on. We are asked to name some things that have been taken from us against our will that are already in the cauldron. This year has been a hard one for many of us. One member lost her home, her extensive art and mythology library, and her book-in-progress in the Oakland fire. Another lost her brother-in-law, her cat, her son's grandfather, and the hard drive in her computer, all in the same week. One member's marriage dissolved. Several of us lost jobs and economic security. We say goodbye to all that has been shattered and lost, never to return, and release it, along with our suffering, to Hekate's cauldron of changes. "Cauldron of changes, blossom of bone, arc of eternity, hole in the stone."

Now for the final ingredients: what would we like to see go back to its elemental beginnings, to compost, releasing its energy to be used for something new? Here the ritual moves from the personal to the planetary. Our personal material is already in the soup. What needs to decay in our larger world and system? Led by our priest, we stand and form our hands and bodies into a DNA spiral in reverse. We are a wand of decomposition. We move as one (counter-clockwise for unwinding) to the altar of each element and call out the names of things we wish to see disintegrate: rigid stances, greed, corruption, nuclear weapons, clear-cutting of forests, addictions, the budget for building more highways, John Sununu's job, uncontained emotions, rape, hatred of women, hatred of men, sloppy thinking, lies, "airy-fairy" ungroundedness, battering, child abuse, pollution, the AIDS virus, and unforgiving, self-righteous attitudes. Be gone! "Down, down, decomposing, recomposing."

We are all in the null space between what was and what will be. This is the moment of limitless possibilities, out of which we may weave reality anew, if we dare. What will we dare? People wander off in silence to contemplate and envision the possible future.

When we reassemble, the DNA wand of hands is reformed, this time moving clockwise, the direction in which energy naturally moves in this hemisphere. Again, we move from altar to altar, naming what we wish to see restored or brought into being: clean air, the ozone layer, caring, commitment, deep feeling, compassion, patience, perseverance, grounding, peace, safety, health, rain! In general, our words are more abstract than in the previous section on disintegration. It is easier to be specific about what already exists that we would like to see gone, than it is to be highly specific about things that do not yet exist that we wish to bring into being. My partner and I are noticeably more concrete. We have big plans and need tools. "Funding!" we call out. "Funding for the Great Earth Survival Revival! And video toasters. And a new audio mixer. A green television network. And railroads, miles and miles of railroads, replacing highways. Birth control clinics throughout the world."

Why are we invoking railroads, clinics, and video toasters instead of peace and clean air? Because it is we humans who are causing the problems. It is we humans who need to wake up and learn to live on this earth in harmony. And it is we humans who are going to have to create the tools and institutions necessary to support the transformation of our relationship to one another and to the planet. How else can we get clean air except by replacing the need for cars with energy-efficient, accessible public transportation? How else can we limit the human population except by providing women with real choices about childbearing? How else will we get the word of the planet out to enough people, except with video and sixteen-channel audio mixers? After years of participating in such rituals I have observed that specificity of imagery increases the odds of the magic's efficacy. Sending John Sununu's job to the recycling bin was a prime example of magic that worked.

The problem that becomes apparent as we try to envision a future of our making is that we lack the moral, thealogical vocabulary to translate our nature-centered paradigm into concrete images and actions at the level of larger systems. How do we get from here to there? Our own lives and work must form the bridge. Just as throwing personal pain or problems into the cauldron is but one step in a larger process of self-transformation, magical envisioning is just one step in the process of social transformation. By itself it is merely wishful thinking.

We speak of the Goddess within, yet we seem unsure of how to be her hands in cocreating the large-scale changes we desire. By envisioning the outcome we want, but not the tools or resources we will need to create it, we seem to be asking for change, rather than guidance, from "above." This comes dangerously close to equating the Goddess with the feminist's nemesis: belief in a magic mommy who can and will fix every little thing.

Where are we humans in this mix? Some Pagans seem to have doubts about our moral right to impose change in any realm beyond the strictly personal, even though at the root of an ecosystem-based worldview is the knowledge that we can't avoid it. There is no such thing as not involved. This understanding has not permeated our liturgy, however, as thoroughly as it might. Too many of us are refugees from the New Age who mouth platitudes about only being able to change ourselves, about transformation lying solely within and through each individual. This common wisdom does not address the nature of social institutions or the reality of systemic, institutionalized evil that is devouring our Mother, Nature, and all Her children. Nor does it empower the moral authority that logically derives from a thealogy of immanence. Unless we can claim the authority of the living planet to say what we believe to be good or evil, unless we use our visions to sustain and inspire our work of fighting evil and healing our world, both within and beyond ourselves; unless we seek resources, strength, and guidance; unless we understand our visualization to be one part of our sustained effort at cocreation—unless we do all these things, our visions will remain disincarnate within a patriarchal model of creation in which ideas give birth by word alone, instantly and without the pain of labor. This is far from a feminist, embodied view of creation or change, and also far from nature's way. Furthermore it gives us no ground from which to view the objective realities of oppression.

Unfortunately we lack a well-developed thealogy of good and evil, a common ground from which to speak and act. Having forsaken the traditional theological language of salvation, sin, and sacrifice, we too often find ourselves in the untenable position of trying to rewrite reality with only visualization and the barrenness of subjectivist psychological vocabulary and paradigm to help us.

This vocabulary and paradigm cannot adequately explain why things are as they are, or how we might be instrumental in changing them, except within a narrow, personal field, because they are based on an atomized view of the individual psyche as casual, at the center of reality. It claims that the social is a mere reflection of the individual. In its inversion of basic feminist theory, it reduces the political to the merely personal. It cannot give us direction because it is morally neutral, patriarchal, and implicitly system-supporting. By reducing rich and important thealogical concepts like "evil," "Goddess," "grace," and "cocreation" to simplistic half-truths like "projecting our shadow," "the inner-feminine," or "creating our own reality," we frame ourselves into an ethic of narcissistic individualism bordering on solipsism. This language and paradigm gives us no moral, conceptual ground from which to judge and intervene in our world. At its worst it is a sort of cosmic, or karmic, Calvinism in which success proves worthiness, thereby blaming the victim for creating the reality of her own oppression.

We need a vocabulary of reciprocal relationality and cocreation with the divine, if we are to find in our liturgy a meaning of our relationships (to the universe and to one another) that is liberating for women, and an ethical system coming out of that understanding that helps us to know how and where to act. It is not our thealogical grounding that is lacking: it is our thealogical language. The language and symbol system of organic evolution, which is inherently relational and processive, as well as diverse, needs to fully inform our understanding of our role in large, systemic change.

It may also be time to selectively reclaim traditional theological language. We need to be able to speak of the redemption of Gaia from those who have her in bondage and are exploiting her unto death. This language shift would redirect our consciousness and actions, putting the onus of liberation on us. We might speak of humanity in this time as a people in need of salvation, having become estranged from our Mother, Nature. This language has depth and power. It is not simply self-absorbed. Our magic would automatically become more concrete, our petition more responsible.

Now that we have completed our major work, we want just to be with each other. We have new stories, poems, and songs to share, as well as insights and visions from our descent that night. And we are monstrously hungry. It is now about 4 A.M. The pot-luck food is brought out from the house, blessed, and we sit comfortably in the circle, eating, drinking, singing, talking, and listening.

This is a remarkable event, this informal sharing in sacred circle. One of the greatest attributes of Pagan thealogy and practice is that it does not separate the sacred from the secular. We do not cast outside the circle certain aspects of life not deemed sufficiently holy. We hold all of life as sacred. Life is w/holy. We honor the sacred in the ordinary. Our laughter, our companionship, our remembrance of Samhains past and friends not present—all are sanctified by their inclusion in our circle.

After a sufficient time of relaxing and informal sharing, we are ready to complete our ritual work: weaving a web of protection. A large web made of many cords is carefully unwrapped in the center of our circle by our church founder. He explains to us that this web was originally woven exactly one year ago in Peru, in a Samhain ritual shared by some of our group members with the indigenous medicine people there. After wearing them for several days, several hosts and visitors had woven their cords together into a symbol of the unification of indigenous, earth-loving people in both Northern and Southern hemispheres. Since then, knots have been added to the web at various conferences and festivals around the country. Each knot in the web stands for a wish or hope for a better world. Now we are invited to add our own wishes to the web's power. Each of us holds one string. This time we are weaving protection into its magic, for what has already been a year of hardship and suffering promises to continue so through the winter. Magic alone does not create reality, but like any form of prayer, it increases or decreases the odds on certain occurrences. By weaving an umbrella of psychic protection, we hope to prevent some of the fallout and backlash from landing on us.

What is it then that we request protection from and for in this elaborated benediction? Do we ask protection from the growing plague of immune disorders and environmental diseases around us, from the devastation of the crashing economy, from the increasing dangers on our streets to ourselves and our children? Also, the solipsistic worldview referred to above once again frames many prayers in such a way that many of our newer members ask for protection from themselves, as if to say, if I can protect myself from myself, all else will be fine; only my own thought forms can harm me. (Our more seasoned members have a more fully developed thealogy and vocabulary and are far less reliant on New Age psychometaphysics for their cosmology.) This denial of evil and of existence outside the self is both dangerous and arrogant. Women lose ground as the language of feminism and interdependence is replaced with the language of addiction and co-dependence.

One woman asks to be protected from the fear that interferes with her relationships; another asks for protection from her addiction; a third from her anger. There is no mention of the real and objective causes for fear and anger, or protection from these. I call out for protection of the Goddess's people from the wrath of right-wing fundamentalists and their God. One feminist petitions for the protection of our right to reproductive choice. Another speaks to the increase of violent crimes against women, and asks that she and her sisters be protected. A masculist predictably responds by asking for protection from male bashing and blame, as if this were comparable. A mother prays for the protection of children from all forms of abuse. Someone else puts a protection on the old-growth redwoods of California's north coast. And so it goes, until we complete the circle and everyone has had an opportunity to speak. In spite of our shortcomings, this is a powerful exercise in group prayer and participatory magic.

When all present have had the opportunity to add their prayers, we visualize a dome of protection surrounding us. We hold the web high above our heads and begin circling clockwise, singing, "We are weaving our power, we are weaving our magic, we are weaving our lives." We circle and sing until the spell is strong in energy, then we ground it in the earth.

The light will return soon. We must finish our ritual and return to the upper world. It is time to thank the God and Goddess of the underworld for gracing our circle, time to say goodbye to our honored guests and ancestors, time to turn things back around. A new year is beginning. Whatever was done tonight is done. The year will tell us what our magic wrought.

We thank the spirits of the earth, air, fire, and water for helping with our magic, and take down the magic circle between the worlds. "All from air into air / let the misty curtain part / All is ended, all is done / What has been must now be gone! / What is done by ancient art/ must merry meet and merry part and merry meet again." (From Faery tradition.)

The circle is open, the ritual is over.

What have we done here and what have we accomplished? We have honored the deities, both female and male, and our departed ancestors. We have offered the old and decaying to the Goddess for breaking down and regeneration. We have shared food, drink, stories, and laughter. We have sung the songs and prayed the prayers. We have honored and said goodbye to the old year and planted seeds for the new one (but we will not know which ones took root until well past winter solstice). We have woven a web to surround and protect us. We have worshiped and communed, touched and been touched, reflected on our lives in the framework of community and of the greater whole.

As I write, I am once again struck by the ancient familiarity of our ritual and by its humanity. It truly reflects us as we are and as we hope to be, in all our frailty and beauty. This is a liturgical tradition that has room for the people in it. Perhaps that is because it is still fresh, in the bloom of its youth, not yet having been codified into doctrine. Perhaps the early Christians told stories and laughed too, as they broke bread in communion. I am sure, however, that pre-Christian people in caves and roundhouses around the Mediterranean and in Northern Europe did so. My bones remember this. They remember too the invasion of the patriarchal hordes, the destruction of the temples, the appropriation and then the defaming of the Goddess's name and her priestesses. Now we are returning.

Is the return of the Goddess, then, good news for women? My answer is: it could be. Or it could be another means by which women are kept in their place, told to be sweet and nurturant, "like the Goddess." It all depends on whether we allow narrow, patriarchal, male-created definitions to circumscribe our ideas about the Goddess. Unless feminists are vigilant in insisting that archetype not be confused with stereotype, Her worship will just become more grist for the patriarchal mill, as happened long ago in patriarchal Greece and Rome,[21] as continues today in India. The patriarchy will grind out ever more subtle and insidious propaganda on the soft power of the inner feminine as an obfuscation of the same old saw of the woman behind the man. Patriarchy will, until its dying breath, which I pray will be soon, use every weapon in its—and our—arsenal to prevent women's power from gaining a foothold. If its agents can turn the movement to reclaim feminine deity in their favor, as an agent of sexism, they will do so, and with the help of many women, in the name of reconciliation, in the name of "balance." If they cannot wipe out all memory of the Goddess, they will try to tame Her, and us, and all the wild, fecund and fetid, unmanageable holy life that whispers Her name.

If on the other hand we recognize the Goddess in all Her aspects and changes, as did our most ancient and gynocentric forebears, if we honor Her solar as well as Her lunar persona, honor Her as warrior as well as midwife, devourer and virgin (woman-for-herself), as well as mother and lover, perhaps our love of her will give us the strength we need to continue to fight for the freedom and dignity of all women and all life, as embodiments of Her.

Notes

1. Mircea Eliade, *A History of Ideas from the Stone Age to the Eleusinian Mysteries* (Chicago: University of Chicago Press, 1978).

2. James Mellaart, *Catal Huyuk: A Neolithic Town in Anatolia* (London: Thames & Hudson, 1967).

3. Elinor Gadon, *The Once and Future Goddess: A Symbol for Our Time* (San Francisco: Harper & Row, 1989), ch. 6.

4. Anodea Judith, "Peruvian Pilgrimage," *The Green Egg*, Vol. 24, no. 93, pp. 20–21.

5. The*a*logy refers to the reflections on a female deity. I have used this form throughout for reasons of affirmative action and consistency.

6. Ernest Klein, *A Comprehensive Etymological Dictionary of the English Language*, Vol. II, L–Z (Amsterdam: Elsevier Publishing Company, 1967).

7. Margot Adler, *Drawing Down the Moon* (Boston: Beacon Press, revised 1986), p. 455.

8. Otter G'Zell, publisher's editorial, *The Green Egg,* Vol. 26, no. 100 (Spring 1993), p. 2. G'Zell was a founder and has been a leader and spokesperson in the Neo-Pagan movement for thirty years. *The Green Egg* is an award-winning quarterly Neo-Pagan journal.

9. While not all Neo-Pagans ordain clergy, a few groups, such as the one described herein, are incorporated as churches and therefore can legally select and ordain people to perform clerical duties. This is a matter of some controversy within the Pagan community.

10. Key argument presented by Sherry Ortner, "Is Female to Male as Nature Is to Culture?" in *Women and Values*, ed. Marilyn Pearsall (Belmont, Calif.: Wadsworth, 1986). See also essays in special issue of *Hypatia*, "Ecological Feminism," ed. Karen J. Warren, Spring 1991, passim.

11. Key argument by Susan Griffin in *Woman and Nature: The Roaring Inside Her* (New York: Harper & Row, 1978). See also essays in *Reweaving the World: The Emergence of Ecofeminism*, ed. Irene Diamond and Gloria Feman Orenstein (San Francisco: Sierra Club Books, 1990).

12. Rick Hamouris, "We Are a Circle," on *Welcome to Annwfn*. Tape by Nemeton Publishing, 1986, side 1.

13. In Pagan ritual, as in no other tradition that I am aware of, it is unusual to have both a priestess and a priest presiding as a matter of course, recognizing both god and goddess. In this particular ritual, the priest takes leadership in a later section.

14. See Gadon, *Once and Future Goddess*, ch. 13: "The Goddess Within: A Source of Empowerment for Women."

15. The seed of modern feminist discourse lies in Simone de Beauvoir's presentation of woman as "other" in *The Second Sex*, ed. H. M. Parshley (New York: Alfred A. Knopf, 1953).

16. See Susan Faludi's *Backlash: The Undeclared War Against American Women* (New York: Crown Publishers, 1991), pp. 300–11, for her critique of men's movement spokesmen Warren Farrell and Robert Bly.

17. Carol Christ, *Diving Deep and Surfacing: Women Writers on Spiritual Quest* (Boston: Beacon Press, 1980). For further discussion see Starhawk, *Dreaming the Dark: Magic, Sex, and Politics* (Boston: Beacon Press, 1982), and Gadon, *Once and Future Goddess*.

18. Marija Gimbutas, *The Goddesses and Gods of Old Europe, 6500 to 3500 B.C.* (Berkeley, Calif.: University of California Press, 1982).

19. Judith Ochshorn, *The Female Experience and the Nature of the Divine* (Bloomington: University of Indiana Press, 1981).

20. Anodea Judith, "The Crone Song," on *Welcome to Annwfn.* Tape by Nemeton Publishing, 1986, side 1.

21. Sarah Pomeroy, *Goddesses, Whores, Wives and Slaves: Women in Classical Antiquity* (New York: Schocken Books, 1975).

10

Women–Church
Transforming Liturgy

Diann L. Neu

Women-church is an international, ecumenical movement of lo
cal Christian feminist spirituality communities that engage in
liturgy and transformation.[1] Women-church feminist liturgies
keep alive the memory and imagination of the community of
women believers and of those children and men who identify
with them. In women-church liturgies we remember those who
engage in liberation from patriarchy. We speak their names, tell
and reinterpret their stories, use their songs and readings, and recognize their power as spirit guides. In women-church liturgies we
image a future where women and those who are marginalized will
be respected, freed, and filled with power. We dream of a new
dawn where, hand in hand, we sweep away oppression. We envision weaving together a huge coat to warm our old people and
our homeless friends. We image cooking a huge dinner to feed all
the hungry of the world. In the meantime, we empower one another and our various communities through feminist liturgies for
social transformation. In women-church, liturgy, justice, and in-
culturation interrelate as friendly companions for feminist change

Women of Fire: A Pentecost Liturgy

"Women of Fire" reclaims for women the traditional Christian feast of Pentecost. This major feast celebrates the birth of the Christian church and the renewal of ministry and community in the Holy Spirit. "Women of Fire" focuses on the power of the Spirit within her people, including women's full participation in ministry and community as church for the transformation of injustice.

The feminist liturgical text that follows celebrates the power of the Spirit received by women. It celebrates women's passion, pain, politics, and promise in a liturgy that includes Eucharist. It names women-spirit crying out for freedom and justice, women-spirit hurting and in pain, women-spirit renewing creation, and women-spirit gathering for Eucharist. It reclaims Pentecost as a time when women-church came to life.

"Women of Fire" closed a weekend conference on feminist spirituality in The Netherlands at de Tiltenberg, the International Grail Center, with more than one hundred women from six countries and various religious and ethnic backgrounds speaking a variety of languages.[2] The original structure was designed by Di-ann L. Neu with Mary E. Hunt and Carol White, the planning team for the weekend. Participants formed liturgy teams to compose readings and blessings, decorate the various spaces, and rehearse individual parts.

Preparation for the Liturgy

The four settings used for each of the four movements of this liturgy were the meadow (passion), the chapel (pain), the library (politics), and the dining room (promise). The meadow, full of nature's gifts, needed no preparation. We rearranged the furniture of the chapel to form a cross that divided the circle into four sections. We gathered a basket and pens and papers, one for each participant, and put them in the chapel. We hung political posters on the walls of the library and lighted a fire in the fireplace. In the center of the dining room, we set a table with the three breads: sourdough, raisin, and an intricately braided spiral loaf. On tables set for eight people we placed a bowl, towel, pitchers of water and wine and juice, and a candle for each participant. The only script that all participants received was music. Everyone gathered in a large circle in the courtyard for music and movement practice before the liturgy started.

Variations of this liturgy have been used for Spirit-Wisdom celebrations with local women-church groups and for Pentecost worship with the National Commission on the Status and Role of Women in the United Methodist Church.

The Liturgical Text

The liturgy begins with the "Call to Celebration" and "Casting a Women-Spirit Circle," in which each woman present names herself as woman-spirit until the circle is complete. After reflections about the meaning of Pentecost for participants, the group moves into the first space, the meadow, the place for passion. One woman proclaims:

> Let the spirit inside you rise like a mighty wind!
> Let the spirit inside you leap like a roaring fire!
> Women-spirit is rising!
> Women-spirit is yearning for spiritual meaning! [3]

An elder invites participants to walk briefly in the meadow, rest, watch, listen, while choosing a symbol—object, poem, song, dance—that represents the voice of Spirit-Wisdom speaking to them of the passion of Pentecost. A bell rings calling the group back together. Each participant then tells the significance of her symbol and shares it with the others.

The group moves in procession to the chapel, where the liturgy focuses on pain. One woman proclaims:

> Let the spirit inside you rage like an angry storm!
> Let the spirit inside you blaze like a fiery torch!
> Women-spirit is hurting and is in pain!
> Women-spirit has been battered and broken!

Following a dramatic reading of a version of Psalm 130,[4] participants reflect on their own pain, name it and write it on a piece of
paper, then share their stories with another if they choose. At the
conclusion of this time, two women perform an exorcism, naming these and other pains suffered by women. This story-telling
ends with participants tearing into pieces the papers with their
pains written on them and placing these bits in a basket. One
woman prays, "Let us transform our crosses into circles, our
stones into bread," whereupon everyone places the chairs in a
ring, singing "Sweet Spirit."[5] The group then moves into the library for the third portion of the liturgy.

In the library the focus shifts to politics, with one woman proclaiming:

> Let the spirit inside you light fires of justice!
> Let the spirit inside you spark revolutions!
> Women-spirit is renewing all of creation!
> Women-spirit is full of power!

As a shared political action, participants burn the scraps of paper,
invoking the spirit of those who have suffered and the spirit of
those who have worked for justice. Carrying candles lighted from
the fire of burning papers, four women lead the group to the dining room to the final movement, promise.

One woman proclaims:

> Let the spirit inside you rise in celebration!
> Let the spirit inside you dance with joy!
> Women-spirit is gathering for Eucharist!
> Women-spirit is fulfilling a promise!

The four women carrying the lighted candles move to the four
corners of the room, saying, "We are the generation that stands
between the fires." Table by table, they light the candles held by
each woman, invoking the power of fire for good. Then follows
the "Blessing of the First Glass." The blesser invites everyone to
pour wine or fruit juice into glasses in a toast to mother earth.

Another woman blesses the sourdough bread as a sign of the "Spirit of Strength." Then all participants wash one another's hands, "as a symbol of women's work" and "as a sign of our care for one another." The second glass of juice or wine is dedicated "to friendship, to courage, to justice, to peace." Another woman blesses the raisin bread as a sign of "women of fire whose energy and passion spread through society like raisins through this bread." Someone else blesses the third glass in honor of all the participants, particularly the hostesses. Two women bless the final bread, an intricately braided loaf, as a sign of the beauty and solidarity of women. One of the hostesses blesses the food for the festive meal, and everyone eats.

After the meal one of the planners commissions participants to

take the Eucharist of Women Church
. . . .
in all directions of the universe
to bless and to embrace,
to forgive and to heal,
to welcome and to sanctify.

During the singing of "Claiming Our Power,"[6] by Marsie Silvestro, the group moves into a centipede-form dance of "passion, pain, politics, and promise": two steps forward, one step back. All are connected, having a good time and singing along with the movement.

Feminist Analysis of "Women of Fire"

The process of planning this women-church liturgy and celebrating it for the first time at de Tiltenberg was life-giving beyond words. The liturgical text alone offered engaged reading. The liturgical celebration provided an exhilarating festivity, expressing feminist values and inviting participation in a feminist way of being and living. It demonstrated feminist spirituality in action.

To analyze this liturgy I will use feminist liturgical principles that I have discovered and named as emerging from a variety of feminist liturgies that women are creating and celebrating. Each of these principles shares equal power, so I do not number them. None is first or last; they interrelate.

Feminist liturgy shares power among all participants. Patterns of leadership and responsibility in creating this liturgy reflected mutuality among all participants, both in the collaborative process of planning and in the community event of celebrating. Each woman chose to use her authority as she wished for the preparation and enactment of this event. Some used their particular gifts and arts to work in teams to design the content for one of the four movements; others created the different liturgical spaces; still others set the tables for the meal; some cooked; some composed the blessings; others chose and played music; some created dances; and others gathered symbols and objects. To make sure that different parts of the liturgy connected, each planning group kept in touch with the other groups by sending someone to listen to and share with them. Finally, when a group's part was ready, one person went to the computer and typed it in as a record of the liturgy.

Mutual ownership was encouraged by the leadership styles used during the planning process and during the celebration. The egalitarian style of rotating leadership among planning groups located power in the community, not in one person. Each part of the liturgy was initiated by those who designed it. Each person started her part when she thought it was appropriate to do so. The written liturgical text described here does not convey the spontaneous nature of words and gestures that leaders used to call forth the spirit of the community.

Participants were invited to share their power throughout the liturgy in spontaneous, self-generated responses. These revealed another expression of the gifts and arts of the community. In the first movement (passion), each woman shared a symbol—an object, song, dance, poem, or fruit of her reflection. In the second movement (pain), each woman thought about and, if she wished, wrote about and shared "from what pain in your life do you wish to be freed?" In the third movement (politics), those who wished to invoke the spirit of justice seekers who worked to renew creation named them and their actions. In the fourth movement (promise), participants were invited to add to the "Commission-ing and Sending Forth."

We chose liturgical spaces that reflected shared power or the lack of it, and we designed each accordingly. We opened the liturgy by "Casting a Women-Spirit Circle," which conveyed shared power residing in the participants, since each person was an equal distance from the center of the circle. Spirit-Wisdom filled the meadow (passion) with gifts of nature that empower each woman in unique ways. We rearranged the furniture in the chapel (pain) to form a cross that divided the circle into four sec-tions and disempowered the community. The cross symbolized suffering, self-sacrifice, and obedience that furthers the victimiza-tion of women. It was rejected because it reinforces violence and abuse, domination and subordination. Spontaneously, as women entered the chapel and encountered the cross, we formed a circle around it, refusing to let it divide us. We hung political posters on the walls of the library (politics) to bring the power of justice makers into our midst. In the center of the dining room (promise) we set a circular table with three breads and around it we set cir-cular tables with place settings for eight people. This meal setting focused the table-sharing power of the Eucharist.

Feminist liturgy honors women in all our diversity as imaging the di-vine and as engaging in divine activity.   This liturgy honored women as embodying divine activity from the opening, when we created our circle as each one spoke her name and said "I am woman-spirit" and "we are women-spirit together," to the closing, when we connected in our "passion, pain, politics, and promise" dance and sang "we are . . . we are women-church." Women's bonds with one another were valued as reflective of divine life. Each line of the call to celebration honored women as embodying Spirit-Wisdom: "Let the spirit inside you rise like a mighty wind!" "Let the spirit inside you rage like an angry storm!" "Let the spirit in-side you light fires of justice!" "Let the spirit inside you dance with joy!"

Throughout the liturgy women interacted with divine life. "Taking a Spirit Journey" into the meadow in the first movement (passion) paralleled the traditional retreat into the wilderness to encounter the Holy One to receive spiritual nourishment and enlightenment. In the song "Ruah," we sang, "The spirit of God within us, crumbles the ancient walls, building a new creation." [7] In "Out of the Depths" we cried out to Mother God, seemingly distant, yet hopefully angry at what has been done to her daughters, sisters, lovers, grandmothers. The "Sweet Spirit" image in the song following the exorcism presented a healing, caring Goddess who catches our tears when we weep because of pain and evil.

The language we used to name the divine moved beyond words like mother or father, she or he. We reclaimed names and attributes for the divine that expressed a variety of aspects of Spirit-Wisdom that women embody, such as Sweet Spirit, Spirit Mother, Spirit of Strength, Creative Spirit, Passionate Spirit, and Spirit of Life.

The names of the divine used in the blessings corresponded to each blessing. For example, in blessing the first bread, after we blessed the strength of the women who went before us, we prayed: "Blessed are you, Spirit of Strength." After blessing raisin bread to symbolize "women of fire whose energy and passion spread through society like the raisins through bread," we prayed: "Blessed are you, Passionate Spirit." After blessing the wonderfully braided spiral bread symbolizing all women as beautiful, we prayed: "Blessed are you, Beautiful Spirit." Using attributes for the Spirit that parallel the blessing expands our concept of Spirit, stretches our imaginations about the divine, and enables us to see ourselves as strong, passionate, and beautiful.

Feminist liturgy uses symbols, gestures, texts, images, and words that emerge from women's ways of knowing. The symbols used throughout this liturgy are ancient ones with a feminist glow. The candles lighted at two different times symbolized the preservation of the soul and the spark of revolution. In the third movement (politics) four women lighted four large candles from the central fire to illuminate the spirit of the justice seekers named in "Invoking the Spirit." In the fourth movement (promise) the fire from the candles reminded us that "we are the generation that stands between the fires" of war, genocide, and destruction. We lighted candles and were given a unique flame to acknowledge the variety of gifts among us. The four candle bearers passed their fire to participants by lighting each one's candle and entrusting her with a gift, saying,"I am the fire from the east and I call forth in you the flame of justice."

The Eucharist celebrated in this liturgy was a communal banquet, the very concrete sharing of a meal in love and justice. As in the communities of gospel times, the common meal was the action whereby the community gathered for memorial and thanksgiving and expressed a sense of common identity.[8] Women-church purposefully reclaims this meal character of Eucharist, which was abandoned in the first century. In this and in all feminist Eucharists we redeem and reclaim the gospel message of table sharing: women bless and eat food, bless and break bread, bless and drink the fruit of the vine, tell stories, give thanks, claim power, and actualize promises "in memory of her."[9] Women-church blesses in Eucharist a variety of breads and drinks because no one bread can feed our hunger, no one drink can quench our thirst. Women-church savors the taste of a variety of powerful foods and savors the community of a variety of powerful people.[10]

The three glasses of this Eucharist were dedicated to mother earth; to friendship, courage, justice, and peace; and to our hostesses, respectively. Each blessing included a clicking of glasses and toasting together by saying the blessing prayer. The three breads—sourdough, raisin, and braided spiral—represented the strength of our foremothers, the energy and passion of women of fire, and the beauty of all women, respectively.

Celebrating the four movements of this liturgy in four different spaces invited the use of procession to move people from place to place. Processions are religious retinues going solemnly in ritual action from one place to another while singing. In procession, we walk with women-spirit on the pilgrimage of life; we draw in spiritual energy; we are challenged to give public witness to our beliefs. Walking with spirit guides, we discover sounds and echoes, moods and music, voices and silences of Spirit-Wisdom. We take Pentecost seriously and turn ourselves and church inside out.

The texts used in this liturgy are works by women. "Out of the Depths" was written by Kathy Galloway of England as a contemporary psalm. The exorcism was composed by a writing team of the participants. "Invoking the Spirit" was written by Chung Hyun Kyung of South Korea for the World Council of Churches meeting in Canberra.[11] The blessings were written by participants for the occasion. The songs were composed by women recording artists. Women's work is plentiful, available, and powerful.

One may ask why scripture was not used. Some scriptural texts are considered abusive to women; therefore, many feminist liturgists do not use scripture. We exercise a hermeneutics of suspicion toward inherited texts. Since the early church did not record most works by women, we do not have them to use now in our liturgies. We must read and sing, create and re-create texts by women to remember our stories and recover feminist collective memory.

Feminist liturgy values women's bodies as vehicles of divine revelation. As a liturgy, "Women of Fire" expressed embodied knowledge through kinesthetic, auditory, and visual pathways. This made it possible and more comfortable for women with disabilities to participate and provided an arena for everyone to experience the divine in her own embodied way. We emphasized embodied action in the language of space, gesture, sound, color, and nature. Delighting in the sensual, we used sight, sound, smell, touch, body movements, and tactile objects to engage participants to embrace the liturgy's meaning. We gave a hand to the person on either side of us as we formed the opening circle. We moved in procession to and from each of the four liturgical places. We rang bells to signal the beginning of each new movement (passion, pain, politics, promise) to announce the beginning of each moment of the Eucharist, and to punctuate the reading, "Out of the Depths."

We included gestures as we sang "Ruah." We exorcised "seeing women's bodies and souls as dirty, sinful, inferior." We added gestures of disgust to each "Be gone! Be gone! Be gone!" in the exorcism. We tore up the papers on which we had written our pains and threw them into the fire to burn. We rearranged into a circle the chairs that were set up in the form of a cross. We smelled the food of Eucharist as well as the flowers and trees in the meadow. We lighted candles. We clicked glasses. We broke bread. We ate food. We danced. The "Blessing of the Third Bread" captured the beauty each woman's body reveals through its shape, size, color, ability. "We women—aren't we beautiful? All women are beautiful. All women are beautiful." We honored the variety and integrity of women's bodies.

Feminist liturgy values women's solidarity with one another and strengthens these bonds in community for overcoming violence. The liturgy challenged women to active engagement on women's behalf in the social and political arena. In the second movement (pain), the tolling of the bell throughout the reading of "Out of the Depths" reverberated through each of us. How many women battered? How many women robbed of their humanity? How many women rejected by their families? How many women weeping in mourning? "Do you hear my voice, O God my Mother? I can sing your song of praise no longer. . . . What is the new life you promise me? I do not want more of the same." As women thought of and wrote down the pain from which they wished to be freed, many wept.

The exorcism that followed was cathartic. We named evils done to women and responded to them by saying, "Be gone! Be gone! Be gone!" in Dutch, German, French, English, Portuguese, Italian, and Spanish, adding gestures of disgust. Our enthusiasm engaged our entire bodies: kicking, shouting, punching, shaking, yelling, and stomping; outcries of injustice and lament. Tearing up our papers of pain, and eventually burning them, symbolized for us how women's collective power casts out forces of evil. Dismantling the cross together became a visible symbol of individual and group power and commitment to counteract violence on behalf of women. When we reached the third movement (politics), we took off our shoes, honoring Holy Ground, and listened to "Invoking the Spirit." We stood in solidarity with those who work to renew all of creation.

When we blessed the third bread we said, "This bread—isn't it beautiful?" And we were. "All parts are connected: A strong bond of solidarity." And we created community.

Feminist liturgy shares with children a feminist faith that models a life stance of love and justice. Children participated in the power of this liturgy. A few nursing children celebrated a Pentecost that will, no doubt, be foundational in their lives. One woman captured everyone's heart when she blessed the bread holding her child in swaddling clothes. During our local women-church liturgies we often provide a time when the children gather separately for a different, yet similar, reading and for an activity that follows the theme of the liturgy, for example, making and decorating a symbol used in the liturgy, drawing a picture that interprets the reading or creating a song about the theme. For this liturgy, there was enough activity and variety that children entered into the entire event.

Feminist liturgy motivates and legitimates social transformation. In this liturgy the unnatural divisions of class, race, sexual orientation, and culture were transformed to remind us of the work we must do. We exorcised the evils of "racism and apartheid" and the "chains of classism, heterosexism, ableism, and ageism that bind women everywhere." In the entire third movement (politics) we listened "to the cries of creation and to the cries of the spirits within it." We remembered the justice seekers from all parts of the world's story who worked to renew creation. The closing "Commissioning and Sending Forth" challenged us to "take the Eucharist of women-church" and rid the world of injustice. These experiences encouraged solidarity beyond this immediate gathering.

The language used throughout this liturgy encourages social change. It shapes a feminist present and future reality that values inclusivity and liberation in all its forms. Since this was a women-celebrated liturgy we spoke of women, and where appropriate, as in the "Commissioning and Sending Forth," we used women and men. When I have used variations on this text with men present, I have spoken of women and men, where appropriate, and named women first to signify a change in power.

We spoke deliberately of two matriarchs, Sarah and Hagar, honoring the one who is often not recognized as a matriarch because she was black and an outcast.[12] We were sensitive to racist words and connotations such as light and dark, replacing them with fire and flame. In the exorcism we named all races: black, brown, red, yellow, and white, and named white last to signify a change in power. In "Kindling the Lights" we spoke of the human race instead of mankind. Aware that words such as "vision" and "hearing" exclude those who do not see or hear, we did not use them, or we used them with qualifications.[13] For example, we spoke of "all" instead of "whole," "dreams" instead of "visions," "insensitivity" instead of "blindness," "indifference" instead of "deafness." Real inclusivity includes communicating in a variety of languages. While the liturgical text is written in English here, many languages—Dutch, French, German, Spanish, Portuguese, Italian, and English—were used in celebrating this liturgy in The Netherlands. Social transformation will come when we can communicate with one another in our own languages.

Conclusion

Women-church feminist liturgies provide a place and a space where women, children, and women-identified men can engage in spiritual renewal and social transformation for ourselves, for religious traditions, and for social change.

For women. Feminist liturgies present women with the blessings of feminist spirituality. They empower us to see ourselves as holy and to deepen our sense of self-esteem and self-worth. They make it possible for women to be church. Women's ways of knowing—thinking, feeling, reacting, and living—become normative in feminist liturgies. Women-church is creating new ceremonies that express women's spiritual experiences. Women-church is reclaiming the feminist origins of religious traditions and symbols. Women-church is bringing feminist concerns to institutional religious services.

Will women take time out of our busy lives to create and record feminist liturgies for ourselves and for the next generations? How will women-church feminist liturgies be generative for women, for religious traditions, for social change? Will feminist liturgical communities embrace our liminal status, or will we compromise our prophecy to keep our footing in established churches, so we can be "acceptable" like everyone else? Or will we go our own way, creating for ourselves our own small world and our own small icons inviting terminal inconsequence?

For religious traditions. The topic of feminist liturgies is challenging and sensitive, transforming and life giving. Feminist liturgies challenge religious traditions to reassess themselves. Feminist liturgical issues are effecting change in each denomination and religious tradition at the levels of parish church congregations; house church communities; neighborhood synagogues; university campuses; ordained priests, rabbis, and ministers, both women and men; and the laity, including women in religious congregations. These changes will influence generations to come. At this time in this world it is feminist liturgical communities in our particular circumstances of oppression and struggle who are called to offer new life to the rest of the church and to those who come after us. Perhaps real liturgical renewal will come from feminists who rename traditional issues and breathe life-giving spirit into lifeless liturgical forms.

Can the institutional churches and synagogues change enough to welcome this new Spirit-Wisdom of women, which invites them to transformation? What contributions can women-church liturgies make to the larger churches and synagogues? Can women-church move from the margin to the center of a church that is life for all of us together?

For social change. Feminist liturgy provides a place where we are filled with real love of ourselves that engages us in the justice issues of our day. In liturgy we get in touch with fundamental experiences of justice or the lack of them. We move from this awareness to action for social transformation. Feminist liturgies interrelate with political action. The liturgical assembly is not gathered for itself only, but for the world also. On the other hand, religious pain is a social problem. Religious institutions often present social problems from their own narrow definitions of ethics.

How will feminist liturgies empower feminist liturgical communities for social change? How will women keep refreshing our energy and focusing it on transforming injustice? How will we know that we have helped create a feminist church and society?

Women-church feminist liturgies are nourishing feminist spirituality communities to keep alive the memory and imagination of
the community of faithful women believers and justice seekers,
and those who identify with them. This model of liturgy holds
promise for the feminist transformation of Christian worship and
for women's empowerment. May the promise be fulfilled in our
lifetime.

Notes

1. The concept of women-church is developed in the works of
Mary E. Hunt, "Defining Women-Church," *WATERwheel*, Vol.
3, no. 2 (Silver Spring, Md.: WATERworks Press, 1990), pp.
1–3; Rosemary Radford Ruether, *Women-Church* (San Francisco:
Harper & Row, 1985); and Elisabeth Schüssler Fiorenza, "Toward a Feminist Biblical Spirituality: The Ekklesia of Women," in
In Memory of Her (New York: Crossroad, 1983), pp. 341–51.

2. For proceedings from the "Women of Fire" conference in
The Netherlands see Diann L. Neu and Mary E. Hunt's *Women of
Fire: A Pentecost Event* (Silver Spring, Md.: WATERworks Press,
1990).

3. This and all other quotations in this chapter, unless otherwise cited, are taken from my liturgical text "Women of Fire,"
written for this event, in Neu and Hunt, *Women of Fire: A Pentecost Event*

4. Kathy Galloway, "Out of the Depths," in *Celebrating
Women,* ed. Janet Morley and Hannah Ward (London: Women in
Theology, 1986), p. 6.

5. Susan R. Beehler, "Sweet Spirit," in *A Shared Journey* (El
Paso, Tex.: self-published booklet, 1984).

6. Marsie Silvestro, "Claiming Our Power," in *Crossing the
Lines* (Cambridge, Mass.: Moonsong Productions, 1987).

7. Colleen Fulmer, "Ruah," in *Cry of Ramah* (Albany, Calif.:
Loretto Spirituality Network, 1985). Movement gestures by
Martha Ann Kirk. Used by permission of Loretto Spirituality
Network.

8. This concept of Eucharist is found in Elisabeth Schüssler

Fiorenza's "Tablesharing and the Celebration of the Eucharist," *Concilium* 152 (1982), pp. 3–12.

9. See my article "Our Name Is Church: The Experience of Catholic-Christian Feminist Liturgies," *Concilium* 152 (1982), pp. 75–84. "In memory of her" is the concept Elisabeth Schüssler Fiorenza reclaims in *In Memory of Her* (New York: Crossroad, 1983).

10. For a more developed blessing of breads, see my liturgy "Blessing of Many Breads," *Daughters of Sarah* 17 (Chicago, 1991), p. 20.

11. Chung Hyun Kyung, "Come Holy Spirit, Renew the Whole Creation," *Women in a Changing World,* no. 31 (Geneva, Switzerland: World Council of Churches, 1991), pp. 12-15.

12. See Renita J. Weems's "A Mistress, a Maid, and No Mercy," in *Just a Sister Away* (San Diego: LuraMedia, 1988), pp.1–21.

13. This form of inclusivity in language and concepts is developed by Valerie C. Jones Stiteler, "Blessing the Darkness: Toward a Feminist Hermeneutic for Worship Which Is Inclusive of Women with Disabilities," unpublished paper delivered to the Feminist Liturgy Seminar of the North American Academy of Liturgy meeting in 1991.

11

Jubilee Ritual:
A Creative Response

Patricia Malarcher

As Ann Patrick Ware approached her fiftieth anniversary as a sister of Loretto, she decided against the traditional celebration of a Jubilee Mass in the midst of her community. Instead she invited the Women's Liturgy Group of New York to plan a ritual and to travel to Kentucky to hold it in the chapel at the Loretto motherhouse on Saturday, April 27, 1991.

Informally known as WLG, the Women's Liturgy Group had been in existence for more than a decade. Ann Patrick Ware had been among four or five Roman Catholic women who, in the spring of 1981, initiated the practice of creating rituals for themselves. Most of them were experienced in planning liturgies around the official scriptural readings for the cycles of the year. This new venture was not meant to parallel standard liturgies, but, rather, to discover the rituals that might emerge from the talents and experience of a group of women.

Originally motivated by their negative reactions to the unrelenting male dominance within their church, their efforts have unfolded as a series of positive encounters with the creative process. Meeting in one another's homes, the women took turns preparing and leading the rituals. Gradually more women, some of them Christian but not Roman Catholic, were attracted to the group.

WLG II was formed when experience proved that a ritual in the intimate setting of a New York apartment was most effective with no more than twelve participants. Some women, wanting to meet more frequently than once a month, belong to both groups. WLG consists of a broad range of professional women. Several have advanced degrees in theology and among those are teachers in seminaries or universities; several others work in the social sciences as therapists or counselors; some are administrators in religious organizations; one member is a medical doctor and another a high school English teacher; there are visual artists, writers, and musicians. Some are, or have been, members of religious orders; most are single, divorced, or widowed; two are married. For some, but not all, WLG is a primary worshiping community.

At the outset, WLG went through a time of trial and error. Although no guidelines were formalized, it was assumed that (1) the rituals would be original; (2) full participation would be the norm, and (3) leadership roles would not conflict with mutuality.

Early on, rituals tended to be self-conscious or timid, overly or underly programmed. Since the group was not adhering to a text, some were thematically arbitrary. The use of objects often lacked real symbolic resonance; selected texts were frequently either too cerebral or too poetic to elicit an authentic response. Furthermore the notion of what constitutes a ritual had to be explored.

Immediately following each ritual the participants evaluated their responses. By analyzing their reactions to the various elements, they found that certain things worked well and others not at all. For example, most of the women objected to movement that seemed contrived, as well as to reading aloud in unison. Through the ongoing process of trimming and shaping, the group arrived at a basic structure: a clear beginning such as a lighting of a candle or the ringing of a bell that sets the time of ritual apart from ordinary time; a spoken introduction that identifies a focus; an exploration of thematic concerns through the text, visual or tactile materials, music, or gesture; a time of reflection followed by a time of sharing; a blessing and a clear ending.

Along with these "building blocks," the women developed a sense of using music in various ways—for example, to establish a mood at the beginning, or to support a time of reflection, or interspersed with words to enliven the texture of a reading, or to express certain feelings. They became attuned to the use of visual components for their metaphorical and symbolic significance as well as for ambience. In addition they became sensitive to pacing and the "feeling tone" of ritual.

Determined by the individual planner or team, the ever-widening spectrum of themes has ranged from abstract concepts such as "courage" and "wisdom" to personal subjects such as "tears"; from international events relevant to women—for example, Corazon Aquino's election to the presidency of the Philippines—to the death of a member's relative; from the liturgical seasons of Christmas and Easter to the natural seasons of winter and summer. Although at first the group had avoided references to their own liturgical heritage, in time they felt free to draw from that as one among many other resources. WLG's own history now provides another rich frame of reference.

In 1987, groups I and II pooled their efforts to present a public ritual for more than one hundred participants in James Chapel at Union Theological Seminary in New York City. Involving several planners over a series of months, this ambitious project served as a precedent for a ritual of larger scale than usual, planned by a committee rather than one or two members. For Ann Patrick Ware's celebration, which would be attended by twenty-one women, who would come from Saint Louis as well as New York, the complexity of that public event would be combined with the intimacy of a normal ritual.

Four members of WLG volunteered to serve as a planning committee; a former member agreed to serve as music consultant. Although her Jubilee was the purpose for the celebration, Ann Patrick Ware asked the planners not to isolate her as the center of attention, but to focus on the group as a whole. She suggested "promise" as the theme, and she made the arrangements for the chapel, but otherwise Ware was not involved in preparations. Three planning meetings over four months were supplemented by many phone calls.

The Loretto motherhouse chapel in Marion County, near Louisville, Kentucky, is a gracefully proportioned late nineteenth-century building stripped to monastic simplicity under the guidance of Frank Kaczmarcyk, a contemporary liturgical designer whose renovations are characterized by austerity. Despite the cloudy April day, the afternoon light was coming through the windows when the ritual began at four o'clock. In an open space between the sanctuary platform and the first row of pews, twenty-one chairs were arranged in a circle—actually more of an oval. In the center, on a low table, a clear crystal punch bowl partly filled with water was surrounded by twenty-one glasses. Also on the table were two pitchers filled with water, an evergreen branch, and a cluster of pebbles. Off to one side, countless lengths of colorful ribbons, no two the same, were draped over a lectern.

Before the ritual formally started, song sheets were distributed. Annette Covatta, the music consultant, led the group through a quick rehearsal of "Salve Regina" in Gregorian chant. After a pause the ritual began with a recording of "Celestial Sodapop," a light, effervescent, contemporary piece that sounded like musical champagne. As this was playing, two women rose from among those seated, took the pitchers and poured water from them into the glasses. The music faded as the last glass was filled. Anne McGlinchey, a member of the planning team, then presented a brief statement of welcome, establishing the focus of ritual and setting a tone:

> We rejoice today with Ann Patrick Ware, who has lived her promise for fifty years as a sister of Loretto. We thank her for having touched our lives in many ways, for encouraging us and for challenging us to live out Promise in our own lives.
>
> In planning this liturgy, we had many discussions around the word "Promise." As with many words in the English language, its meaning ranges from the superficial to the profound.
>
> We commit ourselves to live our whole lives in an unfolding relationship with God, with one another, and with the world around us. It is this deeper meaning of Promise that we reflect upon today.

Immediately following this introduction a series of seven statements attributed to women, each read by a different person, was
presented. Some were excerpts from published writings by promi-
nent authors; some were prepared especially for the ritual. In force-
ful prose, poetry, and allegory, the statements reflected a wide range
of concerns, including Jewish-Christian relationships, women's liberation, feminist philosophy, and courage, in the following order:

> Jew and Christian, as persons, need to continue their dialogue to
> understand one another as children of God. On this basis we can
> talk, accepting our vulnerability and admitting it to each other.
> Since Vatican II quite a lot of progress has been made. To date, this
> attempt at change has been most evident in the teaching at Jewish
> and Christian seminaries. It is hard to figure things out together
> and not against one another.   —Helga Croner[1]

> A small bird on the prison tilts its head upward,
> reaching toward what is beyond itself.
> A woman sits in her cell and from within herself pushes
> her spirit to be free.   —Annette Covatta, WLG

> It takes loving intention, inspired resolution, and willingness to
> risk, to live out one's promise to one's self as a woman and to other
> women: by refusing to internalize male views of women; by having
> the strength to speak out against oppression . . . ; by finding differ-
> ent ways of working with women and for women; by joyfully liv-
> ing the common one day at a time.
>   —Ada María Isasi-Díaz, WLG

> Keep our values keen
> Care fiercely in our struggles with ambiguous situations.
> We need to form our questions the way a poet does;
> Nudge the boundaries; give voice to questions with
> difficult answers, sometimes no answers.
> Allow yourself to feel the bruising edge of a
> conviction discovered in yourself;
> Then Act.   —Claire S. Derway, WLG

"When you say Man," said Oedipus, "you include women too. Everyone knows that."

[The Sphinx] said, "That's what you think."   —Muriel Rukeyser[2]

Life shrinks or expands in proportion to one's courage.

—Anaïs Nin[3]

Courage stems from the conviction deep down in oneself that a certain value is absolutely essential for the integrity of one's own being and that no price is too big to live up to it. Courage is not reckless bravado or mere risk-taking, but it does demand challenging the phoney, the pretentious, and, above all, the inhuman, wherever we see it.   —Ann Patrick Ware[4]

Following the readings, the "Salve Regina" was sung. Mary Ragan, a member of the planning team, then introduced a time of reflection to be followed by a period of sharing:

We started out this ritual by talking about what it means to become oneself, and that this process happens differently for different people. Think about what, in your own life, has helped you become more yourself or what has kept you from being yourself.

She invited the women, one at a time, as each felt moved to do so, to go to the table, pick up a glass of water, sit and reflect on the questions aloud or in silence, go back to the table and pour the water from the glass into the bowl. "The words we speak will be a blessing over the water." Finally, before returning to her seat, each was asked to choose two ribbons from the lectern and take them with her.

A few minutes later, the women began to go forward. Through the course of the reflections the word "promise" was considered from many different angles, like a crystal turned in the sun. It was viewed as both a noun and a verb, as a vow made in the past and as hope for the future. People spoke of connections with their families, friends, professions, and vocations. Each time the water was poured into the bowl, a refrain composed for the ritual by Annette Covatta was sung: "We keep our promises when we become ourselves."

When everyone had finished pouring the water, Eileen King, the fourth planner, introduced the next section of the ritual. After summing up the essence of the sharing, she picked up the stones on the table and dropped them into the bowl:

> I feel that wisdom would suggest that we add a few stones and that we watch them fall because there were times when we were more disturbed than assured. With this bowl of water and its rocky bottom, we acknowledge that life is sometimes turbulent, and that we celebrate that these life realities are the very substance of promise.

She then asked the participants to pick up their ribbons and to hold one between two fingers of each hand.

> There are no knots here because we do not understand promise as something that limits, restricts or confines us. Instead we suggest the cohesion of the rainbow. What binds us in a promise is full of color and full of freedom.

She then dipped the evergreen branch in the bowl and, walking around the inside of the circle, sprinkled everyone individually as she said:"May this shower be a blessing on you as you become most truly yourself . . ." She ended in front of Ann Patrick Ware, and spoke a special blessing over her:

> I will gather water again into this piece of evergreen for a benediction on you by all of us. Please consider these as droplets of love, of courage, of conscience, of honesty, of risk. They are intended to form a shower of goodness returned to you for all that you have lavishly poured out on us.

Ann Patrick Ware then read "Now I Become Myself," a poem by May Sarton,[5] that speaks of a point of fusion, which has "taken time, many years and places," when

> I, the pursued, who madly ran,
> Stand still, stand still, and stop the sun!

To conclude the ritual, participants were invited to stand in a circle, hold hands with their ribbons streaming from between their fingers, and sing "The Best of Times." The last verse was altered to become a toast to Ann Patrick Ware.

The following September, in order to extend the experience to members of Groups I and II who had not gone to Kentucky, the ritual was repeated on an outdoor patio at the home of one of the members. Except for the different environment, the only change (determined by accessibility) was the substitution of Native American flute music for "Celestial Sodapop." However, a qualitative difference occurred in the content of the sharing. In Kentucky, which had been the destination of a pilgrimage, reflections on "promise" seemed to encompass a broad overview of individual lives. Close to home on an ordinary Sunday afternoon, the reflections seemed more related to the immediacy of everyday life. No evaluation had been held in Kentucky, but both presentations of the ritual were discussed critically after the second. Those who were present, including some who had also gone to Kentucky, agreed that the ritual had been a transformative experience.

How did the elements of the ritual work to produce a transformative effect? They can be examined from different perspectives. First, note that "Promise I" was the first WLG ritual to be held in a building consecrated for Roman Catholic worship. Although it took place outside the altar area usually associated with ordained leadership, the space used was generous and organized with its own integrity. In the opening gestures of pouring water, women projected the image of gracious hostesses serving each other, thereby claiming the space for themselves on their own terms.

Considered on a purely sensuous level, the flow of music and text and gesture, the recurring sound of water being poured, the interwoven rhythms of formal and spontaneous segments, the color and movement of the ribbons, all combined to form a self-contained, sense-awakening interval with its own system of internal relations.

The music was an eclectic mix of contemporary and traditional works, with each piece functioning within the total fabric of the ritual. "Celestial Sodapop" established a spirit of celebration at the beginning. "Salve Regina," sung at a lively pace, reminded participants of their roots in a tradition, one in which women have played significant roles. It also suggested the scope of time being celebrated. When Ann Patrick Ware entered Loretto in 1941, Gregorian chant would have been a dominant form of musical expression, but it is now seldom sung. The refrain after each sharing served a dual function: (1) it was affirmation of each individual and (2) it texturally unified an otherwise unstructured portion of the ritual. "The Best of Times," which had been sung at previous rituals, has become part of the group's history. The group has not defined its positive response to this song, but the recurring phrase "the best of times is now" suggests an approach to life that leaves the past behind but does not wait for an illusory future. For some who have left rich, established traditions in order to search beyond them, this affirmation of the present may have additional significance.

The Sarton poem was new to the group, but various works by the same poet have been read at other rituals. Therefore, "Now I Become Myself" not only was appropriate in content but represented a voice to which the group was already attuned.

The ritual also invites examination for its symbolic and metaphorical content. Water, which was established as the central image, is a universal symbol with significance in almost every culture. A substance essential to life, it is a basic Christian sacramental. Among the accumulated, sometimes contradictory, meanings attributed to water over time are destruction and drowning, healing, rebirth and refreshment. Water has also been equated with the female principle, the "mother of all things." In the Christian tradition, the presence of a large bowl of water in a ritual alludes to a baptismal font. Whether the planners intentionally or intuitively made the connection, it is worth noting that the baptismal font has been referred to as a "womb," the birthplace of "spirit."

Although the ritual did not refer to baptism, one might see it as a reinterpretation of the sacramental action of an ordained minister blessing water in a font, then drawing from it to baptize. In "Promise," the bowl was filled with water that first had been breathed upon as women spoke about their lives. The implication was that the water had been blessed by both the women's words and the life force behind them. As the waters commingled in the bowl, the stories could be felt as a gathering of power. The sprinkling invited an assent to what had been invested in the bowl rather than a blessing bestowed by an authority figure.

The ribbons were selected by the planners as "a way of talking about promises that bind without confining." Again there was no direct reference, but one attuned to Christian ritual might also have seen in them an echo of the stole, the official garment of priestly ordination. Unlike stoles, they were not weight added to the shoulders but flowed freely from the fingers. In their variety of colors, and patterns, and in their being chosen freely, they also seemed to celebrate diversity within unity.

If one were to draw a diagram of the ritual, it might show a circle in the center, representing the time of shared reflections, with a path leading toward it opposite a path going from it. The open space finds a metaphorical equivalent in the image of the bowl to be filled. A receptive bowl is a quintessential feminist archetype. Although the image may be rooted in the female unconscious, it is not gender bound. Rather, it could be meaningful to anyone willing to accept openness as opportunity for spiritual empowerment.

For me, a problematic aspect of "Promise" was the series of statements read at the beginning. Although each was profoundly literate, as well as inspirational, they could seem disconnected to one unaware that each reflected a phase or a conviction that had been an important influence on Ann Patrick Ware. For example, because I did not know of her involvement in Jewish-Christian relations, Helga Croner's words seemed peculiarly out of context. I also found the particular mix of pronouncements and more affective pieces to be somewhat jarring because they did not seem inevitably to lead from one to another. On one hand, the statements suggested the question of how text functions in a ritual when it is not drawn from a pool of writings shared in the collective memory of those attending. On the other hand, the selection of texts underscored the fact that, in looking beyond the common Christian story, WLG's use of other resources is only limited by the internal demands of a particular ritual. Any text can have potential spiritual significance. It seems that the implications of different approaches to the use of text could be a point of discussion.

Also somewhat arbitrary was the unexplained water already present in the bowl when the ritual began. What did it mean as itself, and what did it mean when the other waters joined it? Was it purely for visual effect? This is the sort of question that sometimes surfaces after the fact, but which is not raised within the ritual itself. In fact, when asked about it later, none of the planners could offer a reason for it other than the aesthetic concern that the bowl be full at the end.

An obvious question is whether the Kentucky event, as well as other WLG rituals, are actually liturgies. Strictly defined, the term "liturgy" today refers to a public event that expresses a shared system of belief. If WLG gatherings are called "liturgies," this would seem close to the original secular meaning of the word: "a work undertaken on behalf of the people," that is, its early Christian reference to "priestly work," rather than its later, more restrictive reference to eucharistic worship. Although the members of WLG share common roots in Christianity, that tradition seems to serve more as a subliminal foundation from the past than as a blueprint for the future. Having put aside the old story, at least for now, they are building their own. Perhaps more significant than previously emphasized is the fact that at least a third of the women who attended the Kentucky ritual were not members of WLG, and yet participated fully and without hesitation. The implication may be that a post-Christian story is now being lived but is yet to be recorded.

Yet, other questions arise. Apart from whether these rituals are liturgies, are they worship? If so, to whom, or to what? Does WLG represent a set of beliefs? Did "Promise" focus too much on the people present rather than the Other? Finally, is WLG different from any other women's support group?

In regard to worship, WLG has not developed a creed, nor has that been a priority. Members are aware of various ways in which the idea of "god" is being reinterpreted. Although the notion of "goddess" has been introduced from time to time in rituals, the group has not identified exclusively with that or any other image of deity now being scrutinized. Neither, it seems, has the use of the name "God" been examined in depth. However, what the rituals seem to affirm is that, regardless of restrictions from without, women have access to indwelling spiritual power. Furthermore, they reinforce the idea that women can empower one another.

Although WLG may serve, in part, as a support group, its emphasis on ritual gives it a distinctive character. A ritual—a focused period of time organized with a beginning, middle, and end, enhanced by musical and visual elements—is closer to an art form than to group therapy or consciousness raising.

The question that steers the evaluation period is: "Did it work?" That is not the question of a priest after mass, or of a minister after a sermon, but it is the question of artists and critics, concerned with how parts relate to a whole, and how a whole relates to the culture around it. Like a play, or a painting, or a piece of music that works, a ritual that works can be transformative. It seems that, in searching for liberating alternatives to religious restriction, the members of WLG are operating in a mode that is more akin to that of artists than of theologians.

Notes

1. From an interview with Helga Croner conducted by Claire S. Derway, WLG, a member of the planning committee.

2. Muriel Rukeyser, "Myth," in *Cries of the Spirit,* ed. Marilyn Sewell (Boston: Beacon Press, 1991), p. 278.

3. Anaïs Nin, *Diary of Anaïs Nin,* vol. 3 (New York: Harcourt Brace Jovanovich, 1985), p. 125.

4. Ann Patrick Ware, from manuscript.

5. May Sarton, "Now I Become Myself," in *Selected Poems of May Sarton,* ed. Serena Sue Hilsinger and Lois Brynes (New York: W. W. Norton, 1978).

12

On the Birthing Stool:
Mujerista Liturgy

Ada María Isasi-Díaz

LAS HERMANAS is a twenty-year-old national Hispanic women's organization that promotes justice for Hispanic women and our communities in church and society, and enables the development of leadership of Hispanic women. Started by Chicana women in Catholic religious communities in 1971, LAS HERMANAS ("the sisters") soon welcomed lay women and Hispanic women from all national and ethnic backgrounds. Given the marginality and scarcity of financial resources of Hispanic women, lack of funds has kept the organization from carrying out its task as fully as its members have wished. The first half of the 1980s was particularly difficult for the organization. When a group of about one hundred of its members met in 1986 in Denver to celebrate the fifteenth anniversary of the organization (*la quinceañera*), key leaders in the group committed themselves to finding ways to strengthen the organization. In the fall of 1989 a national conference was held in San Antonio in which more than two hundred women participated. The conference was a celebration of the ability of LAS HERMANAS to survive. It was also a celebration of the increasing number of grass-roots Hispanic women who belong to the organization and believe in it. The conference also provided LAS HERMANAS with an opportunity to analyze the issue of power: How has power been used to oppress us? How do we reconceptualize power so it becomes enablement and encouragement instead of control and domination? What power do we have as Hispanic women and how do we claim it as important, as life giving? What organizational power does LAS HERMANAS have? How do we use it and strengthen it?

Since the second half of the 1970s, LAS HERMANAS has struggled with the issue of celebrating mass as part of its conferences and meetings. The issue is not lack of belief in the Eucharist but the exclusion of women from ordained ministry in the Catholic church. Celebration of mass would require bringing in a male priest, something many of us find disempowering. From having mass as a part of the conference schedule, usually with Hispanic women present very actively involved in leadership, including giving the homily, the organization has moved to having a "liturgy" prepared by us, one in which only women have leadership roles.[1] "Liturgy," therefore, in our conferences means a Hispanic women's liturgy in which we celebrate in an autochthonous way who we are, our struggles, our preferred future, and our belief in the divine, in Jesus as a friend and *compañero* in the struggle. For many of us these liturgies are eucharistic; for others they are a prayer service. The goal of the organizers of the LAS HERMANAS conferences during most of the past decade has been not to force anyone to accept our liturgies as Eucharist but rather to enable the participants to develop and experience new forms of liturgical expressions.

It was against this background that we celebrated the "liturgy" that I am using as the framework for articulating some mujerista principles and elements of liturgical celebrations, elements not necessarily unique but distinctively ours. This is indeed a birthing moment, a climbing onto the birthing stool to articulate religious understandings embodied in our Hispanic women's liturgies.

Teología Mujerista

Mujerista theology is a liberative praxis—reflective action that has as its goal the liberation of Hispanic women. Using as its source the lived experience of Hispanic women, mujerista theology seeks to be a platform for our voices. Mujerista theology reflects upon and articulates the religious understandings and practices of Hispanic women. As a communal theological praxis mujerista theology endeavors to enable Hispanic women to be agents of our own history, to enhance our moral agency, and to design and participate in actions that are effective in our daily struggle for survival.[2]

For us liturgy is an intrinsic part of mujerista theology. Therefore, the principles and understandings that undergird our liturgies have to contribute effectively to the liberation of Hispanic women. Liturgy is a powerful means for us to understand and articulate our religious beliefs and practices. Liturgy provides us with opportunities to express and strengthen our values as a community of faith struggling for liberation. Our liturgical celebrations are signs of rebellion, for when the oppressed celebrate, we are telling the oppressor that we have not given up, that we have not been conquered. In our liturgies we affirm who we are and our willingness to risk. Liturgies provide for us an opportunity to share experiences, celebrate the small victories we have, and encourage each other. For us liturgies are hope-providing moments in the daily struggle to survive.

These theological and liturgical understandings and principles have guided us in preparing the liturgy that we here present. They are further elaborated in the explanations and descriptions that follow. It is also these understandings and principles that provide the framework for critiquing the Hispanic women's liturgy that we celebrated at the Las Hermanas Conference in 1989.

A Mujerista Liturgy

Preparación

Four elements were important in preparing our mujerista liturgy:[3] two of us were responsible for designing the liturgy; those of us preparing the liturgy were part of the community gathering for the conference; the liturgical celebration was not the only ritual we had during the conference; the liturgy was understood and conceptualized as an integral part of the conference so its goals were the same as those of the conference.

In LAS HERMANAS we value teamwork and reject hierarchical structures. Very early in the history of the organization we moved from having a president, vice president, and so forth, to a team of national coordinators. We have a small working board, and at its meetings national coordinators as well as staff participate fully in decision making. So when it came time to plan the liturgy it was natural to ask two of us to be responsible for preparing it. We both knew we were expected to (and we wanted to) consult with many of the other women preparing the conference. This was not a perfunctory kind of consultation; their views carried as much weight as ours.

As Hispanic women ourselves, and because both of us responsible for designing the liturgy had worked with grass-roots Hispanic women for many years, we were not strangers to those gathering for the conference. We were all part of the community of Hispanic women—a group of women rich in diversity whose ethnicity works as a common denominator.[4] Besides, between us we knew personally about two thirds of those coming to the conference. More than half of the conference participants were grass-roots Hispanic women, women at the lower end of the economic ladder who work at manual labor and who have limited formal education. The rest of the participants were professional women with relative economic security and a college or postgraduate education.

Because as mujeristas we value rituals, we had decided to use a variety of them at this conference. As has become traditional for LAS HERMANAS, our conference started with an opening ritual telling our organizational story. This time, rather than the "regular" opening prayer service, we used audiovisuals, which was very effective. We then had a wonderful one-woman show: a Hispanic actress did a series of vignettes that put us in touch with and celebrated our tradition of struggle as Hispanic women. A second moment of ritual in the conference was our Saturday night *fiesta,* also a traditional element of our national conferences. This fiesta is an evening of celebrating and recognizing those who have served the organization and provides a rare opportunity for Hispanic women who are gifted as singers, dancers, and comedians to perform in a safe, welcoming environment. Finally, the fiesta is a wonderful time of just having fun, enjoying each other and celebrating.

Since these other two rituals had served to accomplish some of the goals of the conference, the liturgy did not have to carry an undue burden within the design of the conference. We had established from the very beginning that rituals were an important element of the conference; that rituals were key in our attempt to communicate ideas, values, and a vision of our preferred future. Little by little, from the beginning, through rituals, lectures, and group discussion the conference had unfolded the announced theme: power. When the time arrived for the closing liturgy, we had done our analysis of power and had set out concrete strategies on how to proceed. Analyzing and determining strategies are in themselves empowering processes. Even so, though we hoped that the whole conference had achieved this goal, we depended on the liturgy to help the women feel empowered to face the daily struggle for survival with new understandings and renewed strength.

Ambiente y Símbolos

Several understandings and convictions guide us mujeristas in determining the setting for our liturgies. First, it is important for us to claim and affirm as sacred the place where we meet. As Hispanic women we are treated as if we possess a diminished humanity; therefore, it is critical for us to claim as sacred any space where we meet to celebrate ourselves and our struggles and to recommit ourselves to *la lucha* ("the struggle"). It is an important way of asserting our share in the holiness of God, for as Hispanic women we are made in the image and likeness of the divine.

The *ambiente* ("environment") for our liturgies has to remind us of the sacred spaces that many of us carve out even in the humblest of houses. Regardless of economic strata, degree of formal education, or type of job we have, the vast majority of Hispanic women have altars in our homes, or at least pictures of Mary, Jesus, and/or the saints hanging on the walls. Our home altars are full of statues and are a tangible way of making the divine present. It is at home altars that God's presence is invoked, where mutual commitment and responsibility between us and God are established. Our home altars clearly indicate that for us the divine is directly accessible; that we do not have to depend on priests or pastors to relate to the divine.[5]

So for this liturgy, in the center of the room where we had spent most of the conference, we set up an altar like the ones many of us have at home. We had asked conference participants to bring statues or pictures of women who had been significant in their lives. We placed on the altar all that they brought; statues of Mary, the mother of Jesus, represented in different ways; pictures of mothers, grandmothers, sisters, women friends, daughters, nieces, granddaughters; holy cards of women saints, and figures of women dear to their owners because of their artistic value or some other quality.

We also placed candles on the altar. Candles are always present in Hispanic rituals for they carry out three important functions. First, candles stand for us in the presence of God. We light our candles and then go our way, confident that our burning candles represent us before God. Second, candles are an offering to the divine that even the poor can afford. Candles are lighted not only to remind God of us but also to thank God for helping us and as an act of praise to the divine. Third, the warmth and light of the candles remind us of the hearth—the center of the home for Hispanic women, the place that incarnates the deep sense of hospitality that we consider "a test of . . . [our] closeness to God."[6] As we shall see below, candles were on the altar not only because of their symbolic value but also because of their important role in the ritual.

We also placed on the altar bread, chalices containing milk and honey, and dates. Though we wanted to use bread because of its centrality in Christian eucharistic celebrations, we wanted bread to be seen also as food for the road, as sustenance for the struggle ahead of us. That is why we also included dates, which had been brought to the conference by a grass-roots women's group from California. To complete the notion of a meal we needed something to drink, but we did not want to use wine for two reasons.

First, we were not trying in any way to have a mass or to imitate a mass. Second, and perhaps more important, wine is not a common drink among Hispanic women. We decided to use milk and honey. Even though it is uncommon among us, we believed we could imbue it with a symbolism to which the women could relate. We talked during the ritual of the milk our women-bodies produce to sustain life; we explained how the Israelites talked about their preferred future as the land flowing with milk and honey. It was in this sense that milk and honey represented the abiding presence of God with us and among us: it helped us celebrate our women-bodies and to keep always present before us the preferred future for which we struggle.

One more symbol was very important for us: the circle. We wanted to symbolize that we are all equals around the altar, that our liturgies are expressions of a community of faith struggling for liberation. So we symbolized equality and unity by being around the altar in a circle. Since there were several women who could not sit on the floor, we set chairs in the circle for them while the rest of the participants sat on the floor.

Palabra y Canto

Since we come from an oral tradition, our usage of word (*palabra*) is not a matter of reading a prepared text; words arise from the participants as an expression of who they are, a relating of their lived experiences. For us the most important use of words is in song (*canto*). For the LAS HERMANAS Conference in 1989, we were gifted with Rosa Marta Zárate Macías, a *cantadora,* a composer and singer who considers what she does a vocation and who understands her musical talents to be an instrument in the struggle for the liberation of our people. For this liturgy we used three of her songs, well known to most of us, that deal with the central message of our liturgy.[7]

A second use of words was the Bible reading and the sermon. For this we used two guidelines. First, we used a biblical text that would be a "reality check" for Hispanic women. Often what we do is diminished, ignored, or misunderstood. So one of the main roles the Bible plays for us is to help us know that what we have done, what has happened to us, and what we think, is not wrong. Women in the Bible who struggle have lived through the same kind of experience. These texts are salvific for us because they become an effective instrument in our struggle for liberation. Second, the preaching had to be dialogic and engaging, providing women with an opportunity to hear their own voices in this sacred ritual. The homily must not be an attempt to give a single interpretation of a biblical text but rather to enable each one present to do her own articulation, trusting that because there is enough commonality in our lived experience, and because we are all involved in the struggle for liberation, common themes will emerge from the rich variety of articulations. Of course during a short dialogued homily this process cannot be completed, but this was the intention that guided the homily in our service. This affected not only what was said but also the way it was said.[8]

This same principle guided us in two other uses of words during the ritual. During the first part of the liturgy we wanted to lift up the power of the women represented by the images and pictures on our altar. We asked participants to call out the names of powerful women in their lives. This name calling grew in intensity and created a wonderful wave of power in the room. Later in the liturgy, when we asked women to call out the names they give Mary, the Mother of Jesus, the name calling became like a soft chant, a reverential litany, expressing love and care.

After the dialogued homily came the blessing of the food we were to share. We wanted every woman to participate in this blessing but did not think that having everyone read a common text would be conducive to ownership of what was being said. Therefore, we developed a "blessing prayer" in Spanish and English, with seven strophes, each finishing with a short line to be repeated by all of us.[9]

Facilitadoras

Because one of the main objectives of mujerista theology is the enablement of moral agency of Hispanic women, our understanding of leadership is that of facilitation and empowerment. An intrinsic part of this understanding is to have a multiplicity of leaders. There are three reasons for this. First, we want our liturgies to provide opportunity for as many women as possible to have an active role in sacred rituals in order to counter their exclusion from approaching the altar during worship in their churches. Second, we believe that leadership is a function of the community vested in a person for a given function because of her gifts. Leadership is not a permanent state for a few. The development of leadership qualities inherent in many Hispanic women is an important strategy in our struggle for liberation. Third, multiplicity of leaders helps decentralize power. Sharing power means that those who design a liturgy have to let go of it, have to trust it in the hands of others in the community who can, and do, modify it in order to have their voices heard.

We wanted, therefore, as many Hispanic women as possible to have a leadership role in the liturgy. Twenty-five women served in that capacity. This gave us a sense that our liturgical celebration was not so much a distribution of bread as a gathering of the fragments of the bread of the lives of many women—a sharing that was a source of pride in who we are and of joy because of our faithfulness to the struggle and to our communities.

Texto y Secuencia

Following is the text and sequence of the Hispanic women's liturgy celebrated at the Las Hermanas Conference in San Antonio on October 28, 1989.

Opening ritual. Those who have a leadership role in the liturgy sit in silence. As the women come into the room they become aware of the silent atmosphere and join in it. Once the gathered community is ready, one by one different women go to the altar, light a candle, and while holding it on high say one of the following lines.[10]

The power to give life.

The power of being vulnerable without being weak.

The power of believing in a better future.

The power of changing oppressive situations.

The power to face difficult circumstances.

The power of not giving up.

The power of loving and claiming the need for love.

The power of crying.

The power that is ours because we are women.[11]

The community is invited to name the powerful women they have known, who have influenced them, while the rest of the candles on the table are lighted by two women.[12]
Once all the candles are lighted, another woman says:

This space in which we have spent these three days is full of the light of our power. We know we are blessed by God and by Mary. Let us call out the different names we give her.

[Pause for the women to invoke Mary. Once they have finished, a different woman says the following.]

And now I ask you to turn to the person on your right and bless her using whatever words and gestures you want.[13]

Once the women are almost finished blessing each other, the song starts.

Lucha, Poder, y Esperanza

Lucha, Poder, Esperanza	Struggle, power, hope
Mujer Hispana en tu vientre	Hispanic Woman in your womb
llevas semillas del Verbo.	you carry seeds of the Word.
¡Demos vida al continente!	Let's give life to the continent.
Adelante compañeras	Onward, *compañeras,*
que a nuestro pueblo asesinan	they are murdering our people
y a la tierra nuestra madre	and our mother, the earth,
el imperio ultraja y viola.	the empire is ravaging and raping.

Vamos a unirnos, hermanas	Let us come together, sisters
firmes, valientes, ya basta	firmly, bravely, it is enough!
de ser esclavas del miedo	No longer slaves of fear we'll be—
hijas de raza violada.	nor daughters of a raped race.
Al viento nadie lo para	No one stops the wind,
al mar nadie lo encadena	no one chains the sea,
las mujeres solidarias	the women in solidarity
son fuego que nadie apaga.	are a fire no one can extinguish.
Tu causa es causa del Pueblo,	Your cause is the people's cause
tu dignidad es sagrada	your dignity is sacred
mujer color de la tierra	woman, your color is the earth's
árbol de la vida nueva.	you are tree of new life.
Lucha, poder, esperanza	Struggle, power, hope
sea consigna en la batalla	may it be the cry of our struggle
por rescatar la justicia	to rescue justice
nuestra hermana aprisionada.	our imprisoned sister.[14]

La palabra entre nosotras ("the word among us").   A reading of Exodus 1:15–21 is followed by the main points of the dialogued homily—to last no more than ten minutes. The homilist walks around among the women gathered.

1. The homilist asks if there are any midwives present. Who was helped by a midwife to give birth? What was her name? As many women as want are called on to speak.

2. The homilist gives thoughts on the close relationship between women and on giving life.

3. She talks about the need for us to ask ourselves what kind of life we want for our children.

4. She asks, What did Shiphrah and Puah do? Could they speak back to the pharaoh and say, "We will not do

that"? What was more important, to voice their convictions, or to find a way to save the children?

5. She presents thoughts on the value of planning strategies, of keeping the goal of liberation in mind, of doing things together and not alone, the value of analyzing what we can accomplish, given the fact that we are oppressed.

6. She asks, What is the central theme of the book of Exodus? Who is the main character? She says that without the women at the beginning of the exodus story, the main event, the liberation of the people, would not have happened. The midwives were a role model for Moses, of how he should act when he faced the pharaoh, how not to give in, how to always keep in mind the liberation of the people.

Blessing prayer.   Each stanza is read by a different woman from where she is in the circle. Everybody repeats the last line of each stanza.[15]

The power of the seed from which the wheat grows.
El poder de la semilla de la que surje el trigo.
El poder de la semilla.

The power of the earth nurtures the seed and makes it flourish.
El poder de la tierra que nutre la semilla y la hace brotar.
El poder de la tierra.

The power of the sun that gives warmth and light to the wheat.
El poder del sol que le da luz y calor al trigo.
El poder del sol.

The power of the *campesinas, campesinos,* who care for and harvest the wheat.
El poder de las campesinas, los campesinos, que cuidan del trigo y lo cosechan.
El poder de las campesinas.

> The power of the yeast that even if it is small in quantity
> makes all the dough to rise.
> *El poder de la levadura que aunque mínima en cantidad hace que la*
> *masa se alce.*
> *El poder de la levadura.*

> The power of the bread which sustains us and without
> which there is no life.
> *El poder del pan que nos sustenta y sin el cual no hay vida.*
> *El poder del pan.*

One of the campesina women present goes to the altar, lifts the
bread over her head, and breaks the loaf.

> The power of this community which in breaking this bread
> renews its commitment to the people who struggle for
> their liberation.
> *El poder de esta comunidad que en el partir del pan renueva su com-*
> *promiso con el pueblo que lucha por su liberación.*
> *El poder de esta comunidad.*

Another woman goes to the altar and, lifting the cup, says the
following:

> This is the milk which comes from our bodies and nourishes
> life. It is mixed with honey, for milk and honey was the
> symbol for our ancestors of the Promised Land, of a better
> future, of liberation. We bless it by drinking of it for it will
> sustain us in the struggle.

Another woman helps the woman at the altar finish breaking
the bread. They set several stations around the table with cups,
baskets with bread, and plates with dates. Then she says:

> The gifts of God for the people of God, come and eat joy-
> fully, with the resolution and understanding that we will
> continue in the struggle and that God will always sustain us if
> we sustain one another. Come and feast.

While the people go to the table and feed themselves, we sing:

Profetiza

Profetiza, pueblo mío	Prophesy, my people
Profetiza una vez más	Prophesy once again
Que tu voz sea	May your voice be
el eco del clamor	the clamor
De los pueblos en la opresión	Of oppressed peoples
Profetiza pueblo hispano	Prophesy Hispanic people
Profetiza una vez más	Prophesy once again
Anunciándole a los pobres	Announcing to the poor
Una nueva sociedad.	A new society.

1. Profeta te consagro   I consecrate you prophet
   No haya duda y temor   Let there be no doubt nor fear
   En tu andar por la historia   As you walk through history
   Sé fiel a tu misión.   Be faithful to your mission.

2. Anúnciale a los pueblos   Announce to the peoples
   Que Dios renovará   That God will renovate
   Su pacto en la justicia   God's justice-covenant
   Su amor florecerá.   His love will flourish.

3. Denuncia todo aquello   Denounce everything
   Que causa la opresión   That causes oppression
   Para que se convierta   So that it can be converted
   Y vuelva de nuevo a Dios.   And returns once again to God.

4. Esta sea tu esperanza   May this be your hope
   Esta sea tu misión   May this be your mission
   Ser constructor del Reino   Be a builder of the Reign
   Sociedad del Amor.   A society of love.

5. Es hora de mi gracia   This is the hour of my grace
   Sacramento de Dios   Sacrament of God
   Sé signo de mi alianza   Be a sign of my covenant
   Sé luz de un nuevo sol.   Be the light of a new sun.[16]

Closing ritual.   Several women step up to the altar and pull
from underneath the table balls of ribbons that have been tied to

the legs of the table. They throw them to the congregation, asking each to hold on to the ribbon that reaches her and pass the ball on to the person next to her. One of the women says:

> These ribbons are a symbol of our lives and of our renewed commitment with the struggle. Allow these ribbons to connect us and unite us. [Pause until all are holding the ribbons.]
> Now let us cut a piece of this ribbon and take it with us to remember that we are not alone in the struggle. [Scissors are passed out.]

While they are cutting the ribbons the final song starts. Women on the outskirts of the circle throw confetti and serpentine into the middle.

Cántico de Mujer

Bendita mujer	Blessed is the woman
La que sabe ser fiel	Who knows how to be faithful
Al quehacer de implantar	To the work of planting
La justicia y la paz.	Justice and peace.
Dichosa será	Happy will be
La mujer que hace	The woman who makes
opcián	an option
Por la causa de Dios	For God's cause
Por la ley del amor.	For the law of love.

1. Hoy canto al Dios del pueblo en mi guitarra
     Today I sing to the God of my people with my guitar
   Un canto de mujer que se libera.
     A song of a woman who liberates herself.
   Dios se solidariza con mi causa,
     God is in solidarity with my cause,
   Me consagra portador de la esperanza.
     Consecrates me bearer of hope.
   Dios escuchó el clamor de nuestro pueblo,
     God heard the cries of our people,
   Se alía al empobrecido y explotado,
     Is an ally of the impoverished and the exploited,

Y a la mujer libera de cadenas
And frees woman from her chains
Impuestas con crueldad por tantos siglos.
Imposed with cruelty for so many centuries.

2. Harás justicia a todas las mujeres
   You will make justice a reality for all women
   Que firmes no cayeron ante el yugo.
   Who were firm and did not fall when faced with the yoke.
   Nos das la libertad y reivindicas,
   You give us freedom and confirm,
   O Dios, tu semejanza originaria.
   O God, your original likeness.
   Al mal pastor que causa tanto daño,
   The bad pastor who has caused so much damage,
   Al gobernante infiel que vende al pueblo:
   The unfaithful ruler who sells the people:
   A todo quien oprime tú destruyes.
   You destroy all who oppress.
   Sin piedad del poder tú los derrumbas.
   Without mercy because of their power you dethrone them.

3. Nos llamas a gestar en nuestros vientres,
   You call us to gestate in our womb,
   Mujeres y hombres nuevos, pueblo fuerte,
   New women and men, a strong people,
   Nos unges servidoras, profetizas,
   You anoint us servants, prophets,
   Testigos de tu amor que nos redime.
   Witnesses of your redeeming love.
   Has puesto en mi cantar una esperanza.
   You have put in my song a note of hope.
   Seré eco de tu amor que reconcilia.
   I will be an echo of your reconciling love.
   Espada de dos filos sea mi canto,
   May my song be a two-edged sword,
   Pregón de un evangelio libertario.
   A proclamation of your liberating gospel.[17]

Analysis and critique. As I mentioned above, the goal of this conference and of the liturgy was the empowerment of Hispanic women and a celebration of Las Hermanas's power to survive. Those of us responsible for designing the liturgy wanted to provide an experience of celebration of Hispanic women's selves, their commitments, their struggles; we saw the celebration as an affirmation of ourselves that would help us in our *lucha.* At the end of the last song, there was no doubt that we had succeeded. The mood was festive, joyful; there were tears that revealed the depth of the experience we had just had. Women milled around for a long time, embracing each other, saying endlessly, *gracias!* to those of us who had prepared the conference and the liturgy.

In the general design of the conference, we saw the liturgy as a teachable moment in two respects. First, it provided an experience of a different kind of celebration, one to which the majority of Hispanic women have no access. We know that different elements of the ritual have been adapted and used repeatedly by those who participated in the original liturgy. Having a different liturgical experience has provided them with a point of comparison they can use to judge and critique liturgies in their own churches. Second, the reading from Exodus, the homily, the litanies and prayer of blessing, as well as the words of the songs were important teaching texts. They presented theological understandings and strategies for the struggle familiar to those who participated in the conference.

We wanted in a special way to make grass-roots women feel at home. For some of them this was the first time they stayed in a hotel, the first time they were in a conference with only women, the first time they heard a woman preach, the first time it was one of them who broke the bread.[18] We were very happy at how well we were able to "translate" the home altar into an altar for a ritual for two hundred people. It was the sense of home altar that brought the elements of the liturgy together and helped many of the participants feel very comfortable in surroundings quite different from their own.

We intended to use the liturgy to demystify the sacred, for the mystification of the sacred is a control mechanism used by "religious professionals." We wanted to enable Hispanic women to understand that if we believe God became human in the person of Jesus, all of us, not only priests and pastors, participate in the divine. We believe we accomplished this, particularly for the Hispanic women who had a leadership role in the liturgy.

Hispanic *mestizo* Christianity is a mixture of religious understandings and practices brought over by the *conquistadores* and the priests who accompanied them, religious understandings and practices of the Amerindian world they ransacked, and those of the Africans brought over as slaves. Though some of the popular religious practices we used in the liturgy, such as the home altar, statues, and candles, have Amerindian and African influences, our liturgy did not include significant Amerindian and African elements. This is something that we have to tend to in future liturgies.

Para Terminar

Since 1978 LAS HERMANAS has given great attention to rituals. Part of this has to do with how important rituals are for us as Hispanic women. Outward expressions of who we are, what we believe, how we feel, are a key element of our culture. As a matter of fact, one of the great hardships we find in being in an Anglo culture is the unacceptability of expressing genuine emotions. Rituals such as this liturgy become vehicles, then, for being our most authentic selves. These mujerista liturgies are indeed opportunities for self-affirmation; they are moments that fill us with hope since, during our liturgies, we are able to give free rein to our way of being; they are moments of celebration of our preferred future in which our ethnicity is not an impediment but a fundamental element of the society in which we live. Mujerista liturgies help us give birth to ourselves as liberated Hispanic women.

Notes

1. Even today this is not totally without problems for some of the participants. What LAS HERMANAS has done for its last two conferences is to list or announce the schedule of masses for Sunday in a nearby church. We have never discussed openly why we do not

have mass as part of the program. The silence around this issue is not because of the differences among Hispanic women but because an open discussion would become known to the Hispanic hierarchy and clergy and result in difficulty for the work of the organization.

2. For a more complete description of mujerista theology, see Ada María Isasi-Díaz and Yolanda Tarango, *Hispanic Women: Prophetic Voice in the Church* (San Francisco: Harper & Row, 1988).

3. Maria Antonietta Berriozabal and I were the two women responsible for designing the liturgy.

4. Ethnicity here is not just an identification of country of origin but refers to the present social-economic-political-ethnic reality of Hispanic women in this country. For a fuller description of this concept of ethnicity, see Ada María Isasi-Díaz's *En La Lucha— In the Struggle: Elaborating a Hispanic Woman's Liberation Theology* (Minneapolis: Fortress Press, 1993).

5. C. Gilbert Romero, *Hispanic Devotional Piety* (Maryknoll, N.Y.: Orbis Books, 1991), pp. 83–97. See also Isasi-Díaz and Tarango, *Hispanic Women*, pp. 37–38.

6. Romero, *Hispanic Devotional Piety*, p. 84.

7. The lyrics of the three songs are quoted in the "Texto y Secuencia" section.

8. For more about this, see the discussion of the role of leadership in Hispanic women's liturgies in the "Facilitadoras" section.

9. We got the idea for the format and some of the basic ideas for the "blessing prayer" from Carter Heyward's "Blessing the Bread (A Litany for Four Voices)," in *Prayers and Poems, Songs and Stories—Ecumenical Decade 1988–1998: Churches in Solidarity with Women* (Geneva: World Council of Churches Publications, 1988), pp. 79–80.

10. Some of the women chose to say their line in Spanish; some said it in English.

11. Several women at this point decided to add their own statement to the litany.

12. Some of the leaders had been cued to start and also to call out names while other people were doing so in order to create the effect we wanted instead of a one-name-after-the-other approach. There were at least twenty small "vigil" candles on the table.

13. Though we had intended for each woman to bless only one or two of the people closest to her, many took it upon themselves to bless many of the women in the room.

14. This song was composed by Rosa Marta Zárate Macías for this LAS HERMANAS conference. It has not been recorded or released. Used by permission.

15. Heyward, "Blessing the Bread," in *Prayers and Poems,* pp. 79–80.

16. Rosa Marta Zárate Macías, *Profetiza y Cántico de Mujer* (Chicago: GIA Publications, 1991), sound cassette. Used with permission.

17. Zárate Macías, *Profetiza y Cántico,* sound cassette. Used with permission.

18. There was one man present, a very supportive Roman Catholic priest who has come to our last two conferences and who participates fully in a very low-key way. He is on leave from the diocese of San Bernardino after being dismissed from his job by the bishop because of the radicalness and effectiveness of his work.

PART 4

Lingering Questions

The chapters in this part invite discussion rather than offer answers. Christian feminists struggle with traditional images of Jesus and some find no value in the images, while others search for new interpretations that can honor women's experiences and struggles. One place where the image of Jesus has sometimes functioned to empower women is in African-American Protestantism. Delores Williams provides a valuable analysis of the multiple layers of meaning within her experience of that tradition and introduces the idea of "resistance rituals," a proposal that will certainly have resonance beyond African-American Christianity. A lingering question is that of traditional forms of prayer, with assumptions of hierarchical relationships, which often create dissonance for feminists. Some feminists find prayer in any traditional form impossible. Others seek new forms. Eileen King reminds us of the diversity of traditions and practices of prayer, a useful beginning to an understanding of feminist praying.

13

Rituals of Resistance
in Womanist Worship

Delores S. Williams

As various kinds of feminist consciousness have irrupted in cultures around the world, new terms have been coined, including *womanist worship*. What is womanist worship? The answer is both simple and complex. Put simply, womanist worship happens when African-American women's experience is obvious in the leadership, liturgy, and god-talk of the church. Obviously, womanist worship exists as ideal rather than practice in most Christian churches including black churches. On a more complex level, womanist worship is not inclusive of all kinds of African-American woman-experience. There are some definite guidelines that stem from the definition of who a womanist is.[1]

She is committed to the survival and wholeness of a people (female and male) and to the folk stream of African-American heritage, female and male. She contributes to that stream through advice and counsel she gives to her children, especially her daughters. As a woman-child, she is courageous and aggressive and wants to know more than is thought "good" for a woman to know. Womanists are not homophobic: they love women and men, sexually or nonsexually. They celebrate life, nature, struggle, hospitality, and love. But they remember to love themselves. Regardless.

A womanist recognizes her organic tie with both feminism and the black community. She liberates her sisters, her people (including males), and herself. She loves the spirit.

So womanist worship is an event in which black women's freedom of expression is obvious. Women's language, thought, and experiences of survival, struggle, celebration, and liberation inform the sermon as well as the revision of patriarchal scripture lessons. The church's music loudly and continuously praises the feminine (and the masculine) in the community's understanding of God. Black women's ways of knowing and being in the world are reflected in every aspect of the service. Black church worship—understood as celebration of and devotion to the presence of the divine spirit at work in black life—is womanist when all aspects of the Sabbath event, from the pulpit to the door, clearly reflect the presence, power, authority, and experience of black women. Womanist worship is family worship because it is also seriously inclusive of the experience of black men and black children.

It is at the point of liturgy and naming God in the black church that complexity compounds. A patriarchal, "denominational overlay" shrouds an egalitarian religious expression and confession in the black church. This overlay is apparently derived from slave religion, and it is Baptist, Methodist, Presbyterian, Episcopal, and so on. Its source is eighteenth- and nineteenth-century Anglo-American expressions of religion in these denominational bodies, from which most of the contemporary mainline black churches emerged. But from the egalitarian "religious undergarment," sometimes womanist fragments peep through. This has been the case for generations.

For example, when I was a little girl and often attended a black Baptist church in my hometown, a certain scenario was acted there nearly every Sunday morning during worship. The minister, who had a deep and loud and resonant voice, began the service by belting out from the pulpit this question to the congregation: "Who do you say God is?" The huge choir in back of him would respond in song: "God of Gods, King of Kings, Father Everlasting!" The preacher would belt out the question again: "Who do you say God is?" Then Sister Sadie Davis, a domestic worker, would come up front from among the congregation and would sing these words in response to the question: "Poor little Mary's boy, and they nailed him to a tree, and they nailed him to a tree." The preacher would ask the question again: "Who do you say God is?" The choir responded: "God of Gods, King of Kings, Father Everlasting." The preacher asked again: "Who do you say God is?" Sister Davis responded, "Poor little Mary's boy, and she laid him in the grave, and she laid him in the grave." The preacher asked again: "Who do you say God is?" The choir sang again: "God of Gods, King of Kings, Father Everlasting!" Raising his voice to drumlike proportions, the preacher rolled out the question, "I say, who do *you* say God is?" Sister Davis's beautiful contralto voice almost screamed the answer: "Poor little Mary's boy, and he got up from the dead, and *he got up from the dead!*" The preacher would say, "Well, all right!" Of course, by that time the atmosphere in the church would be electric, and several women would be shouting. Many of the women had sons and daughters and close relatives who were trying to get up from the death of despair, depression, and defeat.

Sometimes, after this part of the worship (which I now recognize as an invocation to bring God, Jesus, Spirit, and woman into the liturgy), the choir would sing a spiritual, claiming that "Jesus is my mother, my father, my sister and my brother." Today as I remember this service, I recognize quasi-womanist and genuine womanist fragments momentarily showing themselves in a church service that would finally end in androcentric, patriarchal words from the Bible and in the sermon. The quasi-womanist part of this scenario was Sister Sadie Davis insinuating African-American woman and family experience into the Jesus-pageant in the black church. This was quasi-womanist because Sister Davis's emphasis suggested only black women's sons ("poor little Mary's boy"). There was no language suggesting the tragedies experienced by black women's daughters. But the preacher apparently recognized the loss of the female principle in the Trinity and therefore inserted Sister Sadie Davis and "poor Mary" to make up for the loss. To me this represents an effort to integrate the male and female principle in black people's understanding of God, even though the words left out the plight of Mary's daughters.

The genuine womanist fragment in the service was the spiritual: "Jesus is my mother, my father, my sister and my brother." This is genuine womanist because it makes the divinity a mosaic of gender allusions (i.e., female and male); of age differentials in the family (mother, father, then the younger generation sister and brother); of authority differences in the family (mother and father as compared to sister and brother); of parity relation (as mother and father and then as sister and brother). This genuine womanist fragment was totally inclusive. And it was inclusive at the point of identifying who Jesus is for the community. But the patriarchal overlay enshrouding these fragments would ultimately leave the congregation with emphasis upon and preference for the authority of male divinity as illustrated in the choir's song "God of Gods, King of Kings, Father Everlasting!" The woman-inclusive elements would be lost as the androcentric language of the preacher's sermon and the scripture "proclaimed" the gospel to the black congregation, which was *80 percent female!*

Now, twenty-odd years removed from my southern Kentucky roots and living and teaching theology in New York City, I ask myself: how would a truly womanist worship service today answer the preacher's question "Who do you say God is?" Womanist theologian Kelly Brown provides some clues[2] when she defines the task of womanist theology: it is to

reflect at least two aspects of black women's experience: 1) the complexity of their distinctive oppression, and 2) their ability to survive and even achieve in spite of that oppression. Specifically a womanist interpretation of Jesus Christ must confront those understandings of Jesus which have often aided and abetted the oppression of black women. A womanist Christology must also affirm black women's faith that Jesus has supported them in their struggle to survive and be free.[3]

Brown then identifies ideas about Jesus that are oppressive for black women. She points to "the equation . . . often made in black faith between Jesus and God" and charges that "black church people have consistently made very little distinction between the two." This has prohibited black women from being able to affirm the idea of the feminine face of the divinity, as expressed by the female character in Ntozake Shange's play who said, "I found God in myself, and I love her / I love her fiercely."[4] As evidence, Brown repeats a black church woman's response that "calling God 'she' just doesn't sound right." She resolves the problem by stating that womanist theology must "articulate that Jesus's significance as Christ is tied not to biological characteristics, but to sustaining and liberating activity on behalf of the oppressed." Womanist theology must "emphasize that God's incarnation as Christ does not take the exclusive physical form of the Jewish man from Nazareth. Instead, Christ can be made incarnate wherever there is a movement to sustain and liberate oppressed people."[5]

However, Brown disagrees with womanist theologian Jacqueline Grant, who sees the Christ of faith as a black woman. Grant's position is consistent with a liberation faith that recognizes the image of God as the most oppressed of the oppressed in the African-American community. That would be black women. But Brown finds this "theologically misleading," for it is not consistent with black women's testimonies about Jesus nor with Jesus' own self-understanding as suggested in the New Testament.

As I see it, both Brown's and Grant's work suggests an important response for womanist worship's projection of the identity of God. In the black church the "word" must be about a liberator Christ thoroughly integrated by a female principle affirming black women's freedom and survival struggle. This raises questions, of course, about the sources used in worship to support this notion of God. Are other sources needed in black church liturgy besides the Bible? Sociologist of religion Cheryl Townsend Gilkes writes about an Afrocentric biblical tradition that black Americans have formed over the years *from the Bible,* and this tradition is consciously gender inclusive.[6] She cites as evidence the African-American way of adding to the Psalm 68:5 reference to God as "Father of the fatherless." According to Gilkes, black Americans claim that God is not only father of the fatherless, God is also mother to the motherless, sister to the sisterless, brother to the brotherless. She shows how this tradition of "inclusivising" the female in the black American sacred literature is passed along from generation to generation.

This suggests to me that African-Americans, like the biblical redactors of sources such as "J" and "E," could create a transcribed sacred text (like the Bible but beyond it) composed of the oral literature making up the Afrocentric biblical tradition of which Gilkes speaks. In composing this text, the black redactors need to be conscious of two things. First, early Christian origins for the black community were in the early slave period of African-American history. That was when they began fashioning a worldview out of the biblical images and stories *they selected* as appropriate to their life situation—the biblical material that spoke the good news on male and female terms. That is when and how their testimonies, songs, and narratives say they met Jesus.

The second thing the African-American redactors need remember is that every aspect or idea must be gender inclusive, that is, inclusive of the experience of both women and men. This means that black women's stories and black men's stories and black children's stories about their experience with mother-father God must be used to support the ideas in the African-American sacred text— ideas appropriated, at their foundation, from the Bible. The community would select the stories to be incorporated.

Womanist worship would, then, constantly encourage black congregations to remember the early origins of black Christianity in slavery. Thus the service should provide a new sense of what ought to be celebrated and remembered in the black American church—of what ought to be ritualized beyond the Eucharist. Slaves had to develop resistance strategies in order to worship God and to stay alive. The community needs to remember the hush harbor churches of the slaves[7] and the precautions they had to take so that their owners would not discover them worshiping and therefore punish them. Thus slaves used many devices to keep down the noise of their religious practices. According to church historian Albert Raboteau,

> the most common device for preserving secrecy was an iron pot or kettle turned upside down to catch the sound. The pot was usually placed in the middle of the cabin floor or at the doorstep, then slightly propped up to hold the sound of the praying and singing

from escaping. A variation was to pray or sing softly "with heads together around" the "kettle to deaden the sound."[8]

Some slaves claimed that the overturned pots were also put in front of the doors at the places where the slaves had dancing so that the noise would not go outside. Raboteau suggests that these over-turned pots might have functioned symbolically. "Patsy Hyde, for-mer slave in Tennessee . . . claimed . . . slaves . . . 'would tek dere ole iron cookin' pots en turn dem upside down on de groun' neah dere cabins ter keep dere white folks fum herein' w'at dey was sayin'. Dey claimed dat hit showed dat Gawd waz wid dem.'"[9]

I suggest that the black church and the planners of womanist worship develop "resistance rituals" using such things as overturned pots to remind the people of their ancient belief that God supported them and continues to support them in their resistance struggles. We need ritual in the black church celebrating and remembering important female- and male-led events in the black civil rights struggle when the people believed God was in the struggle with them. We need this ritual in the church to reinforce in our chil-dren's minds, at an early age, a sense of African-American history and faith. These resistance rituals could serve as a powerful force that would help African-Americans give a more indigenous re-sponse to the question of who God is and has been for African-American people. However, in the creation and use of such rituals by the church, female inclusion must be accomplished at all cost, for resistance rituals will also commemorate how black women have resisted sexist oppression as they relied on God, the mother to the motherless . . . sister to the sisterless. Especially do black Ameri-cans need to remember how slave women's faith in God helped them survive and hold on to their self-esteem as they were raped by any white man who felt the inclination. This inseparable relation between faith and resistance in black people's history needs to be the material of ritual composed and enacted in the church right alongside any other rituals that are part of Christian heritage.

It seems to me that all this suggests a definite task for womanist worship: it must be constantly resurrecting, reconstructing, and making visible the egalitarian, inclusive womanist black religion both submerged in and outside of the expressions of patriarchal power now dominating in the African-American denominations. We must begin to accomplish this task so that its effects can be realized in worship events like Sunday morning service.

As I see it, three efforts figure into accomplishing this task. The first is to indicate that there is "African-American scripture" and there is the Bible. Appropriate readings from both should be in the service—appropriate meaning womanist-inclusive. Black Americans had a powerful experience with God during slavery when very few of them could read. They believed that Jesus/God "spoke" to them directly and acted in their behalf. We need the stories from black history testifying to this belief. Second, there must be conscious and intentional incorporation of a didactic piece in the service meant to conjure up, stimulate, and encourage memory of significant events in early African-American Christian heritage. This can be done in woman-inclusive music, dance, and drama. Third, this ancient heritage must be used in a ritualistic way to compose responses to the question of who "God-Jesus-the-Spirit" are for black Americans.

With regard to the biblical image of Jesus projected in womanist worship, I favor the Lukan images because they show Jesus the healer also ministering and relating to women in a positive way. But African-American people's (female and male) testimonies and experiences of Jesus/God should provide the primary images. Black women have a rich visionary history in which they claim Jesus/God came to them and gave them direction for their lives.[10] Nineteenth-century black preaching women Jarena Lee, Zilpha Elaw, Julia Foot, Old Elizabeth, and others tell of their visions, through which God instrumented a call to them to preach, even though sexism in the black church prohibited them from getting ordained. Both the women's visions and their experiences of sexism should become part of the story told in "African-American scripture."

I think the liberation of African-American people cannot be effected until liberated womanist worship becomes the "order of the day" in black Christian churches. The emphatically androcentric content in the churches keeps black women bowing down to male images and keeps the congregations ignorant of black women's powerful contribution to the development and practice of Christian religion in the African-American community. Until the black church develops liberating *womanist* liturgy and until it develops resistance rituals to remember and commemorate its own history of faith and struggle, the black church and black people will remain in bondage. And African-American children, female and male, will continue to be ignorant of the historical foundations of the great spiritual heritage of which they are the recipients.

Notes

1. See the definition of a womanist in Alice Walker's *In Search of Our Mothers' Gardens: Womanist Prose* (New York: Harcourt Brace Jovanovich, 1983), pp. xi–xii. Walker coined the word "womanist" and gave it the definition that undergirds the definition in this article.

2. Kelly Brown, "God Is as Christ Does. Toward a Womanist Theology," *Journal of Religious Thought*, vol. 46, no. 1 (Summer–Fall 1989), pp. 7–16.

3. Ibid., p. 14.

4. Ibid.

5. Ibid.

6. See Cheryl Townsend Gilkes, "Mother to the Motherless, Father to the Fatherless: Power, Gender, and Community in an Afrocentric Biblical Tradition," in *Semeia* 47, 1989.

7. "Hush harbor" churches were the religious gatherings held by slaves in the woods at night. These gatherings were held in defiance of slaveowners' prohibitions of church services by slaves.

8. Albert Raboteau, *Slave Religion: The "Invisible Institution" in the Antebellum South* (New York: Oxford University Press, 1978), p. 217.

9. Ibid., p. 216.

10. For examples of black women's visionary experiences in the nineteenth century, see William L. Andrews, ed., *Sisters of the Spirit* (Bloomington: Indiana University Press, 1986). Also see the memoir of the slave Old Elizabeth in Henry Louis Gates, Jr., ed., *Six Women's Slave Narratives*, in the Schomburg Library of Nineteenth-Century Black Women Writers (New York: Oxford University Press, 1988; first published in Philadelphia by Collins, Printer, 1863).

14

A Lingering Question:
What Is Feminist Prayer?

Eileen King

My consistent observation about feminists is that as soon as they enter a space in which they are going to meet, some members of the group will start rearranging the furniture. If it is immobile, invariably one will ask, "Is there another place we can use?" This refusal to accept things as they are is at the heart of feminist identity. In the activity of pulling chairs and shoving tables women are identifying what they need and how those needs can be met. Women do not assume that a space, just because it is available to them, is suitable. Adjustments are needed.

The Question

The question here—what happens when feminists pray?—becomes a large room filled with lively discussions, unflinching honesty, timorous hesitations, divergent perceptions—whatever emerges that provides for a fuller response. It becomes a room where women who pray and who have questions, ideas, insights about prayer are invited to enter in order to learn from one another. By necessity, the question will linger and it will be altered by each woman as she shapes her response. The vitality of the question lies in its capacity to welcome and encourage women to be particular. As feminism seeks out the particular without the comfort of generalizations or abstractions, the need to sustain diversity and difference becomes its greatest challenge and its strongest growing edge. In this room, "What is . . . ?" is a door that opens the investigation.

To begin this investigation, four participants in a conference call struggled to respond: Marcia Falk,[1] a feminist Jew; Marjorie Procter-Smith, a feminist Christian in the Protestant tradition; Marie Therese Archambault,[2] a Native American Catholic Franciscan sister; and the author, a feminist Catholic. It is not surprising that "What is feminist prayer?" turned into "What is going on when these four feminists pray?"

The image of women trying to make a space hospitable is evocative of the present experiences of feminists at prayer. As feminists search for ways to pray within a given religious tradition, they are exploring various forms for prayer and, in the process, learning how immovable some of them seem to be. Occasionally they discover a hidden possibility. Some feminists are creating totally new prayers that do not relate to mainline religious institutions.

In the conversation generated by this question, deep issues are exposed when one "rearranges" present "furniture" of prayer conventions, or when one moves to another space altogether, or when one attempts to do both. Five deeply interrelated components emerge: search, self, analysis/critique, gift, and difference.

The Search and the Self

Feminists who pray are engaged in a profound search for an understanding of the divine and a way to relate to the divine, to one another, and to all of creation, without the distortion of patriarchy; that is, without any form of domination. The search often begins within one's self because self-understanding is essential and freeing and is part of a feminist commitment to speak the truth about oneself and one's circumstances. For women this process always requires courage and often precipitates pain, especially when a dominant philosophy denies the importance of selfhood for women or when a religious tradition rejects women as in any way godlike.

For women of nonwhite, non-Western, and/or non-Eurocentric traditions, this process is made doubly difficult by the suppression and distortion of their religious and cultural heritages. Feminists are also aware of the hazards of an exaggerated emphasis on autonomy and independence, and they encourage women to find or form communities. Thus women's struggle to name their true selves in the context of a prayerful encounter with the divine is at the heart of what happens when feminists pray. In the effort to pray, we claim ourselves.

My ten-year association with a women's liturgy group confirms that a feminist search for a way to relate to God, one another, and all of creation is a communal endeavor. This group intends to provide a protected space, apart from the dominant culture. It is a space in which members can ask disturbing questions, try out new forms and rituals, analyze our own reactions, and explore our dreams for an inclusive community.

As a group, we determine what is conducive to challenging and supporting one another as we take up the inner and outer struggles of being responsible adult women who want to nourish a spiritual life and share a faith journey. Over time we have been able to name our fears, find strength to change self-understandings that are dangerous, uncover new layers of misconceptions, and allow ourselves to cry when we hurt, to rejoice with one another's growth, and to laugh with abandon at past mistakes and delusions once they have lost their negative power. Each time we risk doing a circle dance, each time we use oils, mirrors, or touch, we consciously include our bodies, not only our words. Slowly we are learning how our female bodies are part of this faith journey.

The search that began with self is rooted in truth telling, and it moves outward and inward: outward when women bring new self-understandings into the public arena and inward when women probe unexamined assumptions. Truth telling can also mean listening to hard-to-hear truths about forms of domination carried out by women because of social inequalities based on class, ethnicity, or race. The search is for authentic self-understanding and right relationships with God, one another, and all of creation.

Analysis/Critique

A second essential piece to feminist prayer is the necessity for developing a critique of our own traditions and a method for recovering the voices in that tradition that have been lost or suppressed.
Issues of ethnicity as well as religious identity emerge here.

Marie Therese Archambault told how Native Americans were
robbed of their identity by U.S. government policies at the turn
of the century that outlawed native religion. These laws were not
revoked until 1978. During all those years many of the Native
American spiritual leaders had disappeared or had been killed.
Another destructive interference in Native American spirituality
goes farther back, to 1868 when President Grant asked thirteen
denominations to divide the Indian Nations among them, desig-
nating tribes as Methodist, Catholic, Mormon, and so on. The
devastating effects on Native American women were revealed in a
seminar held in Denver in October 1991 in which these Native
American women were asked to reflect and share their thoughts
on their self-esteem as Christian women:

> We were all from different denominations, but when asked how
> we felt about being Christian-Indian women, total silence fol-
> lowed. It was clear that we could find no voice to express our-
> selves, or what we felt was hidden from ourselves. Later, in private
> we discussed the fact that many of us were either numb, or did not
> feel good about ourselves within a Christian setting. Frequently,
> our first reactions are silence and passivity. Yet we continue to en-
> gage in Christian religious practices without seeing ourselves in-
> cluded in non-Indian Christian rituals, perhaps without really
> respecting ourselves. Indians have a rich and long history of rituals
> but most often none of these appear in prayer services for Indian
> people, such as the Mass or other non-Indian acts of worship.

To regain her own sense of self, Archambault immerses herself
in the silence of that void which has been created by society's intentional destruction of her identity as a Native American Christian woman. In that silence she searches out what is authentic to
her and her people:

The only way I can pray is to use the Buddhist approach, which is to become mindless and empty in order to find my center. I do not use the name of Jesus, even though Jesus Christ is a powerful reality in my life, because so much violence and injustice was done to native peoples in Jesus' name by Christian missionaries. In nothingness and darkness—that is where I am most myself and can express my yearning for freedom from oppressive images and from negative feelings as a native and as a woman. I direct my prayer to the Creator. I ask for a new song, for a voice to speak for myself, for my people who were killed outright, and for all the rest of us whose only alternative for survival is passivity. It is only in a group of native people in ritual or ceremony that I feel most accepted for who I am. There seems to be something more balanced in the native tradition because women have a place. That tradition is whole, with male and female together.

Working within the Jewish tradition, Marcia Falk brings together the three immutable elements of her person—woman, artist, and Jew. When she translated the *Song of Songs* from the Hebrew Bible into modern English poetry, she came to this realization:

> I believe that the *Song of Songs* is the only book of the Hebrew Bible where women really have a voice. In translating it, I felt I was finding my most ancient female ancestors and models in that poetry.

When she turned to the book of Psalms, she found its appealing celebrations of nature inextricably bound to images of a male god. The theology of the Psalms left her so alienated that she was unable to translate even selections from that biblical book. Instead, she began writing her own Hebrew liturgies. Of this endeavor she says:

> No one is creating new liturgies in Hebrew because, for some Jews, Hebrew is enshrined, ossified. Even people who write new English prayers are loathe to touch the Hebrew. I am writing new *berakhot* [Hebrew blessings], and also translating them into English. These *berakhot* articulate a theology different from that of mainstream rabbinic Judaism, although they often make use of the language of

classical Jewish texts. They tap into another stream in Jewish tradition—the appreciation of divinity as immanence.

Falk and Archambault are intimately linked to their ethnic, religious tradition, but their approaches to confronting the oppressive aspects of those traditions differ. Silence is central to Archambault's prayer, and for Falk it is an important phase in the creative process. Falk's ethnic identity is the same as her religion: she is a Jew. Her struggle as a feminist is not confounded by a split between ethnicity and religion. Archambault, a Lakota Catholic, must work to recover and incorporate her ethnic traditions in her Christian religious practices. In seeking out her Lakota ethnic tradition she expects to find the path to wholeness as a Native American Christian woman.

Archambault is engaged in an in-depth study of Catholic theology because she encountered the transcendent when she encountered Jesus in her life. That encounter was profound for her, and she does not feel it demeaned or diminished her, while at the same time she is critical of the ways in which the name of Jesus has been used against her people and their religious traditions. In the company of her Native American community she is searching for ritual ways that will allow the presence of Jesus to be available in the fullness of ancient Native American traditions, not in their denial or annihilation. Because of the violence done to her people, she feels that her struggle to achieve this goal must be nonviolent, and she has made a personal vow of nonviolence.

Marcia Falk is reconstructing Jewish prayer, working with the Hebrew. She finds the traditional (male) terms for God within Hebrew liturgy idolatrous because "they have replaced the greater whole with a partial view of what divinity is." She is smashing the destructive power of one metaphor by creating a new metaphor with a different kind of power. In the process she avoids any anthropomorphism:

> For me, any personal image for divinity, even a female image, is unsatisfying because I feel the need to break down the hierarchy that has led us to the present world order—an order destructive of all life on the planet. It feels very important to me to stop seeing the human species as at the top of the "great chain" of creation.

The only way to do that is to stop using human images for divinity—male or female. Instead I choose my images from the whole realm of the natural world.

Falk identifies with some of the values expressed by feminists who call themselves polytheists or Goddess worshipers, insofar as they address the need to establish reciprocal relationships that acknowledge our interconnectedness. She calls her own process a feminist reconstruction of monotheism.

As a Jew I feel a need to get beyond the vulgar representation of monotheism by an exclusively male deity and move toward what I think or hope was the original insight of monotheism—that we live in a unified world and participate in a single source of being. In order to do that, we have to stop projecting divinity "out there" and splitting ourselves off from it. I believe that monotheists and polytheists need not be at war within a feminist context. As feminists we are, it seems to me, *all* talking about recognizing diversity and respecting difference, within one world in which we are interdependent.

The need for critique and analysis is also felt by my own feminist liturgy group. In the early stages we often felt as though we were working in a void. The lack of a common women's liturgical tradition was deeply felt. We were uncomfortable with silence, we lacked positive images that didn't feel artificial, we did not know how to claim our women's bodies as holy. It has taken time and some awkward silences before new images could emerge. Now a long period of silence in the heart of a ritual is welcome, and we respect the need for that silence. Now new images feel less artificial. The strength that we have derived from our women's liturgy group feeds the courage required to speak the truth, to oppose unjust structures, to recognize our own ignorance. We are watchful that we keep a sense of balance, a sense of human proportions when we face enormous but ever-present problems like militarism, homelessness, crime, and sexism. We are careful that this scrutiny of ourselves, our attempts to pray, and our society is constructive.

Gift

When we first began, the question was occasionally asked after a ritual, "But was it prayer?" Ten years ago, I felt it was too soon to ask. Now I hear that question as pointing to a dimension of prayer that is best named gift. What we do in our women's liturgy group is prepare a setting, focus on a theme or concern, and provide a way that enables us to uncover a better understanding of ourselves and our society. All of this activity may and sometimes does lead to empowerment and to a deeper insight into the presence and mystery of God.

The fact that this encounter is not an inevitable result of the planning and the questioning leads to a consideration of the idea of prayer as gift. As Marcia Falk commented: "I do not think that one of my blessings becomes a blessing unless something un-willed and un-willable happens. Real blessing is a gift. I am a person who does not receive that gift very often."

There is real power in symbol, image, word, music. Combining these with caring preparation, sensitive facilitation, individual receptivity, and divine initiative—all these contribute to an experience of God's presence and love. But the outcome is not automatic. One waits on the gifts and intentions of the community that comes together, and one waits on the divine. The action of the community is not a nudging of an inattentive deity, but rather the recognition of the inscrutable interdependence between the divine and the human within all of creation. A feminist understanding of this connection between the human and the divine is not the dependency of children but the trust that sustains mutually responsible persons. This perspective also acknowledges an understanding of God as one who reveals because of a desire to be known by each of us individually and all of us in community. Sometimes that revelation, that divine/human interconnection, is experienced when one attempts to pray.

Marjorie Procter-Smith adds to the discussion:

> Traditional interpretations of prayer have often emphasized the passivity of the human over the absolute sovereignty of God. It is notable that feminist understandings of prayer recast this experience as

one of mystery and gift rather than as passivity and control. The notion of the relationship between divine and human as reciprocal is a radical challenge to traditional assertions of God's absolute otherness as well as God's superordination.

Difference

What is the best forum for further exploration of feminist prayer? Can it be conducted in a patriarchal context? How can we deal with the violent reaction some will have to the changes feminists propose? Sometimes the simple statement of the truth feels violent because many people do not want to hear it, as Marcia Falk observed:

> When I published my first essay on writing blessings and talked about smashing the idol of the prayer formula "Lord God King of the Universe," many readers found that to be violent. I was surprised by the reaction, but I came to understand that my talk of "smashing the idols" had threatened, angered, and hurt some people, even though others found it healing. Readers were polarized and took sides as to whether or not it was religiously permissible to do what I was doing. Yet, there is another kind of violence I experience when Orthodox Jewish feminists who use my prayers will not allow them to substitute for traditional prayers. They do not realize how offensive it is to me that they consider the prayers of a Jewish woman today less "real" than the prayers of Jewish men who wrote in earlier times. Words are not divinity. Words are our means, our tools for expression. Words cannot have ultimate power, and when they become enshrined we stifle creativity and bring about our own disempowerment.

What these fragments of our discussion reveal is that there are complex, dynamic forces in tension with one another when feminist women pray. These forces exist within women, between women, and between women and the faith traditions to which they belong. Sometimes the tension is hurtful and draining. When the tension can be sustained, feminists understand it to be creative, life giving, and deeply connected to divine life. A healthy tension among feminists and between feminists and patriarchal institutions will pull the elements of search, self, analysis/critique, gift, and difference in more directions. As feminists continue to explore prayer, more questions are likely to be posed. How does feminist prayer address evil? Can the words that anyone writes (even if that writer is a woman) be voiced by someone else as her own prayer? How does prayer empower action? How do we recognize manipulation in public/community prayer? What do we do about it? What will it take for a patriarchal religious tradition to become engaged with its feminist members in correcting oppressive structures and practices?

Feminists who pray are intent on fundamental change, the transformation of patriarchal society. Marjorie Procter-Smith expresses this dimension thus:

> What we are doing when we pray as feminists in our respective traditions is something very radical in the literal sense of the word, that is, challenging our traditions at the very root. Sometimes we challenge by refusing, by using no words. Sometimes we challenge by creating new words that smash the old words. Both ways are powerful acts of resistance.

"What is feminist prayer?" requires many more discussions. The unified wholeness that Marcia Falk refers to depends on the response of many feminists from other backgrounds. A unified wholeness will require us to stretch our capacity both to hold our own integrity and at the same time be open to the wide range of differences that will necessarily be brought forth. The process of asking "What is . . ." will in itself be transformed into one that is inclusive, and then, perhaps, differences will become something that enrich rather than divide. For all the pain that will necessarily follow, there will be joy: the affirmation that there is wisdom in a group of women struggling to answer their own questions and that this wisdom is with God and has been there since creation.

Notes

1. Marcia Falk, affiliated scholar at Stanford University's Institute for Research on Women and Gender, is a poet, a Bible scholar, and a Jewish feminist liturgist. Her books include *The Song of Songs: A New Translation and Interpretation* (San Francisco: Harper San Francisco, 1990), *With Teeth in the Earth: Selected Poems of Malka Heifetz Tussman* (Detroit: Wayne State University Press, 1992), and *The Book of Blessings: A Feminist-Jewish Reconstruction of Prayer* (forthcoming, HarperCollins).

2. Marie Therese Archambault is urban outreach facilitator for the National Tekakwitha Conference in Great Falls, Montana, the first Catholic national urban outreach program for urban Catholic Native Americans. She received her licentiate in scripture from the Pontifical Biblical Institute in Rome and has also completed degrees in spirituality and theology. She is currently finishing a degree in native religious traditions at the University of Colorado. She was born at Standing Rock Reservation in Fort Yates, North Dakota, and attended Native American mission schools for her early education.

Conclusion

Janet R. Walton

> Once you live any piece of your vision it opens
> you to a constant onslaught. Of necessities, of
> horrors, but of wonders too, of possibilities.
>
> Audre Lorde, *Sister Outsider*

The stories of women's ritual experiences are expressions of visions born of necessity. Our visions are diverse, accentuating various human needs and responses. There is no "right" one; there is instead a rich treasure of differences. Each story recounts what is emerging from within ourselves and the cultures from which we come. They represent our quest to know what is true. The process involves pulling back layer after layer of forms, gestures, and images in order to discover both what restricts or harms us and what empowers us. Nothing can be left unexamined: no stereotype or destructive bias, no possibility for change. The women involved in these stories have committed themselves to name and let go of what is damaging, to empower one another to speak and act in light of the truths we learn and share, and to call forth the beauty and potential in each person.

Our visions enable us to survive in a society that has long discounted significant aspects of women's lives. To name the truths we are discovering, to trust their authenticity, and to claim our authority is at the heart of our collective ritual work. What we know of transcendent life, which some of us name God, Goddess, the Holy, and what we understand of ourselves and all created things emerges in the telling and retelling of human experiences. Each repetition uncovers more layers of the profundity and complexities of relationships, both with each other and with what is holy. Our survival is based on such interdependence. Each person's life affects every other, from the one whose power is commonly unacknowledged and invisible in our society to those who make decisions that touch the rest of us. Each has a piece from which collective truth and transcendent life is known. It is a vision upon which all of us rely.

"Of necessities . . . " As women we grew up knowing only a culture that objectified us. We were conditioned by the patriarchal distortions that damaged all human beings and every kind of organizational system. History and tradition taught us that we were created to bear and care for children, to attend to men's needs, to undergird men's professional advancement and provide for their sexual pleasure. These perceptions began to change when visionaries and pioneers among us helped us to see the damage inflicted by patriarchy. And we learned quickly that any change would come about only through our own initiative.

"Of horrors . . . " We are no strangers to fear, both mild and strong. Our lack of confidence in ourselves (a pervasive bequest of a patriarchal society) leads us to question whether we have something significant to contribute, whether we know enough to speak, whether we have a right to name and structure experiences of the Holy. Will what we do work? Can we give up what we have always known and sometimes loved without immediate substitutes? The judgments of others compound our fears. How will we respond to the cynicism, contempt, and censure that accompany a break from established traditions? Comments such as "These women are just angry hags; they are men-haters" are all-too-frequent responses to women's struggle for freedom.

Other fears come also from our history of being victims of violence, particularly of physical and emotional abuse. Why has it taken so long to recognize such injustice? What will happen when we name and eliminate it? Our dreams and our collaborative efforts at ritualizing are a powerful vehicle for refusing to be controlled by this kind of fear, fear that destroys our lives.

"But of wonders, too, of possibilities." Yet once we have tasted the power of believing in ourselves and of trusting what we feel and think, there is no turning back. To love ourselves, to claim what we know to be true, and to acknowledge what we are not unleashes energy among us, a revelation of what is holy. And we want to tell every human being, female and male, what we have learned.

The rituals in this book offer glimpses into the ways in which women have responded to traditional institutional liturgies and to needs not yet addressed in these contexts. The rituals found here are an invitation to all women and men—including authorities of religious institutions—to join us in this exploration.

A Call to Women

We, the authors, and all the women whose work is reported in these chapters call upon the women who read this book to share our discoveries, our determination, and our exhilaration. We invite you to participate in developing rituals that connect with the truths of our lives. The task includes reshaping traditional institutional worship as well as imagining untested forms. What we have presented is an open-ended story. By sharing these principles and concrete examples, our intention is to invite women to take their lives more seriously, to value what they understand, and to generate rituals that honor their experiences.

The perspectives of women's experiences can be a remarkable force in the revitalization of traditional worship. Women's insistence on leadership that draws out the particularities of many cultures, ages, life-styles, and abilities will challenge metaphors and rules that legislate human and divine revelation. Women's respect for the rhythms and shapes of our bodies will invite us to examine our understanding of the cycles of death and life. They will lead us to treasure the beauty of sexuality and the revelation of our bodies. Our recognition of sexual violence will demand conversation about traditional interpretations that do not account sufficiently for the presence of evil in our lives. The power of women's insights is yet to be realized.

Our call is also to women who do not, for a variety of reasons, find themselves part of any institutional setting. We invite you to draw upon your inner resources and creative skills to develop your own rituals. The experience is at once wonderful and terrifying. It demands an honest attentiveness to yourself and others. It calls for serious reflection and a playful spirit. Sometimes the results are frustrating, but more often they are compelling, irresistible, transforming.

A Call to Men

We invite men also to join with us in this venture. Partnership means listening deeply and patiently. It presumes involvement with what is unfamiliar; it includes acceptance of discomfort, participation without control, without knowing the outcome. It implies recognizing that although both women and men are born of woman, we view the world through gendered lenses, seeing things differently at times. What causes pain, what expresses love, what constitutes sin, what measures success, is not the same for human beings socialized in different ways.

For some women, this invitation to men is a request to honor their choice to be separate. Such women feel that their very survival requires excluding men. Violence has scarred some women permanently. It is impossible for them to trust men or to share with them what is emerging in their lives. For some women it is impossible to work with men on a project as intimate as ritual activity.

For other women the invitation to men is a request to participate with them in new ways of ritualizing. It includes imagining possibilities, experimenting together, evaluating the outcome, rejoicing when rituals are effective.

A Call to Religious Institutions

Of authorities and members of various religious institutions we ask—that you discontinue the debate about the validity of women's claims about our lives and about what connects us to the Holy. The debate keeps both women and men from discovering significant aspects of human experience and divine reality. It delays and often denies access to a variety of understandings of power, compassion, sin, integrity, holiness, and relationships that are critical to the collaboration required in this complex world.

Ritual is about action; thus, we invite religious leaders to join us on a journey in which *doing* is primary. Together let us commit ourselves to examine our rituals, changing them when appropriate to acknowledge the sacredness of every person. Let us invoke the Holy in ritual actions that are courageous and bold. Let us agree to believe people when they say a word, image, metaphor, or gesture is demeaning. Let us declare that no one has an exclusive claim to mediate what is sacred. Let us indeed embody a faith where each person is dependent on the revelation of another.

Clearly, in the process we will make mistakes. But fear of mistakes should not keep us from trying. Mistakes are an inevitable part of the process of any lasting discovery. Of greater importance are the passion, honesty, and persistence that accompany significant, fundamental change.

"Once you live any piece of your vision . . . " there is no turning back. There is no return to worship that hurts women or disregards what we know. Rather, there is an urgency to draw out women's wisdom. Yes, it is for the good of all women, but also for the healing and transformation of our world.[1]

Notes

1. I am grateful to Anne E. Patrick and to Siobhán Garrigan for their careful reading of this conclusion and their helpful suggestions.